Social Skills Training
for Schizophrenia

TREATMENT MANUALS FOR PRACTITIONERS
David H. Barlow, *Editor*

Recent Volumes

SOCIAL SKILLS TRAINING
FOR SCHIZOPHRENIA
A STEP-BY-STEP GUIDE
Alan S. Bellack, Kim T. Mueser,
Susan Gingerich, and Julie Agresta

CHANGING HIV RISK BEHAVIOR
PRACTICAL STRATEGIES
Jeffrey A. Kelly

TREATMENT OF OBSESSIVE
COMPULSIVE DISORDER
Gail S. Steketee

PROBLEM DRINKERS
GUIDED SELF-CHANGE TREATMENT
Mark B. Sobell and Linda C. Sobell

INSOMNIA
PSYCHOLOGICAL ASSESSMENT AND MANAGEMENT
Charles M. Morin

PSYCHOLOGICAL MANAGEMENT OF
CHRONIC HEADACHES
Paul R. Martin

TREATING PTSD
COGNITIVE-BEHAVIORAL STRATEGIES
David W. Foy, *Editor*

PREVENTING PHYSICAL AND EMOTIONAL
ABUSE OF CHILDREN
David A. Wolfe

SEXUAL DYSFUNCTION
A GUIDE FOR ASSESSMENT AND TREATMENT
John P. Wincze and Michael P. Carey

Social Skills Training for Schizophrenia

A Step-by-Step Guide

ALAN S. BELLACK
KIM T. MUESER
SUSAN GINGERICH
JULIE AGRESTA

Series Editor's Note by David H. Barlow

THE GUILFORD PRESS
New York   London

© 1997 The Guilford Press
A Division of Guilford Publications, Inc.
72 Spring Street, New York, NY 10012

Printed in the United States of America

This book is printed on acid-free paper.

Last digit is print number: 9 8 7 6 5 4 3 2

Library of Congress Cataloging-in-Publication Data

Social skills training for schizophrenia: a step-by-step guide /
   Alan S. Bellack . . . [et al.].
       p.   cm. — (Treatment manuals for practitioners)
   Includes bibliographical references and index.
   ISBN 1-57230-177-5
   1. Schizophrenics—Rehabilitation.   2. Social skills—Study and
teaching.   I. Bellack, Alan S.   II. Series.
RC514.S875   1997
616.89′8203—dc21

96-52826
CIP

To Wagner Bridger, MD, our Chairman at what was then Medical College of Pennsylvania, who provided a unique academic environment that made this book and countless other academic ventures possible.

To the staff and clients at Misty Harbor Community Residence, Community Treatment Teams of Philadelphia, Delaware Psychiatric Center, and Holiday House.

To Val and Jon Slott.

Series Editor's Note

The search for biological roots to schizophrenia continues unabated. New discoveries centering on brain functioning or genetic contributions most often make headlines, even if the findings do not hold up under the harsh light of prolonged scientific scrutiny. Ultimately, we will learn much more about neurobiological contributions to schizophrenia, and this new knowledge will facilitate further development of useful pharmacological agents.

Running in parallel to these widely publicized efforts, but receiving considerably less publicity, are notable efforts to develop more efficient and effective psychosocial interventions for schizophrenia. Although many individuals, even among the mental health community, are not aware of it, we now possess powerful psychosocial interventions that, when combined with appropriate medications, can double the therapeutic effect in many cases. Among the pioneers in this important endeavor over the past 25 years have been Alan Bellack, Kim Mueser, and their colleagues who have conducted a model of programmatic research. These clinical scientists have developed and refined their therapeutic strategies over the course of many years of clinical innovation, followed by empirical evaluation, resulting in the most up-to-date program of its kind. The growing realization that effective and powerful psychosocial interventions change not only behavior but also brain functioning will ensure that advances in treatments for schizophrenia, such as the program described in this book, are every bit as valuable, important, and worthy of publicity as new discoveries in psychopharmacology.

DAVID H. BARLOW

Preface

This book is a collaborative product that has evolved from our experiences in teaching social skills to individuals with schizophrenia and in teaching clinicians how to work effectively with their own schizophrenia clients. In many respects, the approach is a direct evolution of techniques originally developed by Michel Hersen and Richard Eisler in Jackson, Mississippi, and by Bob Liberman in Camarillo, California, in the early 1970s, and by Alan S. Bellack, Michel Hersen, and Samuel Turner in Pittsburgh in the late 1970s. The training strategy (*how* we teach) is really quite simple. It is based on well-established principles of social learning and has been crafted in response to the extensive literature on cognitive deficits in schizophrenia. The content of the training (*what* we teach) has evolved from our clinical experience with clients and their relatives and from the input of mental health workers who deal with schizophrenia clients on a day-to-day basis.

We expect that most readers will find the training curricula in Part II and the Appendices to be very helpful in getting groups started but that they will quickly tailor the material to their own clients' needs and interests. We encourage that approach. We are convinced that the manner of training is much more important than the content. The latter changes over time and across settings. For example, we are now engaged in training to reduce substance abuse and increase safe sex behaviors. Ten years ago we couldn't have imagined that those topics would be relevant for our clients, let alone much more critical than conversation skills and basic training in assertiveness. However, we are teaching these new skills using precisely the same techniques: demonstration (modeling), rehearsal (role play), and corrective feedback. We expect that these techniques have been used by effective teachers to teach skills throughout history, albeit without the scientific understanding elucidated over the last 30 years. We offer no magic bullets for curing schizophrenia or rectifying all of our clients' problems in daily living. However, we do promise that faithful adherence to our training strategy will enable diligent clinicians to successfully teach their clients critical life skills.

We would like to express our appreciation to a number of people who made our work possible. First and foremost, thanks to Roland D. Turk, MSW, whose faith in our methods was backed by financial support for an open clinical trial over a number of years. Second, our gratitude to the clients and staff at Misty Harbor and Holiday House, two board-and-care homes in Philadelphia that served as our laboratory. Karen Light, MD, Zia Gajary, MD, and Kerry Arnold, BA, are recognized for their valued clinical suggestions. Finally, we appreciate the patience of Sharon Panulla, Barbara Watkins, and Seymour Weingarten of The Guilford Press and hope they find the wait worthwhile.

Contents

I. PRINCIPLES, FORMAT, AND TECHNIQUES
   FOR SOCIAL SKILLS TRAINING
   OF CLIENTS WITH SCHIZOPHRENIA

1. Schizophrenia and Social Skills   3

   The Behavioral Model of Social Skills, 4 / Summary, 20

2. Assessment of Social Skills   21

   General Issues, 22 / Interviewing Techniques, 24 / Behavioral
   Observation of Role Playing, 26 / Social Problem-Solving
   Battery, 30 / Summary, 43

3. Techniques for Introducing Social Skills   44

   Social Learning Theory, 44 / Steps of Social Skills
   Training, 47 / Summary, 66

4. Techniques for Consolidating Social Skills   67

   Homework, 67 / Pacing of Social Skills Training, 72 /
   Additional Teaching Strategies, 72 / Different Training
   Modalities, 78 / Summary, 79

5. Starting a Skills Group   80

   Practical Considerations When Planning a Group, 80 /
   Selecting Group Leaders, 85 / Selecting Clients for
   Group, 87 / Preparing Clients for Participation in
   Group, 87 / Working with Other Mental Health Professionals
   to Generalize Skills, 89 / Summary, 92

6. Using Curricula for Social Skills Training Groups   93

Using an Existing Curriculum, 93 / Developing a New
Curriculum, 103 / Special Considerations, 105 / Summary, 107

7. Tailoring Skills for Individual Needs   108

The Role of Assessment in Setting Individual Client Goals, 108 /
Using Client Goals to Design Social Skills Training Groups, 110 /
Managing the Range of Skill Levels, 116 / Keeping All Members
Involved in the Group Process, 117 / Ongoing Assessment of
Progress Made in Group, 119 / Summary, 122

8. Troubleshooting I: Common Problems and Problems with
Highly Symptomatic Clients   123

Common Problems in Conducting Social Skills Training
Groups, 123 / Problems Related to Highly Symptomatic
Clients, 130 / Summary, 138

9. Troubleshooting II: Problems with High-Functioning
Clients and Dually Diagnosed Clients   139

Problems Related to Higher-Functioning Clients, 139 /
Problems Related to Clients Who Abuse Drugs or Alcohol, 142 /
Summary, 150

10. Reducing Relapse by Creating a Supportive Environment   152

Recognizing a Stressful Environment, 152 / The Importance of
Family Members and Staff Members in Creating a Supportive
Environment, 154 / Characteristics of Supportive Staff Members
and Family Members, 154 / Characteristics of a Supportive Living
Situation, 158 / Improving Stress Management in the Client's
Environment, 159 / Developing a Social Learning Milieu in a
Residential or Inpatient Program, 163 / Special Considerations
for Family Members, 167 / Summary, 168

II. STEPS FOR TEACHING 48 SPECIFIC
SOCIAL SKILLS: CURRICULAR SKILL SHEETS

Introduction   173

Conversation Skills   177

Listening to Others, 179 / Starting Conversations, 180 /
Maintaining Conversations by Asking Questions, 181 /
Maintaining Conversations by Giving Factual Information, 182 /

Maintaining Conversations by Expressing Feelings, *183* /
Ending Conversations, *184* / Staying on the Topic Set by
Another Person, *185* / What to Do When Someone Goes Off
the Topic, *186* / Getting Your Point Across, *187*

Conflict Management Skills 189

Compromise and Negotiation, *191* / Disagreeing with Another's
Opinion without Arguing, *192* / Responding to Untrue
Accusations, *193* / Leaving Stressful Situations, *194*

Assertiveness Skills 195

Making Requests, *197* / Refusing Requests, *198* / Making
Complaints, *199* / Responding to Complaints, *200* / Expressing
Unpleasant Feelings, *201* / Expressing Angry Feelings, *202* /
Asking for Information, *203* / Making Apologies, *204* / Letting
Someone Know That You Are Afraid, *205* / Refusing Alcohol or
Street Drugs, *206*

Community Living Skills 207

Locating Your Missing Belongings, *209* / What to Do If You
Think Somebody Has Something of Yours, *210* / What to Do
When You Do Not Understand What a Person Is Saying, *211* /
Checking Out Your Beliefs, *212* / Reminding Someone Not to
Spread Germs, *213* / Eating and Drinking Politely, *214*

Friendship and Dating Skills 215

Expressing Positive Feelings, *217* / Giving Compliments, *218* /
Accepting Compliments, *219* / Finding Common Interests, *220* /
Asking Someone for a Date, *221* / Ending a Date, *222* / Expressing
Affection, *223* / Refusing Unwanted Sexual Advances, *224* /
Requesting That Your Partner Use a Condom, *225* / Refusing
Pressure to Engage in High-Risk Sexual Behavior, *226*

Medication Management Skills 227

Making a Doctor's Appointment on the Phone, *229* / Asking
Questions about Medications, *230* / Asking Questions about
Health-Related Concerns, *231*

Vocational/Work Skills 233

Interviewing for a Job, *235* / Asking for Feedback about Job
Performance, *236* / Responding to Criticism, *237* / Following
Verbal Instructions, *238* / Solving Problems, *239* / Joining
Ongoing Conversations at Work, *240*

Epilogue: Tips for Effective Social Skills Training   241

APPENDICES

Appendix A: Materials Useful to Group Leaders   249

Appendix B: Materials Related to Assessment   265

References   279

Index   283

Social Skills Training
for Schizophrenia

I

PRINCIPLES, FORMAT, AND TECHNIQUES FOR SOCIAL SKILLS TRAINING OF CLIENTS WITH SCHIZOPHRENIA

1

Schizophrenia and Social Skills

If asked to define schizophrenia or explain it, you would probably refer to hallucinations and delusions, the prototypical symptoms. But, stop and form an image of a typical patient with schizophrenia. In imagining specific clients and what they are like, you likely think about their appearance and behavior. Even when florid symptomatology is controlled by medication, most individuals with schizophrenia seem a little different, or "off center." It may be difficult to follow their train of thought in a conversation. They may even say some things that sound slightly odd or unrelated to the topic. Their face and voice may be unusually inexpressive, and they may avoid looking at you during the conversation. In fact, you may feel they are not really listening to you. Overall, you are apt to feel a little uncomfortable.

Critical factors that lead to your unease can be subsumed under the rubric of *social skills deficits*. "Social skills" are interpersonal behaviors that are normative and/or socially sanctioned. They include such things as dress and behavior codes, rules about what to say and not to say, and stylistic guidelines about the expression of affect, social reinforcement, interpersonal distance, and so forth. Whether they have never learned social skills or have lost them, most schizophrenia patients have marked skill deficits. These deficits make it difficult for many clients to establish and maintain social relationships, fulfill social roles (e.g., worker, spouse), or to have their needs met.

In this chapter, we present an overview of the behavioral model of social skills and how the model applies to schizophrenia. We describe the specific behaviors that constitute social skills and then discuss other factors that interfere with social behavior in schizophrenia, especially information-processing deficits. We then describe some social situations that are especially difficult for clients with schizophrenia.

The Behavioral Model of Social Skills

Definition of Social Skills

Many definitions of social skills have been developed, but most specific definitions fail to account for the broad array of social behavior.

> Rather than providing a single, global definition of social skill, we prefer a situation-specific conception of social skills. The overriding factor is effectiveness of behavior in social interactions. However, determination of effectiveness depends on the context of the interaction (e.g., returning a faulty appliance, introducing oneself to a prospective date, expressing appreciation to a friend) and, given any context, the parameters of the specific situation (e.g., expression of anger to a spouse, to an employer, or to a stranger). (Hersen & Bellack, 1976, p. 562)

More specifically, social skills involve the

> ability to express both positive and negative feelings in the interpersonal context without suffering consequent loss of social reinforcement. Such skill is demonstrated in a large variety of interpersonal contexts . . . and it involves the coordinated delivery of appropriate verbal and nonverbal responses. In addition, the socially skilled individual is attuned to realities of the situation and is aware when he is likely to be reinforced for his efforts. (Hersen & Bellack, 1976, p. 562)

Two aspects of this definition warrant special mention. First, socially skilled behavior is situationally specific. Few, if any, aspects of interpersonal behavior are universally or invariably appropriate (or inappropriate). Both cultural and situational factors determine social norms. For example, in American society, kissing is sanctioned within families and between lovers, but not between casual acquaintances or in the office. Direct expression of anger is more acceptable within families and toward referees at sporting events than toward an employer. The socially skilled individual must know when, where, and in what form different behaviors are sanctioned. Thus, social skill involves the ability to perceive and analyze subtle cues that define the situation as well as the presence of a repertoire of appropriate responses.

Second, social competence involves the maximization of reinforcement. Marriage, friendship, sexual gratification, employment, service (e.g., in stores, restaurants), and personal rights are all powerful sources of reinforcement that hinge on social skills. The unskilled individual is apt to fail in most or all of these spheres and, consequently, experience anxiety, frustration, and isolation, all of which are especially problematic for schizophrenia patients. Thus, social skills deficits may increase the risk of relapse, whereas enhanced social competence may decrease that risk.

Social Skills and Social Behavior

The following discussion elaborates the elements of the social skills model depicted in Table 1.1. First, interpersonal behavior is based on a distinct set of *skills*. The term "skill" is used to emphasize that social competence is based on a set of *learned* performance abilities, rather than traits, needs, or other "intrapsychic" processes. Conversely, poor social behavior is often the result of social skills deficits. Basic aspects of social are learned in childhood, while more complex behavioral repertoires, such as dating and job interview skills, are acquired in adolescence and young adulthood. It appears as if some elements of social competence, such as the facial expression of affect, are not learned, but are genetically "hard wired" at birth. Nevertheless, research suggests that virtually all social behaviors are *learnable*; that is, they can be modified by experience or training.

As indicated in Table 1.1, social dysfunction results from three circumstances: when the individual does not know how to perform appropriately, when he or she does not use skills in his or her repertoire when they are called for, or when appropriate behavior is undermined by socially inappropriate behavior. The first of these circumstances is especially common in schizophrenia. Individuals with schizophrenia fail to learn appropriate social behaviors for three reasons. First, children who otherwise seem normal but who later develop schizophrenia in adulthood seem to have subtle attention deficits in childhood. These deficits interfere with the development of appropriate social relationships and the acquisition of social skills. Second, schizophrenia often strikes first in late adolescence or young adulthood, a critical period for mastery of adult social roles and skills, such as dating and sexual behaviors, work-related skills, and the ability to form and maintain adult relationships. Many individuals with schizophrenia gradually develop isolated

TABLE 1.1. Social Skills Model

1. Social competence is based on a set of component response skills.
2. These skills are learned or learnable.
3. Social dysfunction results when:
   a. The requisite behaviors are not in the person's behavioral repertoire.
   b. The requisite behaviors are not used at the appropriate time.
   c. The person performs socially inappropriate behaviors.
4. Social dysfunction can be rectified by skills training.

lives, punctuated by lengthy periods in psychiatric hospitals or in community residences. Such events remove clients from their "normal" peer group, provide few opportunities to engage in age-appropriate social roles, and limit social contacts to mental health staff and other severely ill clients. Under such circumstances, clients do not have the opportunity to acquire and practice appropriate adult roles. Moreover, skills mastered earlier in life may be lost because of disuse or lack of reinforcement by the environment.

Other Factors That Affect Social Functioning

Why might a patient not use behaviors that are still in his or her repertoire, as suggested by item 3b in Table 1.1? As indicated in Table 1.2, a number of factors can be expected to influence social behavior in schizophrenia in addition to social skills per se (Bellack & Mueser, 1993).

PSYCHOTIC SYMPTOMS

It should not be surprising that an individual hearing highly intrusive voices, or feeling jeopardized by malevolent forces would be unable to focus on social interactions. Patients can be expected to have difficulty fulfilling social roles and behaving in a socially appropriate manner at the height of acute exacerbations. However, research indicates that schizophrenia patients have marked deficits in social competence even when psychotic symptoms are under control; conversely, many clients can learn more effective ways of inter-

TABLE 1.2. Factors Affecting Social Performance

1. Psychotic symptoms
2. Motivational factors
     Goals
     Expectancies for success and failure
3. Affective states
     Anxiety
     Depression
4. Environmental factors
     Lack of reinforcement for efforts
     Lack of resources
     Social isolation
5. Neurobiological factors
     Information-processing deficits
     Negative symptoms
     Medication side effects

acting even when they have persistent symptoms. Psychotic symptoms may play a limiting role on social performance, but they do not explain the bulk of social disability in this population.

MOTIVATIONAL FACTORS

Many individuals with schizophrenia actively avoid social interactions and appear to have little motivation to develop social relationships. Several factors seem to be involved in this pattern. First, most chronic clients have a history of social failure, rejection, and criticism. As a result, they learn that it may be safer to minimize social interactions than to risk further failure or censure. Second, most clients are engaged in a life-long struggle to find an equilibrium in which they can control their symptoms, limit their experience of negative affect, and maintain the best possible quality of life. While at one level they may desire to have improved social relationships and undertake more demanding social roles, venturing out into the social environment may pose an unmanageable threat.

AFFECTIVE STATES

As indicated above, social interaction often is very anxiety provoking to individuals with schizophrenia and leads to avoidance. Moreover, clients often seek to escape from social interactions initiated by others. Research from our laboratory suggests that clients are particularly sensitive to conflict and criticism and will withdraw from potential conflict situations even when they are being taken advantage of or unjustly accused of things they have not done (Bellack, Mueser, Wade, Sayers, & Morrison, 1992).

ENVIRONMENTAL FACTORS

Three aspects of the environment often make it difficult for schizophrenia patients to use their social skills effectively. First, as their skills tend to be limited, their performance often is odd or imperfect in some way. Unfortunately, many people are not tolerant of idiosyncrasies or social errors and tend to be unsympathetic, impatient, or overtly critical. As a result, clients are not reinforced for their efforts and, in some circumstances, may receive a critical or hostile response. Hence, they tend to become wary of engaging in social interactions. Second, many clients are unemployed and live in harsh economic circumstances. They do not have the resources to participate in social–recreational activities that they might otherwise be able to succeed in and enjoy. Finally, many clients are isolated and do not have good social networks. The illness is stigmatizing, leading others to avoid them. In addition, repeated exacerbations and periods in the hospital disrupt relationships and gradually remove clients from the social environment. Friendships develop from the workplace or school, hobbies, volunteer activities, childrearing, and other activities that individuals with schizophrenia often do not participate in. As a result, social contacts for many clients are limited to other clients, mental health staff, and/or family members.

NEUROBIOLOGICAL FACTORS

Several significant neurobiological factors affect social behavior in schizophrenia. The illness is characterized by significant deficits in information processing: the multiple abilities necessary for thinking, learning, and remembering (Seidman, Cassens, Kremen, & Pepple, 1992). Patients tend to have a variety of problems with attention. They cannot process information as rapidly as others. They have difficulty discriminating important from unimportant stimuli, such as what the interpersonal partner is saying versus voices coming from another conversation or the TV. They have problems concentrating, focusing attention, sustaining attention over time, or focusing in difficult conditions such as when under stress or when presented with a highly complex task. Thus, they may have great difficulty attending to what someone is saying if the person speaks rapidly, presents a lot of complex information, if there are distractions (e.g., other conversations going on in the background), if the person is angry and increasing the patient's level of stress or anxiety, or if the person is providing confusing cues (e.g., subtlety or sarcasm).

Schizophrenia patients also frequently have problems in memory, especially with short-term verbal memory (e.g., what someone said or told them to do) (Mueser, Bellack, Douglas, & Wade, 1991). The problem seems to be less forgetting than in initial learning or accessing information that has been learned (e.g., as when you cannot remember a name). Patients often seem forgetful or distracted, and they may be accused of not paying attention or not caring about important things. In fact, the real problem may be that the information is not presented in a way that adjusts for their attention problems (e.g., slowly, clearly, and with repetition) or that they simply cannot remember what they did hear unless they are provided with reminders or prompts.

A third important information-processing deficit involves higher-level or complex information processing (Gray, Feldon, Rawlins, Hemsley, & Smith, 1991). Patients have trouble in problem solving, in part because they have difficulty drawing abstractions or deducing relationships between events. A related problem involves the ability to draw connections between current and past experience. Whether because they cannot recall past experience, cannot determine when past experience is relevant, or because they simply cannot integrate the diverse processes of memory, attention, and analysis of multiple pieces of information, these individuals have difficulty learning from experience. They also are unable to effectively organize mental efforts, such as initiating and maintaining a plan of action. As a result, their reasoning and problem solving often seem to be disorganized or even random. These various problems are not extreme, such as the memory impairment in Alzheimer's disease, but they can nevertheless disrupt social behavior and the ability to fulfill social roles. The fact that these deficits cause significant problems without their being very noticeable to other people sometimes adds to their negative effects, as family members and others in contact with clients often get frustrated and angry with them when they fail to respond or do things that they appeared to understand (e.g., requests for favors, directions for taking medications). As indicated above, disability is often mistaken for laziness, disrespect, and other undesirable personal attributes.

Another significant neurobiological constraint is negative symptoms (Andreasen, 1982). "Positive symptoms," such as hallucination and delusions, are things that clients experience that normal individuals do not. "Negative symptoms" are things that are deficient compared to normal levels of functioning. Many schizophrenia patients suffer from a variety of such deficits, including avolition and anergia, a generalized lack of motivation, energy, and initiative; anhedonia, an inability to experience pleasure and positive emotions; and alogia, a relative inability to generate conversation. Negative symptoms may result from significant depression or social isolation or from excessive doses of antipsychotic medication. In other cases, they reflect a symptom constellation referred to as the "deficit state," which appears to be a fundamental biological component of the illness. In either case, these symptoms deprive the patient of the motivation and energy to participate in social activity or to enjoy interactions with others. This symptom constellation is one of the most pernicious aspects of the illness and also is the least responsive to medication.

Components of Social Skills

As specified above, social competence is based on a distinct set of component skills (Morrison, 1990). These components can be roughly divided into two broad sets: expressive skills and receptive skills. Table 1.3 provides a list of the most important skills for schizophrenia, including some additional skills that reflect the reciprocal nature of social interaction.

TABLE 1.3. Components of Social Skills

Expressive behaviors
   Speech content
   Paralinguistic features
      Voice volume
      Speech rate
      Pitch
      Intonation
   Nonverbal behaviors
      Eye contact (gaze)
      Posture
      Facial expression
      Proximics
      Kinesics

Receptive behaviors (social perception)
   Attention to and interpretation of relevant cues
   Emotion recognition

Interactive behaviors
   Response timing
   Use of social reinforcers
   Turn taking

Situational factors
   Social "intelligence" (knowledge of social mores and
      demands of the specific situation)

EXPRESSIVE SKILLS

There are three groups or categories of expressive behaviors that contribute to the quality of social performance: verbal behaviors, paralinguistic behaviors, and nonverbal behaviors. "Verbal behavior" refers to what we say: the form, structure, content, and amount of words we emit. Socially skilled individuals are easy to understand. They use vocabulary and sentence structure that are sensible to their audience. Conversely, many schizophrenia patients are difficult to follow, in part because they use language in an odd or confusing manner. They may use common words to mean something very idiosyncratic, use neologisms (words that are not real words), or use sentence structure that omits key elements (e.g., conjunctions), making it difficult for the listener to discern the meaning of what is being said. Moreover, many schizophrenia patients have a paucity of relevant and "interesting" things to say. They often do not work or go to school, they do not read newspapers or attend to current events, and they live relatively restricted lives. Hence, even if they have the desire to converse, they may not have a repertoire of things to talk about. Their conversation may also be dominated by their personal concerns, such as bizarre physical symptoms or delusions.

The manner in which one speaks and presents oneself may be as important as what one says. The term "paralinguistic" refers to characteristics of the voice during speech, including volume, pace, and intonation and pitch. Speech that is very fast is difficult to understand; speech that is very soft may be difficult to hear; speech that is very slow, very loud, or monotonic (as in monotonous) is unpleasant to listen too. High-pitched (e.g., shrill) voices may also be annoying, especially as the volume increases. Speech dysfluencies (e.g., "uh" or "um," stutters) and lengthy pauses may also make it difficult or unpleasant for the listener. These voice and speech characteristics are important for interpreting meaning, as well as for the listener's interest and enjoyment. For example, pace, volume, and intonation are especially important in communicating affect or emotion. Flattened tone, slow pace, and low volume often reflect boredom, depression, or fatigue, but they may also signal a romantic intention (e.g., a slow, deep, sultry voice quality). Loud volume (e.g., "raising one's voice") is associated with anger. Rapid pace and high pitch can reflect excitement or fear. Changes in these characteristics are also important in signaling meaning and feelings. For example, increasing loudness can be used to emphasize a point. Schizophrenia, especially the deficit syndrome, is frequently marked by a relatively monotonic voice quality and slow rate of speech that is unpleasant for the listener and is difficult to interpret. Conversely, excited states can result in pressured, high-pitched speech that is very difficult to follow.

Nonverbal behavior also affects one's interpersonal impact. Facial expression is, perhaps, the primary cue to emotional state: smiling, frowning, grimacing, glowering, and other expressions are substantially reflexive correlates of our mood and feelings. Subtle changes in the muscles around the mouth and eyes signal annoyance, curiosity, surprise, pleasure, or any number of other emotional reactions to what the speaker is saying or doing. The eyes have often been regarded as the primary "window to the soul." Good "eye contact" is associated with strength, authority, anger, and truthfulness. Lovers will look deeply into one another's eyes. Conversely, "shifty" eyes or avoidance of eye contact is thought to reflect anxiety, discomfort, or dishonesty. Wide-open eyes and dilated pupils can signal heightened interest or fear, while narrowed eyes and contracted pupils are associated with suspiciousness, annoyance, or anger. The eyes also play an important role in the flow of conversation. Typically, the speaker looks directly toward the listener's eyes, and the listener moves his or her gaze around the speaker's face. When the speaker is ready to pause and shift the floor to the listener, he or she breaks off eye contact; similarly, the listener wanting to speak tries to "catch" the speaker's eye to signal the desire for a floor shift. Schizophrenia patients tend to be gaze-avoidant. They are uncomfortable in social situations, and seem to be especially sensitive to maintaining eye contact. Of course, paranoid patients may present with an unblinking stare that makes the listener uncomfortable or even fearful.

Posture may denote feelings, interest, and authority. A relaxed posture signals comfort, whereas muscular tension (e.g., balled fist, pursed lips, forward lean) signifies arousal or tension. Similarly, leaning forward while speaking or listening is associated with interest and attention, whereas leaning away may reflect fear or distaste. The latter stance is characteristic of many clients with schizophrenia, who are uncomfortable in social interactions. "Proximics," a related behavioral category, refers to the distance between people during their interactions. There are fairly clear, albeit unwritten, cultural rules for the comfortable and appropriate distance between two people during conversations. The acceptable distances vary according to the nature of the relationship and gender, as well as across cultures. For example, familial and romantic relationships allow closer contact than is permitted between employer and employee, especially when they are of opposite sex. Strangers or casual acquaintances are expected to remain further apart than friends, although the acceptable distances shorten in crowded subway cars or elevators. A male patient who got as close to a female staff member in an office or on the ward as in a crowded elevator would be perceived as threatening and displaying inappropriate behavior; conversely, if the same staff member approached him to take his blood pressure, the interaction would be entirely acceptable. As previously indicated, many schizophrenia patients are uncomfortable in close interpersonal situations and maintain inappropriately large interpersonal distances. Some paranoid clients may be sufficiently threatened to act out when their "personal space" is violated.

These diverse behavioral elements identified above are each important by themselves, but their impact and interpretation generally are a function of their relationship to one another. When the different components are consistent with one another, they serve to reinforce the speaker's message, as when someone says, "I am angry" in a loud and slow voice, makes direct eye contact with the listener, and has a tense posture with balled fist, clenched teeth, and a forward lean. Conversely, when someone says, "I'm not afraid of you," in a rapid and tremulous voice, avoids eye contact, trembles, and leans backward, the verbal content must be interpreted in light of these inconsistent paralinguistic and nonverbal cues.

RECEPTIVE SKILLS

Regardless of the individual's ability to emit socially skillful responses, he or she cannot be effective without accurate perception of the social situation. The socially skillful individual attends to the interpersonal partner, analyzes the situation, and knows when, where, and how to structure his or her response. This combination of attention, analysis, and knowledge is generally referred to as social perception. Not surprisingly, individuals with schizophrenia are thought to have particular difficulty in this area. First, as previously discussed, they have significant difficulties in attention. Effective social perception requires the person to detect a rapidly changing series of facial expressions, verbal content with shifting intonation, and subtle gestural and postural changes. Schizophrenia patients may not be able to pick up all of the relevant cues provided by the partner. In addition, accurate interpretation of these various cues requires the individual to integrate the diverse pieces of information, remember them, be able to integrate current information with previous experience (e.g., does Susan express anger directly, or does she do it indirectly by talking more slowly, looking slightly tense, and calling you "John" instead of "Johnny"?), and abstract the crux of the communication by differentiating important and unimportant details. These are all capacities that are limited in schizophrenia.

In addition, it has been suggested that clients with schizophrenia have a specific deficit in the ability to perceive emotions, especially negative emotions such as anger and sadness (Bellack, Blanchard, & Mueser, 1996). This difficulty is thought to be the result of a specific neurological impairment, akin to receptive aphasia for language or agnosia that prevents the interpretation of visual images. The data on this point are somewhat inconsistent, but the clinician should be attuned to the possibility that an individual client who has difficulty interpreting other peoples' feelings may have a specific, inherited deficit that interferes with the decoding of affect cues.

Social skills depend on the effective use of the constellation of specific elements discussed above, but they are not the simple sum of these molecular behaviors. Rather, the ability to communicate and interact effectively is the result of the smooth integration of these behaviors over time, along with ancillary characteristics such as grooming and hygiene. In essence, the whole is greater than the sum of the parts. Moreover, as discussed in the context of our definition of social skill, social behavior is situationally specific. Each situation presents special demands and constraints, and many situations have specific rules that must be mastered. For example, dealing with a high-pressure car salesman may require a false bravado and less candor than is desirable in most other situations. Similarly, effective performance on a job interview demands a style of behavior that would be very difficult to maintain in everyday interactions and would not be appropriate in informal interactions with peers. We refer to these discrete areas of skill as "behavioral repertoires." Skills training programs involve development of curricula to teach one or more of these repertoires depending on the needs of the specific group of clients and the amount of time available. This issue is elaborated in subsequent chapters; Part II provides an extensive set of such curricula. For illustrative purposes, in the remainder of this chapter, we highlight a few repertoires that we have found to be particularly important for schizophrenia patients: (1) conversational skills; (2) social perception skills; and (3) special problem situations. Remediation strategies for these repertoires are discussed in subsequent chapters.

CONVERSATIONAL SKILLS

The ability to initiate, maintain, and terminate a conversation is central to almost every social interaction. Conversational skill is not simply the ability to engage in repartee at cocktail parties, but the basic medium of communication for interactions as simple as asking directions, ordering in a restaurant, and saying "Thank you" for a simple favor. Conversational skills involve verbal and nonverbal responses employed in (1) starting conversations, (2) maintaining conversations, and (3) ending conversations. We describe first the verbal components, which differ most across the three areas.

A relatively circumscribed repertoire of specific verbal responses can be sufficient for starting and ending most conversations. Responses for initiation include (1) simple greetings, such as "Hi" and "Good morning"; (2) facilitating remarks and open-ended questions, such as "How are you today?", "I haven't seen you in a while, what's new?", "Isn't today a beautiful [miserable] day?", and "Did you listen to the ball game yesterday?"; and (3) remarks for entering ongoing conversations, such as "Mind if I join you?" and " Are you talking about the game [show, etc.] last night?" Ending a conversation or leaving a group is frequently an awkward process, and many chronic clients either leave abruptly or continue ad infinitum. Concluding statements include "I have to go; see you later," "What time is it? I have to meet someone," and "It was nice talking with you. See you tomorrow." Of course, social perception skills (see below) are required to ensure that entry and exit are smooth and appropriately timed.

A somewhat more complex set of skills is required to maintain a conversation effectively and to promote satisfactory and reinforcing relationships. One basic requirement is the ability to ask appropriate questions that facilitate a response by the interpersonal partner and/or secure relevant information. The socially skilled individual generally has two types of questioning strategies at his or her disposal. Open-ended questions serve primarily as response facilitators. Examples include "How are you doing?", "What's new?", "What did you think of the game [show, meeting, etc.] yesterday?", and "Do you really think so?" Frequently, the questioner is less interested in the specific answer to such questions than in the general conversation that follows. Specific information is more effectively secured by close-ended questions, such as: "What was the score of the game yesterday?", "What did you eat last night?", and "Would you like to go downstairs for lunch now?" The individual must also be able to differentiate these two types of questions when they are directed at him or her so as to make an appropriate response. Consider the following reply to the greeting "Hi, what have you been doing?": "Well, I bought a pack of cigarettes this morning, then I went to my group, then I had a hamburger for lunch, and I just went to the bathroom." While this response might ordinarily be ascribed to a schizophrenia patient's "concreteness," it could more profitably be viewed as a manifestation of social skill deficit.

Another factor that is critical for maintaining interactions is periodic reinforcement of the interpersonal partner. Brief interactions can be effectively enacted with an exchange of greetings and/or information, but these minimal responses are not sufficient to maintain longer interactions or to facilitate the development of continuing relationships. Conversational reinforcers include statements of agreement (e.g., "Yeah, you're right," "I agree with you"), approval ("That's a good idea," "I never thought of that, you're right"). Simple verbal facilitators such as "Yeh," "Uh-huh," and "Mm-hmm" have also been shown to have significant reinforcing value. The quality of social interactions is also improved by the appropriate use of social amenities such as "Please," "Thank you," and "Excuse me." The experienced clinician will likely be aware of both the relative infrequency with which most chronic clients emit either reinforcement of amenities and the rather sterile nature of their conversational style.

There are a number of nonverbal response elements that substantially contribute to socially skillful behavior:

1. Eye contact should be maintained intermittently, interspersed by gazing in the direction of the partner. Both constant eye contact (i.e., staring) and the absence of eye contact are generally inappropriate.
2. Voice volume should approximate a "conversational" level, neither too loud nor too low.
3. Voice tone should not be monotonic, but should employ inflection to communicate emphasis, affect, and so on.
4. Response latency to input from the interpersonal partner should generally be brief (see also discussion of timing below). Mediators such as "Let me think about that," and "Hmm" can be employed when a response must be contemplated.
5. Speech rate should coincide with normative conversational style.
6. Speech dysfluencies should be at a minimum.
7. Physical gestures such as head nods, hand movements (for emphasis), and forward leaning all add to the qualitative impact of the individual.
8. Smiles, frowns, and other facial gestures should be employed in conjunction with verbal content.

9. Physical distance should be maintained according to preferred social norms.
10. Posture should be relaxed, rather than wooden.

These response elements undoubtedly have differential importance in different situations. At present, there are no clear data on their comparative contribution to social effectiveness or on the relative importance of the nonverbal and verbal response components. However, it seems likely that they combine to create a "gestalt" impression and that anomalous performance of any of the nonverbal elements (e.g., staring, extremely low voice volume) would have deleterious effects on social interactions.

SOCIAL PERCEPTION SKILLS

Good conversational behavior also requires effective social perception skills. The most relevant social perception skills for chronic clients fall into five general categories: (1) listening; (2) getting clarification; (3) relevance; (4) timing; and (5) identifying emotions.

Listening or attending to the interpersonal partner is the most fundamental requirement for accurate social perception. Many chronic clients exhibit poor interpersonal behavior precisely because their focus of attention is primarily internal, and only intermittently and selectively directed outward. Consequently, they fail to secure sufficient accurate information to make an appropriate response, and they cannot emit social facilitators or reinforcers.

Even if the individual is an adept listener, he or she will periodically "tune out" for brief periods and/or occasionally be confused or uncertain about the message being communicated. The skillful individual can identify this confusion, and will seek *clarification*. Failure either to perceive confusion or to resolve it frequently results in breakdown of the subsequent communication process and the emission of inappropriate responses. Clarification can be secured with such statements as "Excuse me, but I didn't hear that," "I don't understand," and "I'm not sure what you mean (what you're asking, etc.)" A related and somewhat more subtle skill is perception of confusion on the part of the interpersonal partner. Confusion is often communicated by "quizzical" or "vacant" looks, which may include cocking the head to the side, furrowing of forehead and eyebrows, contraction of the pupils, and cessation of social reinforcers (e.g., head nods, and "mm-hmms"). By perceiving the partner's confusion, the skillful individual can avoid noncommunicative rambling.

In order to be appropriate, a response must be *relevant* to the conversation as a whole, as well as to the immediately preceding communication.

Chronic clients are frequently irrelevant in their persistent references to personal problems and family members. Determining relevance is primarily a function of listening to and analysis of the communications. However, relevance can also be increased by self-censoring, such that certain content areas or discrete responses are not emitted in certain types of interactions (or conversely, are allowed only in certain interactions). For example, complaints about ill health, references to idiosyncratic experiences (e.g., hallucinations), and discussion of toileting and sexual behavior are customarily inappropriate other than in conversations with health service providers, family, and close friends.

Timing involves performance of responses at appropriate points in an interaction, as well as with appropriate latency. Effective social interaction involves ebb and flow, including both rapid exchanges and silences. Certain activities and emotional states (e.g., grief) also affect social appropriateness. The content of the conversation and social norms are the primary determinants of appropriate timing, and thus, knowledge of social rules is essential for proper timing. Poor timing is exemplified by interruptions, long latencies to simple close-ended questions, leaving an interaction before some resolution is reached (e.g., ignoring requests for delay such as "Let me finish this first" or "Let me think about that").

The final aspect of social perception involves accurate *perception of emotion*. Emotion is frequently communicated by a subtle combination of verbal and nonverbal cues (most people are not sufficiently assertive to communicate their emotions with clear, direct statements). Given that the emotional status of the interpersonal partner is a critical factor in determining an appropriate response, the socially skilled individual must be able to "read" emotional cues. Minimally, this entails perceiving changes in the nature of the partner's behavior; however, discrimination of emotional states is also necessary. In addition, the skillful individual is able to identify his or her own emotional states, transmit them accurately, and analyze their cause. Such personal perception and analysis enhance accurate communication and are necessary for effective resolution of conflict and distress.

ADDITIONAL PROBLEM SITUATIONS

An individual possessing the full range of conversational and perceptual skills described above will be effective in most social situations. However, some interactions are especially difficult to complete because they are anxiety-provoking or stressful, require great subtlety and nuance, or because they are infrequently encountered. While an exhaustive list of such situations cannot be supplied, there are a number of situations that we have found to be problematic for a great proportion of chronic clients.

Assertiveness Skills

One of the most frequently encountered deficits is inappropriate assertion skill. There are generally considered to be two forms of assertion. Hostile or negative assertion involves the expression of negative feelings, standing up for one's rights, and refusing unreasonable demands. Examples of appropriate negative assertion include returning food (in a restaurant) or merchandise that is unsatisfactory or damaged; standing up to an authority figure (police officer, employer, teacher) who is treating you unfairly or inappropriately; requesting an intruder to get to the back of a line or wait his or her turn at a store counter; and expressing justified anger or annoyance to a repairman who has done faulty work or caused unreasonable delay. Commendatory or positive assertion consists of expression of positive emotions: affection, approval, appreciation, and agreement. This includes, for example, warmly thanking a friend for doing a favor; kissing a spouse and verbalizing affectionate feelings; telling a friend (employee, child, etc.) that he or she has done a really good job; and complimenting someone on his or her appearance, improvement, and so on.

Individuals with schizophrenia tend to avoid or escape from situations in which they may be criticized or in which there may be conflict. The result is that they frequently are taken advantage of. In addition, they often face increased criticism from frustrated family members or mental health staff for failing to deal directly with difficult issues. Appropriate assertiveness is one of the most critical skills for chronic patients to learn in order to avoid and reduce distress and avoid mistreatment. Positive assertion is similarly important for them to be able to develop and sustain friendships. Assertiveness skills, along with conversational skills, are the most common focus of skill training programs.

Heterosocial Skills

In addition to the general conversational and perceptual skills described above, there are a variety of special demands and social norms that pertain to dating, romantic, or sexual interactions. Comparable skills are needed by clients who wish to develop same sex-romantic and sexual relationships. Grooming, cleanliness, social amenities, social reinforcement, and positive assertion are of special importance. Dating etiquette (e.g., telephone calls, planning, and engaging in social activities) must be observed. Finally, the individual must have information about sexual functioning, be somewhat sophisticated about how to make and respond to sexual overtures, and know how to perform sexually to maximize pleasure and minimize discomfort. In addition, all clients need to learn about safe sex practices, including the use of condoms and how to avoid or resist unwanted or dangerous sexual encounters. Assertion skills targeted on condom use and saying "No" are especially important for female clients, who are particularly vulnerable to manipulation and abuse by male acquaintances. Education about HIV and AIDS should be a standard part of any skills curriculum with clients who are sexually active or may otherwise be at risk.

Independent Living Skills

While many clients are unable to compete for employment or even hold jobs in sheltered workshop settings, *job interview skills* are needed by those who are able to look for work. These skills include how to present oneself positively; how to answer questions about experience and abilities; how to ask questions about salary, working conditions, and so forth; and such associated behaviors as grooming, tardiness, and the like. Dealing with one's psychiatric history and long periods of unemployment is particularly important. Clients need to be taught what information *not* to disclose about their history and symptoms, as well as what should be disclosed and how to disclose this information in the most positive light possible. Many clients experience difficulty in making *satisfactory living arrangements*. Issues here include: how to find an apartment; how to speak with a landlord (e.g., what to ask, how to discuss rent); how to make arrangements with a roommate (e.g., sharing rent and chores, visitors); and how to interact with neighbors. A related set of topics, which may or may not be appropriate for social skills training, involves activities of daily living (ADLs), including cooking and grocery shopping, managing money, and using public transportation. Although such training often is covered in vocational rehabilitation, the social skills training technology is particularly effective for teaching these nonsocial skills.

Medication Management

A critical factor in poor posthospitalization adjustment and relapse is failure to follow the prescribed medication regimen. It is our contention that an important factor in this regard is faulty communication between the client and the health service provider. Thus, the client might not effectively communicate about side effects and inconsistent usage or might fail to comprehend the physician's treatment plan or the need to continue with medication. We believe that interacting with health service personnel is a specific social skill and that treatment compliance can be increased if clients are able to communicate their concerns, reactions, expectations, and desires effectively. These various behaviors are referred to as medication management skills, and they include education about medication, its importance, side effects, and so forth, as well as specific conversational and assertiveness skills needed to discuss questions and concerns effectively with physicians and nursing staff (Eckman et al., 1992).

Summary

This chapter has provided an introduction and overview of the social skills model. We defined social skills and gave a detailed description of the elements of social behavior. Expressive skills include verbal behavior, paralinguistic behavior, and nonverbal behavior. Receptive skills, referred to as social perception, refer to the ability to attend to and interpret the cues provided by an interpersonal partner. We also discussed factors that interfere with appropriate social behavior and prevent clients from using skills in their repertoires, including significant deficits in information processing, positive and negative symptoms, motivation and affect, and environmental constraints. Finally, we described some of the basic repertoires that comprise effective social performance, including conversation skill, assertiveness, and skills needed in special situations, such as sexual skills and job interview skills. This material was designed to provide an orientation to the rest of the book, which will discuss the assessment and treatment of social skill deficits. As the reader will see, the basic building blocks and constraints to effective performance introduced in this chapter will be referred to in every subsequent chapter in the volume.

2

Assessment of Social Skills

As indicated in Chapter 1, most clients with schizophrenia have some deficits in social skills and social role functioning. However, there is considerable variability among clients in the precise nature and severity of these deficits. Patients with the deficit syndrome or who suffer from long-term, chronic illness may have broad-based, profound limitations that are readily apparent after a brief conversation. In most other cases, skill deficits are relative. That is, clients retain some skills and are able to perform adequately, albeit not at normative levels, in some situations. Or, they may have more notable deficits in one response domain (e.g., facial and verbal expressiveness) than in others. Younger clients and those with less severe forms of the illness may have fairly good skills and only need refinement in particular problem areas (e.g., explaining their inconsistent work history on job interviews). Hence, it is particularly important to conduct a systematic skills assessment before instituting any treatment. We also feel strongly that some reassessment should be conducted during and after treatment in order to determine the effectiveness of the intervention and appraise the need for continued treatment and/or modification of the training program (e.g., if it is not working!). This chapter provides a blueprint for conducting social skill assessments. We focus here on cost-efficient assessment in the clinic setting, as many other sources are available that discuss the more costly and sensitive techniques employed in research protocols. The process is conceptualized as a funnel in which the clinician first gathers general information (e.g., Does the client have a problem in social role functioning? In what situations? Does it result from a social skills deficit?) and then develops a more detailed picture of the client's skills and skill deficits. The more general questions can best be addressed by interviewing the client and significant others in his or her environment. The more detailed evaluation depends on systematic observation. We first discuss some general issues, and then highlight interview methods and behavioral observation of role playing, the strategies we have found most useful.

General Issues

In assessing a client's social skills, the clinician must answer four questions (Bellack & Morrison, 1982):

1. Does the client manifest some dysfunctional interpersonal behavior?
2. What are the specific circumstances (i.e., situations) in which the dysfunction occurs?
3. What is the (probable) source of the dysfunction (i.e., Does it result from a skill deficit)?
4. What specific social skills deficits does the client have?

These questions are ordered hierarchically, from initial and most general to final and most specific. The answers to each of the first three questions determine whether or not the subsequent questions need be answered, and if so, how they must be examined (e.g., the specific situations in which response elements should be assessed). Of course, in the clinical setting, two or more questions may be answered simultaneously, as when a male client reports not knowing how to meet and talk with women.

Question 1: Does the client manifest some dysfunctional interpersonal behavior? The first question is the most general and may not require specific assessment. The customary clinical evaluation and general observation conducted in most psychiatric settings will often be sufficient to make a cursory identification of clients with some social dysfunction. The clinician and clinical staff need only be attuned to interpersonal behavior and have some conception of the range of normative functioning. Of course, the more severe and generalized the deficit, the easier it will be to answer this question. As suggested above, some higher-functioning clients may not be impaired in casual and low-stress interactions with clinicians, but they may have deficits in specific community situations, or their skills may break down in stressful or demanding situations.

Question 2: What are the specific circumstances in which the dysfunction occurs? As with all other behavior, social skills are situationally specific. For example, chronic psychiatric patients have been shown to be differentially assertive with male and female individuals, with familiar and unfamiliar people, and in situations requiring hostile and commendatory assertion (Hersen, Bellack, & Turner, 1978). The particular situations in which deficits appear will naturally differ across individuals. More importantly, the specific deficits (i.e., response elements) will vary not only across individuals, but across situations for any one individual. Consequently, once it is determined that there is some interpersonal dysfunction, the situations in which the dysfunction is manifested must be identified.

Question 3: What is the (probable) source of the dysfunction? As indicated in Chapter 1, many of the interpersonal difficulties of chronic clients result from social skills deficits, but there are other sources for such dysfunction. Most notably, interpersonal anxiety can inhibit social functioning even though adequate skills are present, depression can reduce the amount and the quality of behavioral output in social situations, and a history of social failure may serve as a disincentive to engage in anything more than minimal interactions. Given that the purpose of assessment is to plan treatment, it must be ascertained whether or not there is some skill deficit in order to determine whether social skills training (or some other intervention) is the appropriate intervention.

It should be emphasized that skills deficits and factors such as anxiety, depression, and disinterest are orthogonal rather than mutually exclusive. For example, consider the conceptual relationship between interpersonal anxiety and social skills deficit portrayed in Figure 2.1. An individual falling in Box A would have low skill and low anxiety; social skills training would be the treatment of choice. Box B represents low anxiety and high skill (i.e., no dysfunction), and no treatment would be necessary. Box C depicts high anxiety and low skill. Social skills training would be needed in order to remediate the skills deficit. While skills training generally helps reduce anxiety by increasing feelings of self-efficacy about social competence, a supplemental anxiety-reduction strategy might also be required if the person was too anxious to try out his new social skills. Box D represents high anxiety and high skill. An individual with this profile would require an anxiety-reduction intervention. Social skills training might be a useful adjunct to increase feelings of self-efficacy, but skills development would not be the primary focus of treatment.

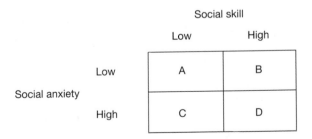

FIGURE 2.1. The relationship between social skill and social anxiety.

Question 4: What specific social skills deficits does the client have? If (a) an interpersonal dysfunction is observed, and (b) the situational determinants are identified, and (c) the dysfunction appears to be associated with a social skills deficit, then (d) the specific parameters of the deficit(s) must be isolated. These include the verbal and nonverbal response elements described in Chapter 1. As might be apparent, this is the most difficult aspect of social skills assessment and requires the most detailed analysis of behavior. Whereas the first three questions can often be answered by interview and informal observation techniques, this question almost invariably requires some systematic observation of the client engaging in a relevant social interaction.

Interviewing Techniques

Interviewing is among the most useful and cost-efficient assessment techniques. It can provide the clinician with a quick "snapshot" of the client, provide information that is otherwise unavailable, and help to differentiate the reasons for poor social performance. Three general categories of information can be secured by interview: (1) interpersonal history, (2) informal observational data, and (3) the perspective of significant others in the client's environment (e.g., parents, staff at a community residence or group home).

The Interpersonal History

The interpersonal history is a retrospective picture about the client's current and past levels of social competence, satisfaction, interests, and motivation. Of special importance is the client's report of situational factors affecting interpersonal competence: where, when, with whom, and under what circumstances do difficulties arise? In addition, the interview can reveal whether the client has ever been able to do something he or she no longer does. Interviewing for interpersonal history can be structured around the clinician's specific knowledge about the individual and his or her difficulties, as well as general sophistication about social skills. Preferred interview style consists of asking somewhat general questions, followed by successively more specific questions, and ending with specific examples. Individuals with schizophrenia also tend to be loath to admit to difficulties, so the interviewer must focus on specific events rather than the person's subjective appraisal of his or her own competence. For example, questions such as "Do you argue much at home?" are apt to be less productive than the following sequence:

1. "Can you remember the last time you had an argument with someone at home?"
   a. "When was that?"
   b. "Can you describe the situation for me?"
   c. "What exactly did you say?"
   d. "Is that usually what happens when you argue with her?"
2. "Can you remember an argument you had recently with someone
   else?"
   a. "When was that?"
   b. "What were you arguing about?"
   c. "What exactly did you say?"

As with any self-report data secured from schizophrenia clients, information gathered in this fashion is potentially incomplete and inaccurate. In
addition to such factors as incomplete observation of the original event and
distorted recall, social perception deficits can obscure important data. For example, if the client cannot properly identify anger, he or she cannot report
accurately on the occurrence and adequacy of hostile assertion. The person
is also likely to be unable to recognize his or her own inappropriate behavior
or unwilling to report it. In any case, data secured in this manner are typically adequate (and vital) for generating initial hypotheses about the nature of
interpersonal dysfunction.

Observational Data

The interviewing process is itself an interpersonal interaction and, as such, is
a valuable source of observational data. On a general level, the interviewer
can appraise his or her own subjective reaction to the client. How easy is the
client to talk with? How comfortable/uncomfortable does he or she make the
interviewer feel? Can rapport be established and with how much difficulty?
Is the individual likable? The interview also provides a sample of the client's
level of verbal and nonverbal skills and interpersonal sensitivity (i.e., social
perception skills, social intelligence). How is the client's eye contact? Does
he or she provide social reinforcers? Does he or she maintain appropriate interpersonal distance? How is his or her conversational timing (e.g., pauses
and turn taking). Although the clinician will ordinarily assess these responses
in a nonsystematic and subjective manner, standardized interviews can be
conducted and audio- or videotaped for subsequent objective ratings.

We have repeatedly emphasized that social skills are situationally specific. The generalizability of behavior during an interview might, thus, be limited. Similarly, problems in other specific situations (e.g., heterosocial, assertion) might not be apparent during an interview. However, the more severe

the deficits, the more likely they are to be manifested across situations. Furthermore, knowledge that the client is able to make appropriate responses in at least one situation (e.g., the interview) is important in treatment planning and suggests a positive prognosis (i.e., the deficit is circumscribed).

The Perspective of Significant Others

Another source of information about the client's social functioning can be provided by interviewing significant figures in the client's environment: parents, spouse, children, roommate, residential staff, and so on. The data provided by such individuals are also potentially biased and inaccurate, but they typically provide a more objective perspective than the client does him- or herself. In addition, observation of these individuals (by the interviewer) can provide valuable input about an important segment of the client's social environment (e.g., Can the environment provide social reinforcement? Will the environment tolerate change? Does the environment model inappropriate behavior?). Interview techniques for collaterals parallel interviewing of the client. Subjective impressions and general statements should be eschewed in favor of specific reports and descriptions.

Behavioral Observation of Role Playing

Self-reports and interviews with either the client or collaterals provide *indirect* evidence about social behavior and social skill. Such evidence can provide a good general picture of the client, but it always has limited fidelity and reliability. That is, most individuals do not observe themselves or other people carefully enough or objectively enough to give detailed, accurate reports. The only way to determine precisely what the client does and does not do in specific situations is to collect *direct* evidence by observing the person in the environment. Unfortunately, direct observation is impractical in most clinical and research settings, especially when the target behavior occurs infrequently (e.g., defending oneself when treated unfairly) or in private (e.g., sexual interactions). The best strategy for dealing with this constraint is to have the client role play in simulated interactions that mimic the natural environment. Role playing is the most widely used strategy for assessing social skill (Bellack, Morrison, Mueser, Wade, & Sayers, 1990). Many variations have been developed, but all essentially follow the same basic plan:

1. A hypothetical social situation is described to the client.
2. The client is asked to imagine that he or she is actually in the situa-

tion and interact with a staff member who will play the role of the other person in the hypothetical interaction.

3. The interaction continues for a time period that might last from 30 second to 10 minutes, depending on what is being assessed.

4. After the designated time period or a fixed number of responses have been exchanged, additional situations are presented in the same manner.

5. The interactions are audiotaped or videotaped to allow detailed ratings of specific behaviors at a later date.

Table 2.1 contains examples of brief role-play scenes and standardized confederate responses. The content and prompts can be varied in any manner desired. There are two general guidelines: (1) scenes should be highly relevant to the clients being assessed; and (2) they should be moderately difficult. Generally, it is not useful to make a role play into a stress test by having the role-play partner be very hostile or critical. In addition, it is useful to begin a role-play assessment with one or two very easy practice scenes, which allow the client to adapt to the role-play format. These items also indicate whether or not the client understands the procedure and can get into role, or if additional instructions are needed.

The most difficult aspect of role-play tests is the objective rating of the client's behavior. It is important to define target behaviors carefully and develop rating procedures that accurately reflect the client's performance *and* that can be rated reliably. For most clinical purposes four to six rating cate-

---

TABLE 2.1. Two Sample Situations from a Role-Play Test

---

1. You have broken a vase belonging to your roommate. It was an accident, but you are blamed for breaking it.

   STAFF MEMBER: Did you break my vase?
   SUBJECT: . . .
   STAFF MEMBER: How can you be so clumsy?
   SUBJECT: . . .
   STAFF MEMBER: You can't be trusted around any of my things.
   SUBJECT: . . .

2. You haven't done laundry for a while, and dirty clothes are piled up in your room. Your mother comments on the mess.

   STAFF MEMBER: Haven't you done laundry for a while?
   SUBJECT: . . .
   STAFF MEMBER: How can you live in this filthy mess?
   SUBJECT: . . .
   STAFF MEMBER: Boy, are you lazy [to have let it pile up like this in the first place].
   SUBJECT: . . .

---

gories should suffice. Several should reflect overall or integrated evalua-
tions, such as Overall Social Skill, Overall Conversational Ability, or Overall Assertiveness. These categories are best rated on 5-point Likert-type
scales. Table 2.2 provides examples of behavioral definitions and the associated Likert scales. Specific behaviors such as eye contact, social reinforcers,
and refusal skills can be rated as occur/nonoccur (i.e., used social reinforcers or did not use social reinforcers), or with Likert scales. Table 2.3
contains examples of these types of ratings. Occur/nonoccur ratings are
much easier to rate reliably and will generally suffice for clinical assessments.

TABLE 2.2. Examples of Likert Scale Ratings

Overall Social Skill

Overall Social Skill (OSS) is a general measure of the subject's social competence. It
subsumes all of the other variables we code, including verbal, nonverbal, and
paralinguistic elements. The person with good social skill is easy to understand,
responds smoothly (e.g., no lengthy pauses or talk overs), and does not engage in
disconcerting behavior. He or she seems to be comfortable or confident in the
situation, even if it is difficult. Affective tone is appropriate and not excessive. The
person is task oriented, but he or she appears to be sensitive to social cues emitted by
the partner and is able to modify his or her behavior when necessary.

OSS is scored on a 5-point scale:

1	2	3	4	5
Very poor social skill	Poor social skill	Neither good nor poor social skill	Good social skill	Very good social skill

Overall Anxiety

Overall Anxiety (OAnx) reflects the subject's general level of anxiety, nervousness,
tension, or discomfort in the situation. Anxiety is reflected in verbal content,
paralinguistic aspects of communication (e.g., speech dysfluencies, stutters,
tremulousness of voice), and nonverbal behavior (motoric tension, "nervous
gestures," body sway or trembling, foot tapping). Nonverbal manifestations of anxiety
are often difficult to distinguish from akathisia (especially when the latter is reflected
in foot tapping, leg bouncing, or hand movements). Do not score such nonverbal
responses if they are not accompanied by verbal or paralinguistic cues. If in doubt,
get confirmation from other sources (e.g., medical record).

OAnx is scored on a 5-point scale:

1	2	3	4	5
Extreme anxiety	Much anxiety	Moderate anxiety	Minimal anxiety	No anxiety

TABLE 2.3. Examples of Behaviors Rated as Occur/Nonoccur

1.1. Expression of Positive Valence: (PV)

Definition: Verbal content expressing feelings of positive valence (e.g., admiration, approval, gratitude or appreciation for some aspect of another person's behavior or manner).

Example: "It's nice to have you at our family affair. I like it when you dress up."

1.2. Positive Affect (PA)

Definition: Positive affective displays with or without specific content.

Example: Laughs, affectionate physical gestures, smiles.

2.1. Negative Valance (NV)

Definition: Verbal content expressing feelings of negative valence (e.g., dissatisfaction, disapproval, or displeasure in regard to the other person's behavior).

Example: "It makes me feel bad when you don't spend time with me. I didn't like the way you did that."

2.2. Negative Affect (NA)

Definition: Negative affect or affective tone with or without explicit verbal content.

Example: Cries, sighs in exasperation, expletives, snarls.

Brief role-play scenes provide information about the client's basic skill capacity: Can he or she emit an adequate verbal response to a simple social stimulus or problem, and does he or she have at least a minimal repertoire of nonverbal and paralinguistic skills? This type of assessment does not indicate how well the client can sustain an interaction or deal with a resistant partner. However, this approach has a number of advantages. It is easy to develop new scenes for specific problem situations, and clients can be presented with 8 to 12 different situations in a relatively brief amount of time. Such brief interactions are particularly useful with very impaired clients, who are unable to sustain long interactions. Brief role plays (like all forms of simulated assessment) do not necessarily reflect *in vivo* behavior, as they tend to be easier than the give-and-take of most real-life conversations; but, they are useful nonetheless, as they provide an excellent measure of behavioral capacity. If the client does well in a role-play test, one knows that he or she has the skill in his or her behavioral repertoire regardless of whether or not the person is willing or able to use the skill in the natural environment. Conversely, if he or she cannot perform adequately on the role-play test, it is very unlikely that he or she will be able to perform adequately under the stress of real-life interactions.

Social Problem-Solving Battery

The brief-format role-play test will generally not be highly informative with recent onset and less-impaired clients. They should be evaluated with a longer, more involved procedure that can assess their ability to stay on task, to modify their behavior in response to variations in what the partner presents, and to carry on an interesting conversation. We have developed the Social Problem-Solving Battery (SPSB) to assess these more difficult behaviors (Sayers, Bellack, Wade, Bennett, & Fong, 1995). The SPSB consists of two tests: the Role-Play Task (RPT) and the Response-Generation Task (RGT). The RPT is an extended role-play test in which the client participates in six 3-minute role plays. It is designed to evaluate the ability to initiate and maintain conversations, to stand up for one's rights, to be persuasive, and to engage in effective negotiation and compromise. The 3-minute format provides a glimpse of the client's ability to adapt to changing behavioral demands, to be persistent, and to generate diverse responses in response to a less than cooperative partner. The RGT taps the client's ability to generate solutions to social problems. It places a premium on social intelligence and reasoning, as opposed to performance capacity.

The following provides a detailed description of our assessment procedure that was systematically developed to yield reliable and valid information about the social functioning of chronic and persistently ill clients. The RPT involves use of audiotape, printed cards, and a confederate. The RGT involves use of a prerecorded videotape. Obviously, it will not be possible to duplicate the exact strategy in many clinical settings. However, we have found that clinicians are better able to conduct useful assessments when they adapt this blueprint to fit their resources and needs then when they attempt to invent their own techniques ad hoc. The critical elements in any assessment are to (1) use a standardized procedure so that clients can be compared to one another and to their own behavior over time; (2) make the content relevant to the client and to situation that is the focus of interest.

General Procedures

The RPT is administered first, followed by the RGT. Clients should be given ample opportunity to acclimate to the testing situation. All instructions should be read slowly, and every effort should be made to ensure that the person understands the task. Clients should be allowed to take breaks, smoke, and so forth, if necessary. This is *not* a stress test. All instructions should be read in order to ensure consistency across experimenters.

Role-Play Task

Whenever possible, the RPT should be videotaped for subsequent ratings. The client should be seated at a comfortable conversational distance from the confederate (about 6 feet). In order to ensure standardization across clients and for repeat assessments over time, instructions should be delivered on audiotape. The RPT may be administered by a clinician who is known by the client, but it is preferable that they have had minimal prior contact to make it easier for the client to assume the designated role.The confederate (i.e., person role playing with the client) should minimize conversation with the client before or during the RPT. During role-played interactions, the confederate should exhibit appropriate, but subdued, affect that is neither excessively hostile nor excessively submissive in assertion scenes, and neither excessively warm nor excessively aloof in the conversation initiation scenes. The prompts included with the scene descriptions below should be modeled to the extent possible. They are general enough to be appropriate in response to a wide range of client comments. However, some flexibility is required. Each scene is subdivided into segments, during which the confederate presents a different, homogeneous set of responses. This systematic variation helps structure the confederate's behavior as well as presents the client with a series of different problems that must be solved. A timer/clock should be situated in the confederate's line of sight to signal when the shifts should occur.

INSTRUCTIONS TO CLIENTS

CONFEDERATE: "You and I will be acting out several situations that might happen to you in real life. The instructions for acting them out are on this tape. Listen carefully as I play it for you. After the instructions, there will be a chance for you to ask me questions about what we will be doing."

AUDIOTAPE: "The purpose of this procedure is to find out how you react to common problem situations. We'll do this by role playing these situations, that is, by acting them out.

"_____ [confederate] will play several different roles. In some cases, he or she will act as your family member. Tell _____ now whom you consider to be the most significant family member in your life [pause tape while client identifies a family member]. In the role plays that involve a family member, _____ will play the part of the significant family member whom you just mentioned. In other situations, she will play the part of a stranger or an acquaintance.

"The situations are, of course, only imaginary, but you should imagine that you are really in the situation and respond as if it were actually happening to you.

"The procedure will be as follows: First, you will read the situation that is typed on a card. Be sure to read it carefully and try to imagine that you are actually in that situation. At that point, _____ will ask you whom he or she will be playing just to make sure that it's clear whom he or she is pretending to be. Then the tape recorder will play a description of the same scene. Be sure to listen carefully as the situation is being described.

"After you have familiarized yourself with the scene by reading the situation card and listening to the tape, you and _____ will act out the situation. _____ will say something to you and you should respond to continue the conversation. Please keep the conversation going back and forth until _____ tells you to stop. You should respond as if you were actually in that situation. In the role plays, you will be playing yourself, responding as if the situation were actually occurring."

"Explain to _____ what you will be doing."

CONFEDERATE: "The first couple of scenes are practice so you can see how the role plays go. Here's the first card. [Go through two practice scenes, giving feedback as needed.] That's exactly what we want you to do. Now let's go on to the others."

TARGET SCENES FOR ROLE-PLAY TASK

Practice Scene 1: 1½ Minutes

Situation: You and a friend have made plans to go out together on Friday night, and now the two of you are trying to decide what to do.

Confederate says: "I'm looking forward to getting together tomorrow night."

The confederate should have the client make suggestions. The confederate should disagree with the first one or two suggestions, saying that activity does not sound like fun or that you have done that recently. The confederate should question as to when and where you could do this activity, as well as how you could get there, how much it will cost, and so forth. The confederate should always try to ask questions that are open-ended, in order to encourage the client to elaborate on answers. The main point of the practice scenes is to encourage the client to be comfortable with talking and pretending to be in a certain situation.

Practice Scene 2 : 1½ Minutes

Situation: You and your family member go to the video store to rent a movie to watch together, and you are trying to decide which movie to rent.

Confederate says: "I'm really in the mood for a movie tonight."

The confederate should have the client suggest types of movies (i.e., comedy, drama, etc.) as well as specific titles of movies. The confederate should disagree with the first one or two suggestions, saying that you do not like that type of movie or you have already seen that movie before. The confederate should question which video store to go to, as well as how you can get there and when you should go.

Scene 1: 3 Minutes (Four 45-Second Segments)

Situation: You have never lived away from home but feel that you are now ready to look for your own apartment. You have been thinking about this for about a year now. You have been working hard at your job and earn enough to pay the rent. Also, you have learned a lot about cooking, house-cleaning, grocery shopping, doing your own laundry, and so forth. You also have a good friend who is planning to move out on his own, and the two of you are thinking of sharing an apartment together. You decide to tell your family member about this.

Confederate says: "I really think that you should stay at home for a few more years."

First segment: Confederate argues that he or she likes having the person living at home. Interaction time with client approximately 45 seconds. Some or all of the following lines can be used:

- "I really like having you live at home."
- "I would really miss you if you moved out."
- "It's just that I like having you live here with me."

Second segment: Conferate raises questions about the roommate/friend. Interaction time with client approximately 45 seconds. Some or all of the following lines can be used.

- "What about this friend you're thinking of moving in with?"
- "Do you think he or she will be good to live with?"
- "How do you know you can trust him or her?"
- "I'm just worried that he or she won't be very good to live with."

Third segment: Confederate argues that he or she doesn't think that things are stable enough at this point.

- "I'm also worried that things aren't stable enough at this point."
- "Are you sure things are stable enough at this point?"

Fourth segment: Confederate invites client to generate solutions. Interaction time with client approximately 45 seconds. Confederate says, "Well, I'm still worried about your plans to move out. How do you think we could settle this?" If the client offers a reasonable solution, the confederate should question it but not reject it. If possible, the confederate should talk with the client on each of the topics for approximately the same amount of time (about 45 seconds each). The confederate can use all of the responses but does not have to. For example, if the client speaks for a long time on the first topic, the confederate may have to skip either the second or the third response in order to have time at the end to generate solutions. The confederate should always leave at least 45 seconds at the end of the interaction for the client to generate solutions.

A Variation on Scene 1

It is possible to encounter a client who cannot imagine or pretend to be moving out on his or her own for the first time. For example, a client who has older children and has named a daughter or a son as the family member with whom he or she has the most contact may not be able to imagine telling the child that he or she is going to move out. In this case, the situation can be changed by the confederate reading the following scenario:

Situation: You haven't lived on your own in a while, but you feel that you are now ready to look for your own apartment. You have been thinking about this for about a year now. You have been working hard at your job, and you earn enough to pay the rent. Also, you have learned a lot about cooking, housecleaning, grocery shopping, doing your own laundry, and so forth. You also have a friend who is planning to move out on his own, and the two of you are thinking of sharing an apartment together. You decide to tell your family member about this.

Confederate says: "I really think that you should stay at the board-and-care home for a few more years."

First segment: Confederate argues that the person has been doing very well at living at the board-and-care home.

Second segment: Confederate argues about trustworthiness of friend.

Third segment: Confederate argues that things aren't stable enough at this point.

Fourth segment: Confederate says, "Well, I'm still worried about you getting your own place. How do you think we could settle this?"

Scene 2: 3 Minutes (Two 90-Second Segments)

Situation: When you left home this morning, you noticed a moving van in front of your apartment building. Your neighbor across the hall recently moved out, and you are wondering if the moving van means you will have a new neighbor. When you return home later in the afternoon, you notice that the door across the hall is open, and an unfamiliar person is standing near the door. You decide to meet your new neighbor.

Confederate says: "Hi."

First 90-second segment: Throughout, confederate responds in a friendly but reserved manner, answers questions, and responds appropriately but keeps responses brief. The client is asked few, if any, questions, and the confederate tolerates long silences. Following 15-second silence, the confederate asks a brief, open-ended question related to the client's last comment.

Second 90-second segment: Confederate asks general questions.

Topics for confederate to discuss:

- "Have you lived here long?"
- "What is the landlord like?"
- "Is there a supermarket/laundry facilities near here?"
- "I'm new to the area. I'm not very familiar with this area."
- "How do you find living here?"
- "Do you work near here?"

Answers to questions that clients may ask:

- "Are you from around here?"
    "No, I'm new to the area."
- "Where did you live before you came here?"
    "I lived in New Jersey, so I'm pretty new to the area."
- "Are you married/have children/have roommate?"
    "No."
- "What kind of work do you do?"
    "I work in the hospital down the street [name an administrative kind of job—personnel department, secretary, etc.]."

Scene 3: 3 Minutes (Four 45-Second Segments)

Situation: You've had your friend Joe come over to your house a couple of times. But after his last visit, your mother said she didn't like having him in the house because he smoked. Joe is the only friend that you feel comfortable with and can talk to easily. You ask your mother if Joe can come over this afternoon.

Confederate says: "You know I don't like having him in the house because he smokes."

First segment: Confederate argues that the smoke smells up the furnishings. Some or all of the following lines may be used:

- "The smoke really bothers me."
- "The smoke gets in the furniture and smells up the whole house."
- "The smell of the smoke stays in the house for days."

Second segment: Confederate argues that Joe is rude/not a good friend.

- It's not just the smoking. I think Joe is a rude guy."
- "He was so impolite the last time he was here."
- "I'm worried that Joe is not a good friend for you."

Third segment: Confederate argues that Joe is using the client.

- "It just seems that Joe only calls or comes by when he wants something from you."
- "I'm just worried that Joe will take advantage of you."
- "I just don't want to see you get hurt."

Fourth segment: Confederate says, "Well, I'm still worried about Joe coming over this afternoon. How do you think we could settle this?" If the client offers a reasonable solution, the confederate should question it, but not reject it. In this situation, the client can name solutions for each of the three arguments. Thus, different responses are needed as solutions are generated. Some common solutions and responses are as follows:

CLIENT: Joe will only smoke in one room/in my room/in the basement.
CONFEDERATE: It's just that the smoke gets in the furniture/travels from one room to the next . . . and it smells up the whole house.

CLIENT: I'll tell Joe not to smoke when he comes over.
CONFEDERATE: Joe seemed like a pretty heavy smoker. I'm worried that he won't be able to keep from smoking when he's here.

CLIENT: Joe can smoke outside.
CONFEDERATE: Do you think Joe would agree to do that?

CLIENT: If Joe was rude to you, I'll talk to him about it.

CONFEDERATE: I'm worried that he will get really mad at you if you talk to him about it.

CLIENT: What did Joe say that was rude?

CONFEDERATE: It's just his manners in general. I don't remember anything specifically.

CLIENT: If Joe was rude to you, why don't you talk to him about it?

CONFEDERATE: I wouldn't feel comfortable talking to Joe about it because he's your friend.

CLIENT: Well, I won't talk to Joe anymore.

CONFEDERATE: I wouldn't want you to lose a good friend.

Scene 4: 3 Minutes (Four 45-Second Segments)

Situation: You called your landlord last week about a slow leak in your ceiling. He said that he would be there in the next day or two to fix it. He has not fixed it yet, nor has he called you to let you know when he will be over to fix it. By now, the leak has become much worse. You decide to call your landlord again.

Confederate says: "Hi, _____. How are you?"

First segment: Confederate argues that he or she hasn't had enough time to get over there to fix it.

Second segment: Confederate argues that he or she has other problems that require his or her attention.

- "I've been very busy."
- "I have a lot of other tenants with a lot of other problems that are ahead of yours."
- "I have a list and you're on the list, but there are other problems that are more important."

Third segment: Confederate argues that he or she aware of the problem.

- "You don't need to call anymore. I'm aware of the problem."
- "You keep calling, but I'm aware of the problem. I'll be there when I can."

Fourth segment: Confederate argues that he or she can't fix the situation at this time: "Well, I don't know what I can do about it right now." If the client offers a reasonable solution, the confederate should question it but not reject it. Some common solutions and responses are as follows:

CLIENT: Just get up here to fix it.
CONFEDERATE: I told you—I'm very busy and I have other things to do.

CLIENT: Send up your assistant to fix it.
CONFEDERATE: I don't have an assistant. It's just me doing all of the repairs.

CLIENT: Call a repairman to fix it/I'll call a repairman to fix it.
CONFEDERATE: He or she won't do it right. I know what to do, I just haven't had the time to get up there to do it. He or she will cost too much/be too expensive.

Scene 5: 3 Minutes (Two 90-Second Segments)

Situation: You have been working at a new job for the past week. So far, none of your new co-workers has approached you or said anything to you. You would like to get to know your co-workers. This morning, as you are punching in at the time clock, one of your co-workers arrives to do the same thing.
Confederate says: "Hi, you're new here, aren't you?"
Throughout the interaction the confederate should respond in a friendly but reserved manner. The confederate should answer questions and respond appropriately but keep responses brief.
First 90-second segment: Confederate puts onus on client by asking few, if any, questions and tolerating long silences. Following 15-second silence, the confederate asks a brief open-ended question related to the client's last comment.
Second 90-second segment: Confederate asks general questions.
Topics for confederate to discuss:

- "Do you live near here?"
- "How do you like the work you're doing here?"
- "What did you do before you came here?"
- "Have you met your supervisor yet? What did you think?"
- "How do you get to work in the morning?"

Answers to questions that clients may ask:

- "How long have you worked here?"
    "About a year."

- "I haven't met many people here. I feel like people are avoiding me."
  "Everybody is busy this time of year."
  "It's hard to get to know people when you're new to a job."
- "Where does everybody eat lunch?"
  "There's a cafeteria down on the ground floor."

Scene 6: 3 Minutes (Four 45-Second Segments)

Situation: You have been involved in a 10-week job training program for the past 2 weeks. You've had a number of problems there since you started. For example, you didn't realize that there was a dress code, and you wore shorts and a T-shirt one day. Then, you were late a couple of times. Now you've been asked to leave the program because you have violated too many rules. This job training program is very important to you, and you feel that you can do a lot better now because you've had a couple of weeks to get adjusted to the program. You decide to ask for another chance and go to your supervisor's office.

Confederate says: "Hi. Can I help you?"

First segment: Confederate argues that person has violated too many rules.

- "Well, you've violated a lot of rules."
- "We have our rules for a reason and we like our employees to follow them."

Second segment: Confederate argues that the person hasn't been trying hard enough.

- "It just seems that you're not trying very hard in the program."
- "It seems that the program isn't very important to you."
- "You broke so many rules it just seems that the program isn't all that important to you."

Third segment: Confederate argues that people in the past have not changed.

- "We've seen in the past that people whom we have given a second chance haven't changed."
- "I'm just worried that I'll give you a second chance, and you won't change."
- "How do I know you'll try harder?"

Fourth segment: Confederate says, "Well, I'm still worried about giving you a second chance in the program. How do you think we could settle this?"

After 3 minutes: The scene should end positively. The confederate should agree with the client's solution or offer an alternative one, for example, "What if I give you a 2-week probation?" If the client offers a reasonable solution, the confederate should question it but not reject it. Some common solutions and responses are as follows:

CLIENT: We could give it a trial period of _____.
CONFEDERATE: Well, that's a pretty long time, especially if you continue to break the rules.

CLIENT: You could watch me carefully and tell me when I'm breaking the rules.
CONFEDERATE: I don't have the extra time to watch you when you work.

CLIENT: Just give me a chance, and I'll prove myself to you.
CONFEDERATE: I'm just very worried about giving you a second chance.

Response-Generation Task

The Response-Generation Task (RGT) can usually be administered immediately after the RPT, but it can be administered at another point if the client is fatigued or time does not permit. As with the RPT, it is preferable to have all of the instructions audiotaped to ensure standardization. The basic procedure involves playing a taped conversation of two people having a problem and asking the client a standardized series of questions:

1. What is the problem in this situation?
2. What is _____'s goal in this situation?
3. What could _____ do to achieve his or her goal of _____?
4. What could _____ do if that doesn't work?
5. Which solution do you think has the best chance of working? Which one do you think is the best?
6. For the best solution:
    What do think could go wrong with that?
    Why might that not work?
7. For the second solution proposed (or the first if the second was selected as the best):
    What do you think could go wrong if the person tried _____?

The staff person should try to get the patient to generate two solutions. If the second solution is not different from the previous response, he or she should ask (once): "Is there anything else the person could do in this situation?"

The following set of instructions assumes the problems presented to the client are standardized and presented on a videotape. In clinical settings, useful information can be collected without this degree of formality. The clinician can type the problem situations on cards and have the client read the card aloud. If he or she has difficulty reading or with reading comprehension, the clinician can read the situation to him or her. The key aspects of this assessment task are to present the client with a relevant problem situation and to see if he or she can identify the problem, goal, and potential solutions. It will not be useful if the clinician paraphrases the situations and/or provides paralinguistic emphases that make it too easy or too difficult. That is why we prefer to deliver the material on tape.

INSTRUCTIONS TO CLIENTS

"In this task, we are interested in how people solve problems. You will watch a videotape of a person having a conversation with either a family member or a friend. Before each interaction, a narrator will describe the situation. You will then see one person on the screen talk to another person who is not shown on the screen. (You won't see the second person.) After each segment, I will ask you some questions about the person you saw on the screen.

"The way the task will work is this: For each scene, you will hear a narrator describe a situation. Listen carefully so that you understand the situation clearly. Next, you will see a person on the screen talking to a person off screen. I want you to watch and listen to the person on the screen carefully, so that you can clearly understand and describe the problem. After the situation is acted out on the screen, I'll stop the tape and ask you to describe the problem in the situation. I will then ask you to think of ways that the person on the screen could solve the problem.

"Do you have any questions? Let's try a practice scene so you can see how they go."

TARGET SCENES FOR RESPONSE-GENERATION TASK

Practice Scene 1

Barb is in a store buying some lottery tickets. Each ticket costs 1 dollar, and Barb gives the salesperson a 5-dollar bill in order to buy five tickets. Barb specifically asks for five tickets, but the salesperson only gives her four.

Practice Scene 2

Barb is watching her favorite television show. Her roommate suddenly comes in and changes the channel.

Scene 1

Jane's parents have been giving her a weekly allowance from her Social Security checks and putting the rest in a bank account. However, since Jane has started taking classes at the local community college, her allowance hasn't been enough to cover her bus fare and meals. As a result, she has had to skip lunch on a couple of days. Her parents have never agreed to an increase to her allowance in the past, but she realizes that her current weekly allowance just isn't enough to cover her basic expenses. The next time Jane visits, she decides to talk to her mother about it.

Scene 2

Earlier this morning, Ted was in a bad mood. When his mother asked him if he could help her take out the trash, he yelled at her to do it herself and slammed the door as he walked out of the house. Now, he is sorry that he lost his temper, and he decides to say something to his mother. When he walks back into the house, his mother is finishing up some of the household chores.

Scene 3

Jennifer's father has been in the hospital for the past week, and no one—including her father—has told her why. Each time she visits him, he says, "It's nothing serious. Nothing to worry yourself about." However, Jennifer is worried because he looks pale and weak. She wants to find out more about her father's illness. The next time she visits her father in the hospital, she decides to talk to him about it again.

Scene 4

When Jennifer first started her job as a dishwasher in a local diner, her boss promised that he would train her to assist the cooks in the kitchen after she had worked for 6 months. More than 6 months have passed, and her boss has not said anything to her, but he has been training others to work with the cooks. Jennifer decides to talk to him about it when he gives her her paycheck.

Scene 5

Ted's next door neighbor, Mrs. Reilly, is a cheerful, elderly lady who always waves hello to Ted as she sits in her rocking chair on her front porch. When he walks by her house today, she does not wave to him, and he notices that she is not smiling as usual. Ted is concerned that something is wrong and decides to ask her if she is okay.

Scene 6

Jane is feeling hungry for something sweet to eat. She goes to the refrigerator and hopes that there is a piece of chocolate cake left over from dinner. Just as she gets to the refrigerator, her brother comes in, also wanting some chocolate cake. Jane discovers that there is only one piece left, and both of them want it.

Summary

This chapter has provided an overview of the assessment of social skills. Assessment is a necessary precursor for social skills treatment. We have described some strategies for conducting this detailed evaluation that emphasize role play and presented specific procedures and scenarios. Although these techniques have been standardized to yield reliable data, a somewhat less-structured approach will often be required for use in clinical settings.

3

Techniques for Introducing
Social Skills

Deficits in social skills are important components of social dysfunction in schizophrenia. Poor skills, such as the inability to initiate conversations, express feelings, and resolve conflicts, may be determined by a variety of factors in schizophrenia. These include biological factors, lack of access to good role models, loss of skills because of low morale, and chronic psychotic symptoms. Despite the multiple origins of skills deficits, clinical techniques based on social learning theory can be effective for teaching new social skills to clients.

In this chapter and the next, we describe the techniques involved in social skills training. The specific methods used to train skills are based upon several learning concepts. We discuss those first then detail the Journal techniques for introducing new skills. Chapter 4 then describes the techniques for consolidating learning of skills.

Social Learning Theory

Social learning theory (Bandura, 1969) refers to a set of observations and principles concerning the natural development and learning of social behavior. According to this theory, social behaviors are acquired through a combination of observing actions of others and the naturally occurring consequences (both positive and negative) of one's own actions. Social learning theory builds upon the earlier work of Skinner (1938, 1953) on the effects of positive and negative consequences (*operant conditioning*) on behavior. Five principles derived from social learning theory are incorporated into social skills training: modeling, reinforcement, shaping, overlearning, and generalization.

Modeling

Modeling refers to the process of observational learning, in which a person learns a new social skill by watching someone else use that skill. Although good social skills are modeled in many individual and group therapy treatments for schizophrenia, social skills training is unique in its emphasis on explicit and frequent modeling of social skills for clients. In social skills training, therapists frequently model specific social skills in role plays, directly drawing the attention of the participants to the process and discussing the specific steps of skills that are demonstrated.

Group leaders liberally use modeling in role plays to demonstrate targeted social skills, which are then practiced by clients in role plays. Thus, the learning that takes place from observing the behavior of the leaders is crucial to the success of social skills training. The power of modeling is that many clients have difficulty changing their behavior based on the verbal feedback of others, but they are capable of behavior change after observing skills modeled by group leaders.

Reinforcement

Reinforcement refers to the positive consequences following a behavior that increases the likelihood of that behavior occurring again. Two types of reinforcement can be identified: positive reinforcement and negative reinforcement. Positive reinforcement involves the provision of some valued or desired outcome (e.g., verbal praise, food) following a behavior. Negative reinforcement refers to the removal or reduction of some unpleasant stimulus (e.g., criticism, a noxious noise) following a behavior. Positive reinforcement in the form of verbal praise from the leaders and other group participants is used in social skills training to reinforce both effort in the group and the performance of specific components of social skill. Throughout each social skills session, leaders provide and elicit from other group members abundant amounts of positive feedback about specific social skills performance to help each member improve his or her skill level. The high level of positive reinforcement in social skills groups and strict avoidance of "put-downs" or criticism make participation in the group an enjoyable, nonthreatening learning experience.

Positive reinforcement can also be used to encourage attendance at social skills training groups. For example, providing refreshments or linking privileges to attendance at the group may foster participation.

Shaping

Shaping is the reinforcement of successive steps toward a desired goal. Most skills that are taught in social skills training are too complex and difficult for clients to learn in a single trial. By breaking down complex skills into component steps and teaching them one at a time over multiple trials, effective social skills can gradually be shaped over time.

The progress of social skills for patients with schizophrenia often occurs in small increments. The ability to shape gradual changes in clients' social skills requires that leaders be attentive to even very small, seemingly insignificant changes in behavior. By providing specific reinforcement for these small changes, additional improvements can be made, and work can begin on other component behaviors. By adopting a "shaping attitude," social skills trainers recognize that changes in social behavior occur gradually over time, with ample encouragement provided each step along the way.

Overlearning

Overlearning refers to the process of repeatedly practicing a skill to the point where it becomes automatic. In social skills training, clients repeatedly practice targeted social skills in role plays in the group as well as for homework assignments outside of the group. Familiarity with specific social skills is not sufficient for learning, however. The leaders' goal is to provide group members with so many opportunities to practice the skill that it becomes second nature to use the skills in the appropriate situations. For this reason, behavior rehearsals and role plays are frequently used in social skills training to facilitate overlearning.

Generalization

Generalization is the transfer of skills acquired in one setting to another, novel setting. Clearly, in order for social skills training to be effective, clients must both learn specific social skills and be able to use these skills in their naturally occurring encounters. The generalization of social skills is the ultimate test of skills training. Therefore, skills training methods are designed in order to maximize the ability of group members to transfer skills learned in the session to outside of the session.

Generalization of skills is programmed using two methods. First, after being taught a skill in the session, members are given homework assignments to practice the skill outside the session in their natural environment. Homework assignments are then reviewed in the subsequent skills training session. Second, clients may be prompted to use targeted skills in the natural setting by the skills trainer or another involved person. This *in vivo* prompting of specific social skills can take place in the context of planned trips (e.g., community outings) or spontaneously, as occasions arise. Programming the generalization of social skills is a critical ingredient in skills training that necessarily takes place outside of the traditional group or individual therapy session. Furthermore, as will be discussed later, attending to issues of generalization often requires the involvement of other people in the client's immediate environment to ensure that targeted skills will be reinforced when they occur.

Steps of Social Skills Training

Social skills training is a structured format for teaching interpersonal skills that follows a specific sequence of steps. These specific steps, followed on a routine basis within and across sessions, are what distinguishes social skills training from other treatment approaches. The steps of social skills training include (1) establishing a rationale for learning the skill, (2) discussing the component steps of the skill, (3) modeling the skill in a role play and reviewing the role play with the client(s), (4) engaging a client in a role play, (5) providing positive feedback, (6) providing corrective feedback, (7) engaging the client in a second role play of the same situation, (8) providing additional feedback, and (9) assigning homework.

We describe each of these steps in detail below. For ease of communication, we describe the use of skills training in a group format with two leaders. However, later in this chapter, we also address how to apply social skills training to other formats as well.

Establishing a Rationale

In order to motivate group members to learn a new skill, a rationale for its importance must first be established. Broadly speaking, there are two strategies for establishing the rationale for learning a new skill: The clinician can elicit the rationale from group members, and he or she can provide reasons for the importance of the skill. With most groups, a combination of both strategies is most effective.

The reasons for learning a new skill can be elicited from group members by asking leading questions about the importance of the skill. For example, when teaching the skill Starting Conversations, the leader can pose questions such as "Why might it be helpful to be able to start a conversation with somebody?" or "What's so important about being able to start a conversation?" Typical responses to these questions include "That's how you get to know other people" and "If you want to make new friends, you have to know how to start a conversation." For another example, when introducing the skill Expressing Positive Feelings, the leader can raise questions such as "Why is it helpful to be able to express positive feelings to another person?" and "What happens when you express a positive feeling to someone else about a specific behavior he or she did?" These questions tend to elicit answers such as "It makes other people feel good" and "If you let people know what they did that you liked, maybe they will do it again."

When eliciting the rationale from group members, it may be helpful to ask questions regarding the disadvantages of *not* using a specific skill. For example, when developing the rationale for giving other people compliments, the leader might pose the question "What happens if you like someone a lot, but you never compliment that person about anything? How does it make him or her feel?" Asking group members about the disadvantages of not using a skill is another way of helping them see the advantages of learning that skill.

In most groups, the importance of learning a specific social skill can be addressed by asking the group members suggestive questions. The leader may also choose to amplify reasons given by group members or provide additional reasons. In some groups of clients, however, cognitive impairments may limit their ability to generate reasons for learning a particular skill. In groups such as these, the leader may elect to provide the rationale for the skill directly, rather than to elicit it from the group members.

When explaining the importance of a social skill, the leader should make his or her explanation as brief as possible. Then, to check on the understanding of group members, the leader should prompt members to paraphrase the rationale. Correct understanding can be reinforced, misperceptions can be corrected, and the leader can then move on to the next step of skills training. Part II contains a wide variety of skills that can be taught using social skills training. For each skill, a specific rationale is provided, and the component steps are listed.

An example of providing a rationale for the skill Expressing Unpleasant Feelings is provided below.

LEADER: Today we are going to work on the skill of Expressing Unpleasant Feelings. By "unpleasant" I mean feelings that are difficult or that don't feel good to have. Can anyone give me an example of an unpleasant feeling?

BOB: Mad.

LEADER: Yes, Bob. Feeling mad or angry is a good example of an unpleasant feeling. (*The leader writes down "anger" on the posterboard, and adds to the list as group members add other feelings.*) What are some other examples?

JUANITA: Feeling scared?

LEADER: Yes, feeling scared, or frightened, or anxious are examples of unpleasant feelings. Can you think of any other examples?

LIONEL: Boredom.

LEADER: You're right, Lionel, feeling bored is another example of an unpleasant feeling. Any other examples?

YOKO: Like when I want to hit someone.

LEADER: How do you feel when you want to hit someone, Yoko?

YOKO: Pissed off.

LEADER: Right, feeling pissed off or angry is another good example of an unpleasant feeling. You all came up with some good examples of unpleasant feelings: anger, anxiety, boredom. What happens when you have an unpleasant feeling, such as anger, and you hold it inside of yourself for as long as you can?

YOKO: You feel even worse.

LIONEL: You explode.

LEADER: Yes. Holding unpleasant feelings inside you for a long time often feels real bad. And sometimes when you hold it in too long, one tiny little thing will just set you off. It's like the straw that breaks the camel's back. What happens if you're feeling really upset about something and you just fly off the handle, like you yell or shout or scream, or even hit someone?

BOB: Trouble.

LEADER: Right, Bob. Yoko, what happens when you lose control over your anger?

YOKO: I lose privileges or get the other person mad at me.

LEADER: Good point, Yoko. Negative consequences often happen if you express your anger in a destructive or hostile way. What happens if you have an unpleasant feeling about something and you express it in a *constructive* way to someone else?

BOB: It's better.

LEADER: That's right, Bob. What about the situation? What if somebody's done something that annoys you, and you try to express an unpleasant feeling constructively to that person, telling the person what he or she did that annoyed you?

JUANITA: Maybe he'll change.

LEADER: Yes, Juanita, letting someone know what he or she has done that's upset you can help that person change his or her behavior, and maybe that situation will be prevented from happening in the future. So we can see that never expressing unpleasant feelings or expressing them in a hostile way has lots of disadvantages, but there are a number of advantages to expressing unpleasant feelings in a constructive way.

Discussing the Steps of the Skill

When the rationale for learning the skill has been established, the leader introduces and discusses each step of the skill. The purpose of breaking a skill down into its component steps is to facilitate the teaching process by helping members focus on improving one step at a time. The steps of the skill should be written down and posted in a prominent location in the room so that all participants can see it.

The leader briefly discusses each step of the skill, eliciting from group members the importance of each step or directly explaining it. When discussing the steps, the leader points to the step on the poster or flip chart. The discussion of the different steps of the skill requires only a few minutes.

We provide below an example of discussing the steps of the skill, following the same group working on Expressing Unpleasant Feelings.

LEADER: When learning how to express unpleasant feelings constructively, it can be helpful to break the skill down into a number of steps. The first step of expressing an unpleasant feeling is to look at the person and to speak in a firm voice tone. Why do you think it can be important to look at a person?

JUANITA: So you know they're listening.

LEADER: Right, you want to look at the person to make sure you have his or her attention. What's so important about speaking in a firm voice tone?

LIONEL: Then that person really knows you mean business.

LEADER: That's right, Lionel. If you have an unpleasant feeling about something and you express it with a meek, quiet voice tone, then the other person might not think you really mean what you're saying.

The next step is to tell the other person what you're upset about. What's important here is to make sure that you're as specific as possible. Why do you think that might be important, Bob?

BOB: So the other person know what you're mad about?

LEADER: Yes. If you tell the other person exactly what you're upset about, it will help him or her to understand better.

The next step is to tell the other person how it made you feel. What we are talking about here is making a specific feeling statement, such as "I felt mad," or "I felt angry," or "I was upset." Why do you think making a feeling statement might be important, Yoko?

YOKO: So the person knows how you felt.

LEADER: Yes, making a clear feeling statement helps the other person know exactly how his or her behavior affected you. Being as specific as possible helps the other person understand better.

The last step of Expressing Unpleasant Feelings is to suggest a way of preventing the situation from happening again in the future. Why is this an important step?

JUANITA: That way you could change the situation.

LEADER: Right.

YOKO: But what if the person doesn't want to change?

LEADER: Telling the other person how he or she could change the situation in a constructive way often works very well. However, you're right Yoko, it doesn't work *every* time. I have found that if you use these steps, though, the chances are good that you can change the situation. There are some other strategies that we can talk about later that you can use when dealing with somebody who doesn't want to change a problem situation.

YOKO: Okay.

Modeling the Skill in a Role Play

Discussion of the steps of the skill is immediately followed by the leaders modeling the skill in a role play. This demonstration is intended to help participants see how the different components of the skill fit together into an overall performance that is socially effective. Demonstrating the skill helps translate the abstract steps of the skill into a concrete reality.

It is best if the leaders plan in advance of the session the role-play scenario they will model in the group. Role-play situations should be selected that have high relevance to the participants, may occur frequently, and are realistic. The role play should be brief and to the point. Many role plays for basic skills, such as Expressing Unpleasant Feelings, Making Requests, and Starting Conversations, may last as little as 15 to 45 seconds. More complicated skills, such as Compromise and Negotiation, Maintaining Conversations, or Listening to Others, may require longer role plays. If the group is conducted by two leaders, then both of them should participate in the role play, with one of them demonstrating the skill and the other taking the role of the partner. When the group is conducted by a single leader, he or she should enlist a group member to play the role of the partner in the role play. In the latter case, a participant should be selected who is cooperative and likely to respond appropriately to the leader during the role play.

Prior to beginning the role play, the leader instructs the group members that he or she will demonstrate the skill and that their task is to observe which steps of the skill they see the leader use. The role play, is then conducted. Immediately after the role play the leader reviews the different steps of the skill with group members, eliciting for each step whether it was performed. After reviewing the different steps, group members are asked to provide an overall evaluation of whether the leader was an effective communicator during the interaction.

Patients with schizophrenia sometimes get confused when observing or participating in role plays. This confusion can be due to a lack of clarity regarding when a role play begins and ends. In order to help clients differentiate between "pretend" and real interactions in the group, it is helpful if the leader explicitly points out the beginning and the end of each role play.

There are several strategies the leader can use to signify the beginning and end of a role play; usually some combination of strategies works best. First, the leader can make a clear verbal statement to initiate and terminate the role play, such as "Let's begin the role play now" and "Stop, let's end the role play here." Second, the leader can use hand signals to signify the beginning and end of role plays. For example forming a "T" with one's hands, the signal used to stop a game for "time" in many professional sports games, can be used to indicate the end of a role play. Third, having the role-play participants change positions in the group for the role play can help to make it clear when a role play begins and ends. For example, the two-role play participants can stand or sit in the middle or in front of the group during the role play and then return to their seats after the role play is completed. Thus, a specific physical space in the group is reserved for active role playing. The strategy of repositioning role-play participants has the added advantage of introducing an element of theater or drama. By increasing the theatrical quality of role plays, the leader can attract the attention of less interested or cognitively impaired clients. Finally, encouraging participants in role plays to get up and move around the room can be energizing for all group members.

We provide an example of modeling the skill below.

LEADER A: Now that we've talked about the different steps of expressing an unpleasant feeling, we'd like to demonstrate this skill for you in a role play. In this role play, we are going to pretend that I'm watching a TV program that I enjoy. In the middle of watching this TV program, someone comes in and changes the channel to watch a different program. Sandra [Leader B] will be playing the role of the person who comes in and changes the TV channel. I'm going to express an unpleasant feeling to Sandra about her changing the TV program. What I'd like you to do is to see which steps of the skill you see me do. (*Points to poster with steps of skill.*) Any questions?

JUANITA: No.

LEADER A: Okay. (*Moves two seats to the center of the group and positions a third seat opposite from him for the imaginary TV.*) Let's pretend that I'm sitting here watching TV. (*Points to the empty seat to designate the "TV."*) Let's pretend I'm watching a baseball game. Sandra, I'd like you to come in and change the channel. This can be your seat (*pointing to the adjacent seat*). Let's start the role play *now*. (*Sits back in his chair and pretends to enjoy watching TV.*)

LEADER B: (*Walks up to TV.*) Oh, a boring sports program. I think I'd like to see what's on the news. (*Changes the channel.*)

LEADER A: Hey, Sandra! You just changed the TV channel that I was watching. It annoys me when you change the TV station like that without checking it out with me ahead of time. I'd appreciate your talking to me first if you want to change the station. Then maybe we can work something out.

LEADER B: I'm sorry. I didn't realize you were really watching it.

LEADER A: Well, I was. I would like you to turn it back to the game.

LEADER B: Okay. (*Turns back channel.*)

LEADER A: Let's stop the role play *now*. (*turning to group members*) Let's talk about what you saw in that role play. (*Points to poster with steps of skill.*) How about my eye contact? Was I looking at Sandra just then?

LIONEL: Yes, you were looking at her.

LEADER A: Right, and how about my voice tone? Did I speak with a firm voice tone?

JUANITA: Yes, you sounded pretty firm to me.

LEADER A: Good. How about telling her what I was upset about? Was it clear what I was upset about?

LIONEL: Yes.

LEADER A: What did I actually say I was upset about, Bob?

BOB: Changing the channel.

LEADER A: Right. And how about telling her how I felt? Did I make a feeling statement?

JUANITA: Yes you did.

LEADER A: What was the specific feeling statement I made, Yoko?

YOKO: You were annoyed.

LEADER A: Right. And did I suggest a way of preventing this from happening in the future?

YOKO: You told her to check with you before changing the channel.

LEADER A: That's right. Overall, was I effective in getting my point across?

BOB: Yes.

LEADER A: Did I sound hostile, Yoko?

YOKO: No, you did a pretty good job.

LEADER A: Good. That was an example of how to constructively express an unpleasant feeling.

Engaging a Client in a Role Play

The modeling of a specific skill is always followed immediately by a role-play rehearsal of the same skill by a group member. The leader explains that he or she would like each group participant to have a chance to practice the skill. A role play is then set up with group member and a leader. Instructions are given to the member, and the role play is conducted.

When a skill is introduced for the first time, it is preferable for participants to practice the skill using the same role-play situation that was modeled by the leaders. The purpose of these initial role plays is to familiarize participants with the specific steps of the skill, while minimizing the adaptations necessary to use the skill in different situations. Thus, it is best at this point not to modify the role-play situation significantly. Minor alterations can be made, however, such as having the participant identify a specific TV program that he or she could pretend to be watching during the role play.

When engaging clients in role plays, the leaders begin with an individual who is likely to be cooperative and more skilled. This will enable more skilled group members to serve as role models for less skilled group members who practice the skill in role plays later in the group. We recommend making a direct request to the client to do a role play rather than offering the open-ended question "Who wants to do a role play?" Making a direct request, such as "I would like you to try a role play," is usually more effective at engaging clients than leaving the decision up to the group members themselves.

An example of the step of engaging clients in role plays is provided below.

LEADER A: I would like each of you to have a chance to practice this skill in a role play. Juanita, let's start with you. I'd like you to do a role play of this same situation with the TV.

JUANITA: Okay.

LEADER A: Good. Let's set up this role situation the same way we did before. (*Helps Juanita position her chair in the middle of the group with an empty chair for the "TV."*) Let's pretend you're watching a TV program. Juanita, what's a TV program that you like to watch?

JUANITA: *Jeopardy*.

LEADER A: Okay, let's pretend that you're watching *Jeopardy*, and Sandra is going to come into the room and change the channel. When Sandra changes the channel, I'd like you to express an unpleasant feeling to her, using the steps of the skill the way I just did. Any questions?

JUANITA: I guess not.

LEADER A: Good. Let's start the role play *now*.

LEADER B: (*Walks in the room and looks at the TV.*) I think I'd like to watch the news. (*Changes channel.*)

JUANITA: What did you do that for?!

LEADER B: I just wanted to watch a different program.

JUANITA: Well I was watching that program, and you changed the channel. Change it back!

LEADER B: But I wanted to see something different.

JUANITA: Well you just can't do that.

LEADER A: Let's stop the role play now. You did a good job on that role play, Juanita. Let's get you some feedback.

It is important to end the role play with a brief, positive statement about the participant's performance. The imperfections in Jaunita's role play will be addressed in the step of Providing Corrective Feedback.

Providing Positive Feedback

Role-play rehearsals by group participants are always immediately followed by positive feedback about what specifically the person did well. Something genuinely positive must be found in even the poorest role-play performance. Although it is important to encourage effort in participating in role plays, specific feedback about the participant's performance is necessary if behavior change is to take place.

Positive feedback can be provided both by eliciting it from other group participants and by providing it directly to the participants. To elicit positive feedback from other group members, it can be helpful after the role play is completed to inquire, "What did you like about the way _____ did that skill just now?" and "Which steps of the skill did you see _____ doing?" Specific feedback about aspects of the skill that were performed well are then given directly to the participant by other group members. The positive feedback provided by group members can then be supplemented by additional positive feedback from the leader.

The leader must be vigilant to ensure that all feedback given at this stage is positive. Negative or corrective feedback is immediately cut off. The goal at this stage of feedback is to reinforce the group member's effort in the role play and to prove some specific feedback about what was done well. Group members in social skills training soon learn that positive feedback always proceeds corrective or negative feedback, and this rapidly becomes accepted as a group norm.

Positive feedback should be as behaviorally specific as possible. The feedback may pertain to the specific steps of the skill identified on the poster or other specific nonverbal and paralinguistic skills. If the group member's role-play performance was rather poor, and the leader is concerned that group members will have difficulty identifying aspects of the role play to praise, the leader can steer the group toward providing feedback about a specific aspect of the performance that was done well. For example, the leader could ask, "What did you like about _____'s *eye contact* in that role play?" The process of providing positive feedback after a role play is usually relatively brief, lasting between 30 seconds and a couple of minutes. An example of this step of social skills training is provided below.

LEADER A: (*speaking to group*) What did you like about how Juanita did that role play just then?

LIONEL: She spoke her mind!

LEADER A: Yes, she did seem to speak her mind. Lionel, what did you think of Juanita's voice tone? Was she firm?

LIONEL: Yes, she was pretty firm.

LEADER A: And what about her eye contact? Yoko, was Juanita looking at Leader B during that role play?

YOKO: Yes, she was looking right at him.

LEADER A: That's right. Juanita, you spoke pretty firmly, and you had good eye contact in that role play. Bob, did Juanita make it clear what she was upset about?

BOB: I thought so.

LEADER A: What was she upset about?

BOB: She didn't like it when Leader B changed the channel on her.

LEADER A: That's right. (*speaking to Juanita*) You did a good job in that role play. Your eye contact and voice tone were good, and you made it clear that you were concerned when Leader B changed the TV channel while you were watching the TV.

Just as the feedback must strive to be both specific and genuine, leaders should be careful to avoid "hedging" their compliments by using phrases such as "pretty good" and "not bad."

Providing Corrective Feedback

Providing positive feedback immediately after the role play sets the stage for giving corrective feedback aimed at improving the participant's performance in the next role play. Corrective feedback should be brief, noncritical, to the point, and as behaviorally specific as possible. The aim is to identify the most critical aspects of the role-play interaction that need to be changed in order to enhance overall performance.

As with positive feedback, corrective feedback can be elicited from other group members and provided by the leader as well. At times it may be preferable for the leader alone to provide corrective feedback in order to maximize the member's ability to focus on those critical elements. Corrective feedback should not include an exhaustive list of all the problems in the group member's performance. Rather, it should focus on one or two of the most critical components of the skill.

Using phrases such as "Your role play would be even better . . ." can be helpful in suggesting modifications in a role play. Similarly, constructive feedback can be obtained from other group members by asking phrases such as "Are there ways that _____ could improve his or her skill in this role play?"

An example of providing corrective feedback is provided below.

LEADER: How do you think that Juanita could have done a better job of expressing an unpleasant feeling in this situation?

YOKO: She sounded a little bit hostile.

LEADER: What do other group members think? Did Juanita sound really mad?

BOB: Yes, I think so.

LEADER: Did Juanita make a specific verbal feeling statement about how she felt when the TV channel got changed?

YOKO: I can't remember.

LIONEL: No, she didn't.

LEADER: Juanita, I didn't notice that you made a feeling statement in that role play. Making a specific feeling statement can be helpful when expressing unpleasant feelings, because it lets the other person know exactly how you felt when they did something.

The leader might have also addressed Jaunita's hostility in the role play. However, it is common for patients to sound more hostile when they are not *verbally* expressing their feelings. Use of verbal feeling statements, such as "annoyed," "angry," and "upset" often make people actually sound less hostile. Therefore, the leader decided to focus on teaching Juanita to make a verbal feeling statement, with the expectation that it would make her sound less hostile and would be less likely to lead to an argument. In addition, it is desirable to limit the amount of corrective feedback to just a few points.

Engaging the Client in Another Role Play of the Same Situation

Identifying the specific components of a social skill that were deficient in a role play leads naturally to making suggestions for improving performance in a subsequent role play. In this step of social skills training, the participant is engaged in another role play of the same situation and is requested to make one or two small changes based on the corrective feedback that has just been given. Although corrective feedback may be given about a number of different components of social skills, the specific instructions given to the participant before the next role play are limited to one or two components that are most salient and that the client is most likely to be able to change.

In providing feedback to group members about their role-play performance, contributions are elicited from group members and provided by the leaders. However, only the leader provides specific instructions to the participant about which social skill components to change in the next role play. This ensures that the instructions given to the participant about how to improve his or her performance in the next role play are clear and within the realm of that participant's capability. As when engaging group members in role plays, it is best if the instructions for the second role play are made in the form of a request (e.g., "I would like you to . . ."), instead of a question (e.g., "Would you mind . . . ?").

An example of how to engage the patient in a second role play of the same situation is provided below.

LEADER A: Juanita, I would like you to try another role play of this same situation. As before, I would like you to practice expressing an unpleasant feeling when Leader B changes the TV channel while you're watching your program. What I'd like you to do a little bit differently this time, however, is to include a specific verbal feeling statement about how you felt when the channel was changed.

JUANITA: I thought I made my feelings pretty clear just then.

LEADER A: Your voice tone and facial expression did communicate some unpleasant feelings. However, I'd like you to be even more clear in explaining how you felt by also using words to describe your feelings.

JUANITA: Okay.

LEADER A: How would you feel if somebody changed the channel while you were in the middle of watching a program? (*Points to posterboard with different feeling statements.*)

JUANITA: I'd feel mad.

LEADER A: Good. Then what I'd like you to do in the next role play is to include the statement that you feel mad when someone changes the channel like that. Any questions?

JUANITA: No.

LEADER A: Okay, let's set up this role play like before. (*Juanita and Leader B get up out of their seats and position themselves in the center of the room.*) All right, let's start the role play now.

LEADER B: (*Walks in the room and looks at TV.*) I think I'd like to watch the news. (*Changes channel.*)

JUANITA: Hey, you changed the channel.

LEADER B: I thought I'd watch a different program.

JUANITA: I was watching that channel. It really makes me mad when you just go up and change the channel like that. Change it back!

LEADER B: Sorry about that.

LEADER A: Good. Let's stop the role play now.

Providing More Positive and Corrective Feedback

As in the group member's first role play, the second role play is immediately followed by the provision of positive and corrective feedback. When providing positive feedback, it is best to first praise the group member for any improvements he or she made in response to the specific suggestions made by the leader immediately prior to the role play. For example, if the leader requested the individual to speak more loudly in the next role play, and she succeeded in improving her voice volume, the leader would first provide positive feedback to the participant about her improved loudness.

After providing positive feedback for specifically targeted social skill components, the leader provides or elicits other positive feedback for steps of the skill that were performed well. As always, feedback should be behaviorally specific, to the point, and sincere. If the participant did not show improvement in the specific component of the skill targeted by the leader, then positive feedback is provided for other components of the skill that were performed well. Corrective feedback for the second role play should also be stated in constructive terms and be as behaviorally specific as possible. Corrective feedback is most helpful when it is provided sparingly, with an eye toward improving social skill performance still further in another role play. Too much corrective feedback can be discouraging to the participant, who may have difficulty remembering it all.

At this juncture in social skills training, the leader must make a decision about whether to engage the individual in a third (or even fourth) role play of the same situation, or whether to move on to the next group member. Several factors must be weighed in making this decision. The first and most critical factor is whether any improvement has taken place from the first to the second role play. If absolutely no improvement has occurred across the two role plays, then no demonstrated learning has taken place, and it is essential to engage the group member in another role play. Supplemental skills training techniques, described in the next chapter, can be used in subsequent role plays to maximize the chances of improving the member's performance.

The second factor in determining the need for an additional role play is cooperation. If the participant was easily engaged in the role play and has made clear progress, but still needs to improve further, he or she can readily be engaged in additional role plays to make further gains. The third factor is whether there is enough time to permit more then two role plays while still allowing for engagement with the other group members in two role plays as well. If time permits, the group member is willing, and insufficient improvement was made after the second role play, the leader should try to engage the member in a third role play, and even possibly a fourth role play.

When engaging an individual in a series of role plays, it is best to work on changing one component first, then to move on to changing a second and even third component of the skill. When group members are able to experience gradual improvement in their performance of the social skill, and positive feedback is used to reinforce these gains, participants often feel rewarded for their hard work and experience a greater sense of self-efficacy that they can learn the skill. Even when several role plays are required to improve a single component of a social skill, participants usually do not feel discouraged, because positive change is duly noted, and abundant reinforcement is provided. Through the process of repeated role plays and feedback, more effective social behavior is shaped.

When the group member has engaged in a final role play and the leader has decided not to do another role play of the same situation, a little more corrective feedback may be given. However, it is not necessary to give corrective feedback after the last role play. The primary purpose of giving corrective feedback is to make specific suggestions for how to improve social skill performance. These suggestions are most likely to be useful when they are immediately followed by an opportunity to practice the skill again in a role play. Therefore, corrective feedback serves less of a purpose for the final role play. After the final role play, it may be helpful to the participant for the leader to praise his or her effort in the role plays and to point out improvements that were made over the succession of behavior rehearsals.

An example of the step of giving additional feedback is provided below.

LEADER A: Juanita, I really like the way you included the specific feeling statement in that role play. Bob, do you remember what feeling statement Juanita made?

BOB: I think she said she felt "mad."

LEADER A: That's right. I thought you made it very clear how you felt when Leader B changed the TV channel. (*turning to other group members*) What else did you like about the way Juanita expressed an unpleasant feeling in that role play?

YOKO: She was clear about what she was upset about.

LEADER A: And what was that?

YOKO: She didn't like it when the TV channel got changed in the middle of her program.

LEADER A: Yes. What else did you like about Juanita's role play? Was her voice tone firm?

LIONEL: You bet! I wouldn't mess with her.

LEADER A: Yes, Juanita, you did have a pretty firm voice tone. How about Juanita's facial expression? Bob?

BOB: She looked pretty serious.

LEADER A: Yes, I thought so too, Bob. (*turning to Juanita*) Juanita, I think that you did a really good job in that role play just then. You had a serious facial expression and spoke in a firm voice tone. You were clear about what you were upset about, and you made a specific feeling statement.

JUANITA: I guess I did.

LEADER A: (*turning to other group members*) Does anyone have a suggestion for how Juanita could do an even better job in that situation?

LIONEL: She let it be known: "Don't mess with me!"

LEADER A: I agree, Lionel, Juanita was pretty clear about her feelings. How about the way she ended the role play? Does anyone remember what she said?

YOKO: She said, "Change it back!"

JUANITA: Yes, I told Leader B to "Turn the channel back."

LEADER A: Yes, that's what I remember, too. What do other group members think about that? Do you think that would be an effective way to get Leader B to change the channel back?

YOKO: I don't know; it might turn off the other person.

LEADER A: How come?

YOKO: Well, I thought she sounded a little hostile, like she was saying, "Turn it off *or else!*"

LEADER A: That's a good point, Yoko. If you want someone to change their behavior, sometimes it's more effective to make a request than to demand something. What do other people think? Would it be better to make a request?

BOB: Yes.

LIONEL: Maybe, but that might not work either.

LEADER A: That's true Lionel, but I've found that people tend to be more responsive to requests than demands. (*turning to Juanita*) Juanita, I'd like you to try one more role play of this situation. I'd like you to do it just the way you did it last time, with one exception. At the end I'd like you to make a request for Leader B to change the channel back rather than a demand. Okay?

JUANITA: Okay.

LEADER A: So what are you going to try to do in this role play?

JUANITA: Express an unpleasant feeling and not be so demanding.

LEADER A: That's right. I'd like you to make a request that Leader B change the channel, not a demand.

JUANITA: Right.

LEADER A: Let's set up the role play again. (*Juanita and Leader B move into their positions.*) Let's start the role play now.

LEADER B: (*Walks up to imaginary TV.*) I think I'd like to watch the news now. (*Changes channel.*)

JUANITA: Hey, you changed the TV channel, and I was in the middle of watching something.

LEADER B: So?

JUANITA: It really makes me mad when you change the channel when I'm watching a program.

LEADER B: Sorry about that.

JUANITA: I'd like you to change the TV channel back to the program I was watching.

LEADER B: Okay.

LEADER A: Let's stop the role play now. (*turning to group members*) What did you notice that Juanita did differently in that role play compared to the previous one?

LIONEL: She made a request.

LEADER: Yes, you did make a request, Juanita. I thought you stated it in a positive, effective manner. (*turning to group members*) What else did you like about Juanita's role play just then?

YOKO: I thought she was pretty clear, and she didn't sound as hostile this time.

LEADER: I agree, Yoko. (*turning to Juanita*) I thought you made it clear that you were upset, but you did not sound hostile.

JUANITA: It seemed a little more polite.

LEADER: Yes. Bob, did you think that Juanita was clear about what she was upset about?

BOB: Yes, changing the TV.

LEADER: That's good feedback, Bob. (*turning to Leader B*) Leader B, you were on the receiving end of those different role plays. Which one did you like the most?

LEADER B: Juanita, I liked your last role play the most. You were clear what you were upset about, you made a specific feeling statement, and you made a suggestion about what I could do to correct the situation.

JUANITA: Okay.

LEADER A: You did a nice job with those role plays, Juanita. I thought you really got your point across in that role play very effectively without sounding hostile.

JUANITA: I didn't really feel hostile — maybe a little bit mad.

LEADER: You did a good job, Juanita. Let's move on, and give someone else a chance to practice this skill.

Engaging Other Members in Role Plays, Positive Feedback, and Corrective Feedback

The social skills training format is established with the first group member and continues with each of the other members of the group. The same principles of role plays, behaviorally specific feedback, and abundant praise for even small improvements apply to each group member. For the initial role play, we recommend beginning with a member who is either more socially skilled or more cooperative than the others. However, we caution against engaging subsequent group members based on these criteria. Overall, in the life of a group, it is best if no particular order is followed for engaging members in role plays.

Assigning Homework

At the end of the session, the leader gives the group members a homework assignment to practice the skill before the next skills training session. The importance of homework can not be overemphasized. While role plays in the group give members the opportunity to practice new social skills, generalizing these skills to "real-world" settings is crucial to the success of social skills training. Therefore, homework assignments to practice targeted social skills are given at the end of every social skills training session, and difficulties completing homework assignments are addressed immediately as they arise.

When homework is assigned, it is important that participants understand the rationale behind an assignment. This can be explained in a straightforward manner, such as by saying, "Now that you have had an opportunity to practice this skill in some role plays here in the group, it's important for you to try the skill on your own in situations you naturally encounter in your day-to-day interactions. It's very helpful for me to know which steps you're having a success with and which ones are a problem for you. For this reason, I will be very interested in learning what happens when you try to use the skill outside the group." Once the rationale for homework has been established, it need not be repeated in every group. However, when confronted with noncompliance on homework assignments, the leader should first ask questions to assess the group member's understanding of the rationale for giving homework.

In order to maximize the chances that a homework assignment will be completed, it is important that the assignment be clear, as specific as possible, and within the realm of the person's capability. When possible, individualizing homework assignments can facilitate follow-through. For example, asking group members to identify specific situations in which they could practice the skill is more effective than instructing them in a general way to practice the skill on their own. A final consideration is the use of written materials or other documentation regarding the completion of homework assignments. Some social skills trainers find it helpful to provide homework sheets for participants to record completion of their homework assignments. These sheets are distributed at the end of each group, and group members bring the completed sheets back to the next group. The use of homework sheets is often appropriate in working with higher-functioning participants. Cognitively impaired or highly symptomatic individuals, however, often have difficulty keeping track of the sheets and completing them appropriately.

An example of providing a homework assignment is provided below.

LEADER: I'm very pleased that all of you did such a good job working on this skill today. Before we meet next time, I would like you to do a homework assignment. The assignment is to find at least one situation where you could try out the skill of expressing unpleasant feelings. Remember that skills training can only be effective if you try the skills we practice here in the group in real situations you encounter on your own. Do you have any questions about this assignment?

YOKO: Leader B was always nice and friendly in the role plays we did in group. But people aren't always like that. What do we do if the other person gets on our case?

LEADER: That's a good question, Yoko. I have found that if you try to express an unpleasant feeling in a constructive manner and avoid getting hostile, that most people will respond positively and will hear you out. That doesn't mean that they'll always do what you ask them to, but it usually doesn't worsen the situation.

LIONEL: But what if it does?

LEADER: In general, it is best to avoid getting into an argument with someone who is hostile to you when you express your feelings. If this happens, we'll see if anybody can come up with some good ideas on how to handle that type of a difficult situation.

LIONEL: Okay.

LEADER: Let's talk a little bit about some situations where you might be able to use the skill of expressing unpleasant feelings. Bob, what is a situation that might happen in the next couple of days where you might be able to use this skill?

BOB: I'm not sure.

LEADER: Are there any people you sometimes have conflicts with, or issues that come up again and again? Such as with your roommate?

BOB: My roommate sometimes bothers me when he listens to the radio too loud.

LEADER: That's a good example, Bob. For your homework assignment, I'd like you to express an unpleasant feeling to your roommate about his playing the stereo too loud. When might be a good time to talk to him about this, Bob?

BOB: Over dinner?

LEADER: That sounds like a good time to me. At our next group meeting, Bob, I'll be interested in hearing how your conversation with your roommate went.

BOB: Okay.

LEADER: Juanita, how about you? What is a situation you might encounter in the next few days where you could express an unpleasant feeling? . . .

Table 3.1 summarizes the 10 basic steps for teaching a social skill. They are the foundation for introducing a new skill as described in this chapter. They are also the foundation for consolodating the skill in subsequent sessions as described in the chapter that follows.

TABLE 3.1. Social Skills Training

---

1. *Establish rationale for the skill.*
   - Elicit reasons for learning the skill from group participants.
   - Acknowledge all contributions.
   - Provide additional reasons not mentioned by group members.

2. *Discuss the steps of the skill.*
   - Break down the skill into three or four steps.
   - Write the steps on a board or poster.
   - Discuss the reason for each step.
   - Check for understanding of each step.

3. *Model the skill in a role play.*
   - Plan out the role play in advance.
   - Explain that you will demonstrate the skill in a role play.
   - Use two leaders to model the skill.
   - Keep the role play simple.

4. *Review the role play with the participants.*
   - Discuss whether each step of the skill was used in the role play.
   - Ask group members to evaluate the effectiveness of the role model.
   - Keep the review brief and to the point.

5. *Engage a group member in a role play of the same situation.*
   - Start with an individual who is more skilled or is likely to be compliant.
   - Request the client to try the skill in a role play with one of the leaders.
   - Ask the client questions to make sure he or she understands his or her goal.
   - Instruct group members to observe the client.

6. *Provide positive feedback.*
   - Elicit positive feedback from group members about the group member's skills.
   - Encourage feedback that is specific.
   - Cut off any negative feedback.
   - Praise effort and provide hints to group members about good performance.

7. *Provide corrective feedback.*
   - Elicit suggestions for how group member could do the skill better next time.
   - Limit the feedback to one or two suggestions.
   - Strive to communicate the suggestions in a positive, upbeat manner.

8. *Engage the group member in another role play of the same situation.*
   - Request that the group member change one behavior in the role play.
   - Ask the member questions to check on his or her understanding of the suggestion.
   - Try to work on behaviors that are most critical and changeable.

9. *Provide additional feedback.*
   - Be generous but specific when providing positive feedback.
   - Focus first on the behavior that the individual was requested to change.
   - Engage group member in two to four role plays with feedback after each one.
   - Use other behavior-shaping strategies to improve skills, such as coaching, prompting, and supplemental modeling.

10. *Assign homework.*
    - When possible, tailor the assignment to each individual's level of skill.
    - Give an assignment to practice the skill.
    - Ask group members to identify situations in which they could use the skill.

Summary

Social skills training is a set of teaching strategies, based on social learning theory, designed to systematically help individuals develop more effective skills for interacting with others. Skills training techniques are based on a number of learning principles, including *modeling* (observational learning), *reinforcement* (verbal praise for effective components of social skill), *shaping* (reinforcing successive approximations toward a desired goal), *overlearning* (repeatedly practicing the skill untill it becomes automatic), and *generalization* (the transfer of skills from the training setting to another setting via homework).

Social skills can be taught in a variety of different formats, ranging from group treatment, individual psychotherapy, or family or couple therapy. Social skills training is taught following a sequence of steps: (1) establish a rationale for learning the skill; (2) discuss the component steps of the skill; (3) model (demonstrate) the positive feedback; (6) provide corrective feedback; (7) engage the client in another role play of the same situation; (8) provide more positive and corrective feedback; (9) if working with a group, engage other clients in role plays, positive feedback, and corrective feedback; and (10) assign homework to practice the skill.

4

Techniques for Consolidating
Social Skills

In the previous chapter we described the format for the first session in which a social skill is introduced. However, because more than one session is usually devoted to teaching a particular skill, it is important to review the format for continuing to work on the skill. In this chapter we describe the format for conducting sessions after the first one in which a skill was introduced. A flow-chart is presented in Table 4.1.

Homework

Except for the very first social skills training session, all sessions begin with a review of the homework assignment given at the end of the previous session. The review of homework serves several purposes. It provides information about whether group members were able to identify appropriate situations in which the targeted skill could be used and whether the person was successful in using that skill. In addition, the homework assignment helps to identify real-life situations that can be used in role plays in the group to continue working on the skill. The overall strategy for the group is to first acquaint members with the steps of the skill by using standardized role-play situations. Then, in subsequent sessions, real-life situations that group members have encountered or expect to encounter are practiced in the group.

The review of homework begins with the leader asking group members about specific situations when they tried to use the particular skill. During the homework review, leaders assess both whether group members are able to identify appropriate situations in which they could use the skill as well as the members' ability to use the skill effectively. The individual group member is then instructed either to show what happened in the situation (if he or

TABLE 4.1. Flow within sessions

Time	Training activity
First 5 minutes	Review homework and reinforce effort.
Next 5–15 minutes	Engage each client in role plays, feedback, corrective instructions, etc., based on homework or other real-life situations.
Next 20–30 minutes	Continue work on the same skill with additional role plays of different situations *or* start a new skill by establishing a rationale, modeling, role playing, feedback, etc.
Last 5–10 minutes	Assign homework, individually tailoring assignments when possible.

she tried to use the skill) or to try practicing how they might have used the skill (if the person forgot to use the skill). The leader encourages the participant to describe the situation in sufficient detail that it can be determined if it is suitable for using the skill. It is preferable to avoid a full recitation of what happened in the situation and to focus instead on getting the participant to show what happened in a role play. After the role play is completed, positive and corrective feedback are given, and if further improvements can be made, additional role plays of that situation are conducted.

When the participant reports that he or she has successfully used the skill, and demonstrates good performance of the skill in the role play, the leader inquires as to whether the participant's goals in the situation were achieved. Positive consequences of using the skill are pointed out and the group member's effort at using the skill is recognized. If the group member used the skill but did not meet with success, the leader can lead a brief discussion focused on identifying other strategies that might have been used to achieve the goal in the situation.

When reviewing homework, the leader is sometimes confronted with the problem of individuals who did not follow through on the assignment. With these group members, the goal is to help them identify appropriate situations that they have encountered or may encounter in the near future in which they could use the skill. These situations are then used to set up role plays in which the member practices the skill in the group. At the end of the session, when providing the next homework assignment, the leader explores obstacles to completing homework with those individuals who did not do their homework and arrives at a plan for circumventing those obstacles.

An example is provided below of how homework is reviewed and how role plays in the group can be structured based on the homework. This vignette is with the same group as the previous vignettes in the preceding chapter, but it takes place in the session after the skill Expressing Unpleasant Feelings was first introduced.

LEADER: I'd like to start by finding out how your homework assignment went. I asked each of you to try to find at least one situation where you could use the skill of expressing unpleasant feelings. What kind of situations did you come up with?

YOKO: I got into a fight with my mother.

LEADER: That sounds like that might be a good situation to use the skill, Yoko. Could you tell us a little bit more about what happened?

YOKO: Well, my mother keeps saying we'll go out for lunch, but then every time it comes around to the date, she calls up and cancels. She always says, "Something else came up."

LEADER: That's certainly an appropriate situation in which to express an unpleasant feeling. Did you try to express a unpleasant feeling to your mother about this?

YOKO: I tried, but it didn't work out very well.

LEADER: Let's set up a role play of this situation and see what happened. Yoko, who would be a good person to play your mother in this role play?

YOKO: Juanita.

LEADER: Okay. Juanita, I'd like you to play the role of Yoko's mother. Yoko, where did this situation take place?

YOKO: Over the telephone. She called me at 11:30 yesterday and said she couldn't make our lunch appointment.

LEADER: All right, so in this role play, your mother, played by Juanita, will call you to tell you she can't make lunch. Yoko, I'd like you to respond just the way you responded to your mother yesterday when she called. Any questions?

YOKO: No.

JUANITA: No.

LEADER: I'd like both of you to pretend to be talking on the telephone. Juanita, you start the role play by calling Yoko and telling her you can't make your lunch appointment. (*Sets up role play.*) Let's start the role play now.

JUANITA: (*Pretends to talk on the telephone.*) Hello, Yoko. I'm sorry, but I can't make lunch today. Something's come up.

YOKO: You have to cancel lunch again?! Something always seems to come up! Why don't I ever count? Why can't you think of somebody other than yourself?

JUANITA: I'm sorry, Yoko, but you're not the only person in the world.

YOKO: But I should count!

LEADER: Okay, let's stop the role play now. Let's give Yoko some feedback. What do you like about the way Yoko handled that situation?

LIONEL: (*to Yoko*) I thought you came right out and told your mother what you were unhappy about.

LEADER: That's true, Yoko, you got to the point. Bob, what did you think about Yoko's voice tone? Did she sound firm?

BOB: Yes, she did.

LEADER: Yes, I thought you sounded quite firm, Yoko. Was this role play similar to the situation that occurred?

YOKO: It was a little bit similar, but I got madder when it really happened.

LEADER: And how did your mother react?

YOKO: She got madder, too, and then I hung up on her.

LEADER: I see. I noticed that in this last role play you didn't make a specific feeling statement about how you felt when your mother canceled your lunch appointment.

YOKO: I guess I never said how I really felt. But she knew I was mad.

LEADER: I'd like you to do a second role play of the situation, Yoko, and this time include a very clear feeling statement to your Mom about her canceling your lunch appointment.

YOKO: Okay.

LEADER: Are you ready to do another role play, Juanita?

JUANITA: Yes.

LEADER: Okay. Let's start the role play now.

JUANITA: (*Pretends to talk on the telephone.*) Yoko, I'm calling to tell you I can't make our lunch appointment. I'll have to reschedule.

YOKO: Mom, it really makes me mad when you cancel our lunch appointments like this.

JUANITA: I'm sorry, Yoko. Something just came up.

YOKO: Well it makes me feel mad.

JUANITA: Sorry.

LEADER: Let's stop the role play now. What did you notice that Yoko did differently in the second role play compared to the first one?

BOB: She said she felt "mad."

LEADER: That's right, Bob. (*turning to Yoko*) You made a very clear feeling statement to your mother about how you felt when she canceled your lunch appointment. I thought you did a good job making your feelings known just then.

I'd like you to try this role play just one more time, Yoko, and this time make one more small change. When you have an unpleasant feeling about a situation, sometimes it's helpful to suggest a way for the other person to prevent the situation from happening again, like in the last step of this skill. In this next role play, I'd like you to make a suggestion to your mother about how to prevent the situation from happening again.

YOKO: All right.

LEADER: Good. When you express an unpleasant feeling to your mother in this role play, make a clear feeling statement like you did before, and also suggest how to prevent the situation from happening again. Are you ready, Juanita?

JUANITA: Yes.

LEADER: Okay, let's start the role play now.

JUANITA: (*Pretends to talk on the telephone.*) Yoko, honey, I'm sorry I can't make our lunch appointment today.

YOKO: Mom, I really feel mad when you keep canceling our lunch appointments like this.

JUANITA: I'm sorry, Yoko, something just came up.

YOKO: Well I still feel mad, Mom. Next time I'd like to set up a time to get together where nothing can interfere with our plans.

JUANITA: That sounds like a good idea, Yoko. Lunch time is often busy. Maybe we should get together for dinner.

YOKO: I'd like that.

LEADER: Let's stop the role play now. You did a great job, Yoko. What did you like about Yoko's last role play?

LIONEL: She tried to solve the problem.

LEADER: That's right. I thought that talking to your mother about how to prevent the situation from happening again was very constructive. How about the other steps of this skill? Did Yoko speak in a firm voice tone?

BOB: Yes.

LEADER: And did she make a clear feeling statement?

BOB: Yes.

LEADER: And was she clear about what upset her?

LIONEL: She didn't like her mother canceling her lunch appointment.

LEADER: That's right. Juanita, what did you think about Yoko's last role play?

JUANITA: I thought she sounded real serious and that she got her message across. But at the same time, she didn't put me off. She seemed to want to try to change the situation, and I liked that.

LEADER: Yes. Yoko, I agree with Juanita. You came across that you were upset about the situation, but you tried to take steps to prevent it from happening again. Nice job, Yoko.

Bob, in our last session we gave you a homework assignment to express an unpleasant feeling to your roommate about playing his stereo too loud. I'd like to know how that went. . . .

When engaging group members in role plays based on actual situations they have encountered, the leader may allow them to participate in role plays with each other, rather than with one of the leaders. An advantage of this is that it allows members a little more leeway in structuring role plays that are similar to the actual situations they experienced, because they can select any person in the group who reminds them of the other person in the situation. A disadvantage is that the leader retains less control over the role play when it involves two clients rather than just one. Clinical judgment must be exercised when one is determining whether or not to allow members to participate in role plays together. When the role play involves two group members, the leader can give instructions to the second one about how to respond in the situation.

Pacing of Social Skills Training

There is no golden rule to determine how long to spend teaching each skill over the course of social skills training. Several different factors must be weighed in determining when it is best to introduce a new skill. First, it is important that all or most group members demonstrate some improvement in the social skill that has been the focus of training. Second, the amount of interest generated by continued work on a skill needs to be considered. If group members are beginning to feel restless when working on a particular skill, and definite gains have been made, it may be time to move on, even if there is still room for some improvements. Third, the overall level of client functioning has some bearing on how long to spend on each skill. More-impaired clients typically require more time and practice to acquire targeted social skills.

Most groups of clients benefit from spending at least two or three sessions working on a particular social skill, and some may require as many as six to 10 sessions. However, after the group has moved on to new skills, old skills should be reviewed on a periodic basis to ensure that gains made do not dissipate.

Additional Teaching Strategies

Up to this point we've described how social skills are taught using a combination of leader modeling, role-play rehearsal, positive and corrective feedback, verbal instructions, and more role-play rehearsal and feedback. These methods are the core of social skills training. However, additional teaching strategies can be useful in helping group members learn skills when verbal instructions alone are ineffective at producing behavior change. These strategies should be used as frequently as necessary to facilitate skill development. The primary goal is to ensure that some improvement in social skill takes place within each social skills training session. Four different teaching strategies are described below: supplementary modeling, discrimination modeling, coaching, and prompting.

Supplementary Modeling

Modeling is one of the most powerful teaching tools available to clinicians. In addition to leaders modeling to demonstrate a newly introduced skill, they can provide *supplementary modeling* at any time throughout the group. The primary distinction between initial and supplementary modeling is that the latter is provided for an individual member, and the leader plays the role of that client in a role play.

Supplementary modeling is usually employed when verbal instructions to change a particular social skill component do not result in the desired change. Rather than relying on additional verbal instructions, the leader explains to the participant that he or she would like to demonstrate what he or she means in a role play. The participant is instructed to pay close attention to the specific component of the skill that is demonstrated in the role play. The leader explains that he or she will play the role of the client in the role play. When the role play has been completed, the leader gets feedback from the participant about the specific component skill that was demonstrated. This is immediately followed by the participant practicing the skill in a role play, with special attention paid to the targeted component skill. When the group member has completed the role play, positive and corrective feedback are provided as usual.

An example of supplemental modeling is provided below, using the group member Bob. He has just completed his second role play of the skill Expressing Unpleasant Feelings. Before this role play, the leader instructed him to make a clear verbal feeling statement in the role play. However, Bob forgot to include this specific feeling statement in the second role play. The leader has elicited positive feedback for aspects of the skill that Bob performed well. The example begins with the leader providing corrective feedback to Bob, followed by the use of supplemental modeling to demonstrate the skill for him.

LEADER A: I noticed in your role play, Bob, that you did not include a feeling statement about how you felt when Leader B changed the TV channel.

BOB: I guess I forgot.

LEADER A: Yes, that sometimes happens. I would like to show you what I mean by making a feeling statement. In this role play, I'm going to play the part of you, and Leader B is going to play the same role she played before; that is, she's going to change the channel while I'm watching it. I would like you to watch me during this role play, and pay particular attention to the feeling statement that I make. Do you have any questions?

BOB: No.

LEADER A: What are you going to look for real closely in this role play?

BOB: To see if you make a feeling statement.

LEADER A: Right! Okay, let's set up this role play. (*Exchanges places with Bob in order to take his part in the role play. Chairs are rearranged accordingly, and the role play commences.*)

LEADER B: I think I'd like to watch the news now. (*Changes TV channel.*)

LEADER A: Excuse me, I was watching my TV program. It really annoys me when you change the TV station in the middle of a program that I'm watching. I would appreciate it if you would check with me first before changing the station while I'm watching TV.

LEADER B: All right, sorry about that.

LEADER A: All right, let's stop this role play now. (*Leaders move out of their positions.*)

LEADER A: Bob, did you notice what feeling statement I made in that role play?

BOB: You said you felt annoyed.

LEADER A: Good! That's right. How about the other steps of the skill? Were my voice tone and eye contact good?

BOB: Yes.

LEADER A: Did I make it clear what I was upset about?

BOB: Yes, changing the channel.

LEADER A: And did I suggest how the situation could be changed?

BOB: Yes, you told her to check with you first.

LEADER A: Right. Now, Bob, I'd like you to do this role play one more time and to make a clear feeling statement, just like you saw me do in this role play just now. (*Bob and Leader B move back into the center of the group, and the role play begins.*)

Discrimination Modeling

Discrimination modeling refers to a method of highlighting a specific component of a social skill by modeling the skill in two role plays, one immediately following the other. The role plays are identical except for the one component to be highlighted. This component is performed poorly in the first role play and competently in the second role play. Group members are asked to observe both role plays and to attend to which component skill is different.

Discrimination modeling can be a useful strategy when one is discussing with group members the specific components of the social skill. It can also be used when a group member has difficulty modifying a particular component skill based on verbal feedback from the leader or other group members. In addition to asking group members to identify which component skill is different across the two role plays, group members can be asked to judge which of the two role plays was more effective.

Discrimination modeling can also be a very effective method for highlighting the importance of specific nonverbal and paralinguistic behaviors, such as eye contact and voice volume. By exaggerating poor performance of these component skills, in contrast to good performance, the value of the skill can be easily appreciated by all the group members. Discrimination modeling can also be used to highlight verbal steps of the skill, but it is most effective for the nonverbal and paralinguistic elements.

An example of how discrimination modeling can be introduced follows.

LEADER: We've talked about how voice tone and loudness can be an important part of social skill. We would like to demonstrate this importance in a couple of role plays. We're going to do two role plays of the same situation. We would like you to pay attention to how my behavior in the two role plays is different. When we are done with the two role plays, we will ask you to explain how they were different, and whether I was a more effective communicator in one role play than in the other.

After this introduction, the leader would first demonstrate poor voice tone in a role play by speaking very quitely and meekly. Then, in the second role play, he or she would strive to speak in a strong, clear, assertive voice tone.

After the two role plays are completed, the leader can stimulate a brief discussion among group members by asking questions such as "What did I do differently in the second role play compared to the first one?"; "Was I more effective in one role play than another? Why?"; "What did you think about how I came across in the first role play?"; "How was this different in the second role play?"; "Which role play did you like better? Why?" The discussion of the two role plays need not be an extended one. Usually several minutes are sufficient to underscore the importance of the skill component in question.

Coaching

Coaching refers to the use of verbal prompts to the participant during a role play to perform specific components of a social skill. Coaching is most often used when verbal instructions before the role play are unsuccessful in producing the desired change in social skill. Rather than simply providing additional verbal instructions and hoping that the participant will be able to do better in the next role play, the leader helps the participant through the role play by providing verbal prompts as necessary.

Coaching can be done spontaneously when it is apparent that the group member has forgotten a step of the social skill in the role play. The member can be prompted to use a specific skill by whispering the reminder in the his or her ear during the role play. After the participant has completed the role play, feedback is provided as usual. Then, the participant is engaged in another role play of the same situation, this time without the coaching (or a lessened amount of coaching). The basic goals of coaching are to enable the participant to perform the skill with help and then to decrease the amount of help provided in subsequent role plays.

The first time coaching is used, the group member may express some surprise, and it may evoke mild laughter from other group members. However, members quickly become accustomed to coaching and appreciate the help they receive in performing the skill. It is preferable if coaching is used *after* verbal instructions alone have not resulted in behavior change. Otherwise, overreliance on coaching can interfere with the assessment of the member's ability to perform the skill. Also, certain highly symptomatic individuals are not good candidates for coaching because of their paranoid reactions to someone speaking in their ear.

An example of how to coach is provided below. In this example, Lionel is practicing the skill of expressing an unpleasant feeling. In the first role play, Lionel forgot to make a feeling statement. The leader instructed Lionel to make a feeling statement before the second role play, but Lionel forgot to include this statement. The example begins right before the third role play.

LEADER A: Lionel, I would like you to try another role play of this situation. In this role play, I'd like you to pay special attention to expressing your feelings about the TV channel being changed. How do you feel when someone changes the channel while you're in the middle of watching a program?

LIONEL: I don't know. It bothers me I guess.

LEADER A: Good. In this role play I'd like you to tell Leader B that it bothers you when she changes the channel. Okay?

LIONEL: Okay.

LEADER A: (*Lionel and Leader B move to the center of the room, and chairs are rearranged accordingly.*) Let's begin the role play now.

LEADER B: I think I'd like to watch the news now. (*Pretends to change TV channel.*)

LIONEL: Hey what did you do that for?

LEADER B: I wanted to watch the news.

LIONEL: You can't do that, I was in the middle of watching my program.

LEADER B: I wanted to see something else.

LIONEL: You can't do that.

LEADER B: Why not?

LIONEL: Because I was watching something. (*Leader A kneels down next to Lionel and whispers into his ear, "It bothers me. . . ."*) It bothers me when you change the channel.

LEADER B: I'm sorry.

LIONEL: Would you change it back?

LEADER B: Okay.

LEADER A: Let's stop the role play now. Lionel, I really liked the fact that you made a clear verbal statement in that last role play. You told Leader B that it bothered you when she changed the channel like that. I'd like you to try this role play one more time, and this time I'm not going to coach you. I'd like you to remember to include a feeling statement, just the way you did in this last role play. Any questions? . . .

Prompting

Prompting is the use of nonverbal signals during a role play to improve a component of social skill. Prompting is most useful for changing nonverbal and paralinguistic features of social skill, such as eye contact and voice volume. Unlike coaching, the meaning of specific prompts may not be clear to the participant unless they are discussed prior to the role play. Therefore, immediately before the role play, the leader discusses the specific prompt he or she will use in the role play and how the participant should respond.

One common hand signal used in prompting is for the leader to point to his or her eye to indicate that the participant should increase eye contact during the role play. Another common hand signal is to motion one's thumb upward to indicate that the participant should speak more loudly during the role play. Both of these hand signals are provided as needed throughout the role play, with the leader standing directly behind the person with whom the group member is interacting in the role play. As with coaching, prompting is used to facilitate performance during the role play and is then faded in subsequent role plays. An example of how to set up a role play with prompting is provided below.

LEADER: Bob, I noticed that it is sometimes hard for you to speak loudly enough in your role play.

BOB: Yes.

LEADER: For the next role play, I would like to arrange a signal to help you to remember to speak up. During this role play I'm going to stand behind Leader B where you can see me. Whenever I want you to speak up, I'll point my thumb up, and I'll keep doing that until you speaking loudly enough. (*Demonstrates signal.*) If your voice trails off again, then I'll just use the same signal again. Is that clear?

BOB: I understand.

Different Training Modalities

Thus far in this chapter we have described how to conduct social skills training in a group format. Although there are obvious advantages to the group format, other formats for skills training can be suitable as well. Social skills training conducted with individuals, families, or couples can be an excellent way of supplementing or improving the generalization of group-based social skills training. Some considerations for addressing these other formats for social skills training are addressed below.

Individual Format

Individual social skills training can be used either to supplement group-based training or alone. It can also be used in combination with other therapeutic techniques, such as psychoeducation and stress management training. Sometimes individuals are reluctant to attend social skills training groups, and a limited number of individual skills training sessions can help prepare them for participating in the group. In such cases, it can be beneficial for the individual therapist, if he or she is not the group leader, to attend some of the early group sessions with the individuals. This strategy can gradually ease the participant into the group with the minimum amount of stress.

When individual skills training is conducted on a long-term basis, several modifications in skills training procedures may be necessary. To avoid the repetition of the therapist always engaging in role plays with the individual, it can be useful to elicit the occasional help of another person to participate in the role plays. Trips with the therapist into the community to practice social skills may also provide necessary variations in the training procedures.

Another consideration when using an individual format is the content of the session. In group skills training, sessions are devoted exclusively to training specific social skills. In individual skills training, sessions may also focus on skill development, but they may address other topics as well. For example, skills training sessions can address topics such as education about the psychiatric illness, strategies to manage stress (e.g., relaxation techniques), methods for coping with persistent symptoms, or leisure and recreational activities. Thus, social skills training can either be the dominant form of therapy provided or one of a variety of strategies in a clinician's armamentarium of techniques.

Couple and Family Format

Social skills training for couples or families can be an effective strategy for improving communication and decreasing stress. It has been well established that patients with schizophrenia are highly susceptible to the negative effects of critical and emotionally laden communications from family members ("expressed emotion"; Kavanagh, 1992). More effective communication skills can be taught using skills training techniques, thereby decreasing the stress on everyone in the family.

Treatment manuals are available that describe the rudiments of social skills training with families and couples (Falloon, Boyd, & McGill, 1984; Mueser & Glynn, 1995). Typically, skills training approaches with families emphasize work on conflict resolution and skills for expressing positive feelings and making requests. The emphasis is on developing more effective communication skills using the same procedures as when one is conducting social skills training groups. Skills training with families is usually combined with other therapeutic techniques, such as psychoeducation.

When one is working with families, the primary focus is on *all* family members, not just the client. Since family sessions usually occur on a weekly basis or less frequently, participants tend to acquire skills at a slow rate. Therefore, family-based social skills training is usually not a satisfactory alternative to more intensive group-based social skills training. However, family and couple sessions can provide a useful complement to group skills training. Furthermore, when relatives review the skills that are taught in group sessions, they can then prompt and reinforce patients' use of these skills in their day-to-day interactions. Meeting regularly with relatives and other significant persons to review the skills taught in groups is an effective strategy for programming the generalization of social skills to the natural environment.

Summary

In addition to the teaching strategies described in Chapter 3, skills trainers may utilize a number of additional methods for helping clients acquire better social skills, including *supplementary modeling* (modeling the skill in additional role plays for the client), *discrimination modeling* (modeling good vs. poor performance of the skill in subsequent role plays to highlight differences), *coaching* (providing verbal prompts to the client during the role play), and *prompting* (providing verbal prompts to the client during the role play).

Social skills training incorporates a diverse set of clinically based strategies into a structured teaching format. The methods can be adapted to teach skills to a wide variety of schizophrenia patients, while ensuring that the learning process is both rewarding as well as not stressful.

5

Starting a Skills Group

As described in Chapters 3 and 4, social skills training utilizes a structured format that can be adapted for use with individuals, couples, families, and groups. Providing social skills training to people with schizophrenia in a group format has several advantages. For example, groups can provide clients with a variety of models as they see both group leaders and peers practicing the skills being taught. Clients also receive support and feedback from both of these sources. Another advantage of the group setting is that it can encourage clients to socialize with their peers. This is particularly important for individuals with schizophrenia because their symptoms often make it difficult for them to interact with others. Participating in a group can help foster a sense of community among the clients that may, in turn, reduce the sense of social isolation that many feel and provide an opportunity for friendships to develop that may be pursued outside of the group setting. In addition, social skills training in groups is both an efficient and cost-effective approach to rehabilitation, as several clients can participate in a group led by two leaders. This chapter provides practical advice necessary for beginning a social skills group.

Practical Considerations When Planning a Group

The importance of preparation for the group cannot be overemphasized. In the planning phase of any project, one must begin by clarifying a rationale for its creation. Planning for a social skills group is no different; it is important to be clear as to why there is a need for such a group and what its objectives will be. Paying careful attention to pregroup tasks and concerns will greatly increase the likelihood of having a successful group. The following questions are important to consider when one is planning a social skills group.

1. Who will participate in the group? Clients with the same skill deficits or those with different deficits? Clients in the hospital or those living in the community? Higher- or lower-functioning clients? Clients with or without a substance use disorder?
2. What are the goals of the group? What will clients gain by participating in it?
3. How long will the group be conducted? Will it be time-limited or open-ended?
4. How many clients will be in the group? Where will the group meet? How often will it meet? How long will each meeting last?
5. What characteristics and background are you looking for in a group leader? Who will lead the group, and how will the responsibilities of leading be divided?
6. What client screening and selection procedures will be used? What is the rationale for using these procedures?
7. How will clients be prepared for participation in the group? How will leaders articulate the group goals to clients? How will clients set individual goals. What ground rules will be established by the group leaders at the onset?
8. What evaluation procedures will be used? What follow-up procedures?
9. How will other staff be involved in reinforcing the skills taught in group? How can they encourage generalization of skills to outside the group?

The answers to these questions will depend on a number of factors including the group composition, size, setting, frequency, duration, and logistics. Guidelines for addressing these and other issues related to starting a group will be provided in the remainder of this chapter.

Group Composition

It is usually easier to conduct social skills training when group members function at a similar level. Group leaders should make every effort to identify clients with similar deficits during the assessment process, as a group will run more smoothly when its members are focusing on related goals.

However, often it is not feasible to match all clients on skill level. Clients can still benefit from being in groups with members with differing abilities. Therefore, it is important for the leaders to learn ways to balance the needs of all the members of the group regardless of skill level. For example, clients who are making progress slowly in group can learn from, and be encouraged by, the improvement being made by more advanced clients. The more advanced clients often experience the satisfaction of helping out others having difficulty, boosting their self-esteem, and providing valuable practice using the skills with others. Further strategies for tailoring the group to meet the specific needs of all of its members are discussed in Chapter 7.

Group Size

The ideal size for a group is between four and 10 clients, with size determined mainly by the functional level of impairment (e.g., severity of positive or negative symptoms, level of independent living). Small group size allows leaders to provide more focused teaching, including more explanation about role plays, modeling, and role-play rehearsal for clients who may have difficulty concentrating due to symptoms or cognitive deficits. On the other hand, if the group consists of primarily less-impaired clients, then up to 10 clients can be accomodated. The limiting factor in group size is that group leaders must ensure that all clients have ample opportunity to practice targeted skills, as well as to reap the benefits of having a variety of models to observe.

Duration of Groups

Deciding how long a group should run and whether it will be time-limited or ongoing requires that the group leaders take several factors into account. External constraints must be considered, such as the type of facility they are working in, whether the group members are in a hospital setting or living in the community, the length of time clients are available, as well as their level of functioning. In addition, group leaders need to determine the breadth of the group's focus. Will it be a group that is designed to improve clients' general social skills functioning, or will it be focused on a specific goal, such as improving friendship skills?

For example, leaders conducting groups in long-term inpatient facilities may have greater flexibility to work on improving a broad range of social skills. On the other hand, a short-term group that takes place in a day hospital and is designed to improve client assertiveness cannot work on a range of skills. In addition, the level of client functioning will also impact on the leaders' ability to work on a range of skills. Leaders working with highly impaired clients will need to focus on basic skills such as Listening to Others, Making Requests, and Expressing Unpleasant Feelings, while those working with less-impaired clients have freedom to work on a greater number of skills.

Frequency and Length of Meetings

When determining how many times a week to hold group meetings, it is important for group leaders once again to ask themselves the following questions: What is the focus of the group? Will it be time-limited or on-going? How impaired are the group members? As a rule, it is best if time-limited groups meet two or more times a week. This provides clients with ample opportunities to practice the skills being taught. The more time clients spend in groups practicing the skills, the greater the likelihood that they will be able to incorporate the skills and use them outside of the group. Ongoing groups may also provide multiple weekly training sessions, or in some cases, they may employ weekly sessions as a maintenance or "booster" strategy.

Determining how long each group meeting should last depends primarily on the level of impairment of the group members. Meetings should be shorter for highly symptomatic or cognitively impaired clients than for less symptomatic ones. For example, a group comprised of highly symptomatic clients who can be expected to have difficulties concentrating may last only 20 minutes, whereas a less symptomatic group may last up to 1 hour or longer. In a group with clients of varying levels of symptomatology, group leaders must be sensitive to the individuals' needs at any given meeting. Such a group could be scheduled for 1 hour, but it could shortened if necessary.

Logistics

The major logistics that need to be considered when one is planning a social skills group include the setting and timing of the group.

SETTING

As a rule, it is wise to hold meetings within a naturally occurring group setting such as an inpatient unit, a day treatment program, or a structured living residence. In this way, the group members will already be at the location of the meeting and will not require that any additional support services be coordinated, such as transportation and the supervision for transport. In addition, clients are usually more relaxed and comfortable in these familiar surroundings.

When groups are held where clients spend much of their time, the leaders can also incorporate the setting into role-play scenarios. Practicing role plays in familiar surroundings may also increase the chances that clients will connect what was taught in group with events happening outside of the group in the same environment. The closer the role plays mirror real life, the greater the likelihood that clients will be able to use the skills outside of the group setting.

Choosing a room that is conducive to learning social skills is another task that requires some foresight on the part of the group leaders. The room should be far enough away from "high traffic" areas, such as the day room of a hospital, so as to shield group participants from distractions. Ideally, the room should have a door that closes it off from the rest of the facility and be large enough that group members can participate in role plays without feeling closed in or cramped.

TIMING

When deciding upon a time to hold the group meetings, it is important that the group leaders choose a time that does not conflict with other scheduled activities that the clients are involved in, especially recreational activities. Social skills training should be used to enhance clients' skills when they participate in other activities. Clients need to be encouraged to take part in activities outside of the group so that they can practice what they have learned. Also, early mornings are usually not good times for many clients.

Once a location and time are chosen, it is best not to change them. Frequent changes in the time and location can be disorienting and quite stressful for some clients. The group needs to enhance these patients' level of comfort by providing a sense of structure and continuity, which may enable them to participate more fully in the group.

Incentives for Participation

All of the time and energy focused on planning for the group will have been of little value if leaders cannot get clients to attend the groups. Therefore, building in incentives for client participation is an important consideration when planning for a group. Some incentives that have been successfully used include providing special privileges for those who regularly attend the group, holding a monthly pizza party, or scheduling special recreational activities for those who actively participate in the groups. Coffee, soft drinks, and cookies can be served at the conclusion of each session as an ongoing incentive. Leaders can tailor the incentives to meet the needs and desires of the group members.

Selecting Group Leaders

Group leaders can come from a variety of clinical backgrounds. Counselors, activity therapists, occupational therapists, case managers, social workers, nurses, psychologists, and psychiatrists have been successfully trained to lead social skills groups. The formal degrees and job titles of the group leaders appear to be less important than other characteristics, such as warmth, clinical experience, and an interest in the clients served.

Highly structured teaching techniques are employed by group leaders. Leaders take an active role throughout the group by modeling the skill being taught, role playing with group members, and providing feedback to group members. The leaders do not focus their attention on "group process" or encourage the general "sharing of feelings," unless they are directly related to the skills being taught. The emphasis is on helping clients develop new skills through experiential learning and group feedback.

The qualities that are needed to successfully lead a group fall into two categories. The first category is comprised of qualities that are not specific to social skills training but are required of any person who works with psychiatric clients, such as warmth, empathy, enthusiasm, flexibility, good social skills, willingness to listen, and the ability to provide structure and reinforcement. The second category includes skills that are more specific to social skills training with clients who have schizophrenia. Leaders function more like teachers or coaches than psychotherapists. They must be comfortable imposing and sticking to a structure. Most important of all is the ability to persistently focus on small units of behavior without losing patience. Other specific skills include the following:

1. Knowledge of basic behavior principles.
2. Knowledge of schizophrenia, including characteristic symptoms and related impairments.
3. Ability to present material in an easy-to-understand format.
4. Ability to plan and present role-play scenarios.
5. Ability to engage group members in behavioral rehearsals.
6. Ability to elicit and provide specific feedback about verbal content, and about nonverbal and paralinguistic elements of the role plays.
7. Ability to be active and directive in coaching and prompting clients to make desired changes in role plays.
8. Ability to assign homework that is tailored to the individual needs of the clients.
9. Ability to manage problematic behaviors that may occur during group.

Co-Leading Groups

It is preferable that social skills groups be conducted by two leaders, since it is challenging for one person to teach the skills, set the pace, and maintain control of the group on a continual basis. In addition, the use of co-leaders can greatly facilitate the demonstration and modeling of new skills, as well as aid in the coaching of clients during role plays.

Conducting social skills training is demanding and requires that the group leaders complete a number of tasks. Table 5.1 provides a list of tasks that need to be accomplished during groups. These tasks can be grouped under two specific headings: group facilitator tasks and role-play confederate tasks. Usually the co-leader who takes on the role of facilitator is responsible for structuring and pacing the session, introducing the skill being taught, and assigning homework. The leader who takes on the job of the role-play confederate is responsible for participating in role plays with group members as well as providing an overview of the group, reviewing group rules and expectations, and introducing new group members. Leaders should meet before each session to agree on tasks and go over strategies for conducting the particular group. Leaders often find it helpful to alternate between the two roles (within or across sessions) to prevent boredom and burnout.

Leader Training

Written materials and didactic presentations are helpful in training prospective group leaders. Another important component of their training, however, is the direct experience of both observing and co-leading groups with an experienced therapist. Although it is advisable that prospective group leaders participate in supervision during their training period, it may not be feasible. Therefore, prospective group leaders should become familiar with the infor-

---

TABLE 5.1. Tasks for Group Leaders

1. Review group rules and expectations.
2. Provide group rationale and format.
3. Introduce new group members.
4. Introduce the skill to be taught.
5. Structure and pace the session (i.e., set up role-play scenarios, elicit feedback about role-play performance, monitor group participation and disruptive behaviors, etc.).
6. Model the skill for the group and participate in role plays as the confederate.
7. Assign homework.

---

mation provided in this book so that they can incorporate its many suggestions into their repertoire and then use the book as a reference guide.

Selecting Clients for Group

Almost any client who exhibits difficulties in interpersonal situations is a potential candidate for social skills training. Determining which clients will be able to successfully participate in group requires that the leaders consider several issues. First, it is important that the clients' symptoms be as stable as possible. Group members who are actively experiencing hallucinations or delusions may be distracted and have more difficulty following what is being taught in groups especially if those symptoms are temporarily exacerbated. If the symptoms are particularly distressing, these clients may even become disoriented or disruptive. Second, it is desireable if clients are able to interact in a small group setting without talking to themselves, pacing, being disruptive, or exhibiting other problem behaviors. Finally, it is best if clients are able to communicate using simple sentences, focus their attention for at least a few minutes without interrupting, and follow simple instructions.

Some clients, however, will not be able to meet the demands that participation in the group requires. Since schizophrenia is an illness characterized by periodic symptom exacerbations, it is not uncommon for previously stabilized clients to have episodes of increased symptomatology. During these periods, it is the group leaders' responsibility to weigh the needs of the individual client with those of the group as a whole. If a symptomatic client becomes so disruptive that one or both of the leaders are primarily focused on managing his or her behavior and cannot accomplish the group goals for the day, then the client should be asked to take a break from group until the symptoms are better under control. In many cases, both individual and group needs can be accomodated. For instance, a client who has become agitated and is unable to remain seated, but who is quiet, may be able to remain in group. The group leader can arrange the seating so that the agitated client can come and go as he or she needs without interrupting the group. However, a client who is delusional and is prone to loud outbursts about his or her delusions will require more intensive supervision and frequent redirection and is, therefore, less likely to be able to remain in group.

Preparing Clients for Participation in Group

It is important that the group leaders meet with prospective members prior to their beginning group. The leaders' goals for this meeting are to orient the clients to social skills training and to assist them in setting individual goals for the group. In addition, therapists can use this meeting as an opportunity to build rapport with the client and screen out clients who may not be ready to attend group. Because building rapport is important for both co-leaders, it is preferable for both to be present at the initial meeting with the client.

Group leaders should plan to spend anywhere between 15 to 30 minutes meeting with each client. If a client has a difficult time concentrating for that period of time, two shorter meetings can be arranged. The first few minutes of the meeting can be spent making small talk in order to put the client at ease and begin to build rapport. The leaders can then describe the rationale for skills training. Appendix A provides an example of some of the information that the leader will want to convey. Leaders should bear in mind that not all clients will be able to absorb the same amount of information when the group is described; the leaders must be able to gauge for each client how much information to provide and at what level the language should be.

After the leaders have described the rationale and feel confident that the client has understood, they should begin the process of helping the client to set goals for the group. Prior to the meeting, therapists should familiarize themselves with previous assessments of each client's functioning, particularly regarding interpersonal and expressive deficits. Armed with this information, the leader is in a good position to guide the client in choosing appropriate and realistic goals. Questions such as those in Table 5.2 can be used to guide the leaders in the goal-setting process.

Not all clients will be able to identify specific goals to work on. Therefore, before meeting with the clients, the group leaders should consult staff or family about goals they would set based on their observations of the patient's behavior and review client charts for any goals already set by the treatment team. It is helpful for the therapists to come to the meeting with a mental list of common goals that are relevant to most clients, such as living independently and having more money.

Other clients, however, may identify very ambitious goals, such as finding a girlfriend, getting a skilled job, getting married, and buying a house all within the upcoming year. In these cases, the leaders' job will be to assist the client with breaking the goal down into manageable steps, such as assessing conversational and friendship skills and targeting areas that the client needs to improve before being able to achieve these goals. It is important that leaders not discourage clients from pursuing their goals, even ones that are very ambitious. However, leaders need to be alert for goals that appear to be delusional, such as becoming the CEO of a large corporation or a rock star. Leaders must become adept at compassionately steering clients away from those goals that they deem to be delusional while assisting them in breaking the more ambitious goals down into manageable steps.

Occasionally leaders will meet with clients who are not yet ready to at-

TABLE 5.2. Individual Goal Assessment

Name: _____

Date: _____ Age: _____ Sex: _____

Education (highest level completed): _____

Current occupation: _____

Work history: _____

What activities are you involved in on a daily or weekly basis? _____

Are there any activities that you are currently not participating in but would like to?

Who are the people you spend most of your time with? _____

Are there people whom you do not currently spend time with but would like to?

Identify two goals that you would like to achieve within the next 6 months (short-term goals). _____

Identify two goals that you would like to achieve within the next year (long-term goals).

tend group. When this occurs, the leaders should stay in contact with the client until he or she is stabilized enough to benefit from treatment. Regular contact can take the form of a brief informal conversation with the client at around the time of the group session. Group leaders should also maintain frequent contact with staff members, mental health providers, or family members who have regular contact with the client so they can receive their input as to the clients progress toward attending group.

Working with Other Mental Health Professionals to Generalize Skills

One of the primary goals of social skills training is to get clients to generalize the skills learned in group to situations outside of the group. This is a particularly difficult task for clients with schizophrenia, who have significant cognitive and attentional deficits. For these clients, participation in groups alone is rarely sufficient for the skills to be generalized outside of the group setting. For maximal skill acquisition to take place, clients need help practicing the targeted skills in their everyday environment. In order to accomplish this, others who are involved in the client's care must be included as part of the greater "social skills training team," such as mental health professionals, family members, and other support staff.

Clients with schizophrenia often have difficulty independently identifying situations outside of the group where they can use the new social skills. Other mental health professionals who have frequent contact with the client, such as case managers, inpatient staff members, employment counselors, and other staff at community residences, can help clients identify situations where it is appropriate to use the specific skills and can help them implement what they have learned. Therefore, staff working with clients need to be kept abreast of the skills taught in group. In order to accomplish this, it is essential to establish a collaborative relationship with professionals and agencies involved in the day-to-day treatment of the clients participating in a social skills group.

Establishing relationships with other professionals is a rewarding, but not always easy, task. It requires patience, flexibility, and commitment on the part of the leaders. In many cases, the integration of social skills training into a hospital, day treatment program, or supervised living situation requires a formal orientation of the staff to the program. As with the introduction of any new therapeutic intervention, it is not unusual for there to be some resistance or suspicion on the part of the staff. The leaders must address directly any discomforts or concerns that may arise among the staff and work toward building enthusiasm among staff members for the skills training approach.

The leaders should explain how social skills training and the techniques involved can be useful not only in addressing clients' skill deficits, but also in helping staff respond to clients' problematic behaviors. It is also helpful for group leaders to have an idea of what problems the staff are currently experiencing working with the clients and then be able to explain how skills training can be used to specifically address those problems. Some common problems facing staff at community residences include frequent arguments among the clients and refusal to do chores or to take prescribed medication. These problems, although common, make the staffs' job more stressful, and any assistance in managing them are usually very well received.

There are many ways that group leaders can orient staff to the philosophy and principles of social skills training. Appendix A provides an example of what might be covered in a written overview of social skills training. In addition, supplementary readings on behavioral principles and social skills training are helpful; however, these should not be the only avenue used to orient the staff. Workshops outlining the principles of behavioral training and social skills techniques are an interactive and efficient way to provide information to the staff. It is usually most effective to combine instructive workshops with written materials. Outlines for possible workshops and a list of supplemental readings can be found in Appendix A.

Group leaders should remain in contact with the staff through regularly scheduled meetings. The group leaders can use these meetings as a way to monitor how well the staff is integrating what is being taught in group with what is happening outside of the group. It is important that the leaders set the expectation from the start that the staff will be practicing the skills with the clients. These meetings can also be used to tell the staff about the topics being covered in group and other behaviors that occurred in group that might be of some interest to them. In addition, these meetings can be used as times when staff can bring up any issues or problems that they may be experiencing relating to the skills training or ask questions about how to handle problems that arise in their setting. Table 5.3 provides the format around which the staff meetings can be structured.

Leaders will find that the type of relationship they establish with other professionals working with the clients in their group can often determine whether a group ends up a success or failure. Developing and maintaining a collaborative relationship with other professionals is a critical component of

TABLE 5.3. Staff Meetings

---

1. Discuss the skill that the clients were taught during last week's group. Identify positive aspects of each client's performance and suggest areas for improvement.

2. Review the need for *in vivo* practice to help clients generalize the skill they are learning in group. Discuss situations for prompting and how to set up role plays if the relevant situations do not spontaneously arise.

3. Discuss any new skill that will be taught before the next staff meeting. Hand out copies of the steps of the skill and role play an example of using the skill. Describe how the skill can be modeled by the staff members themselves.

4. Discuss opportunities for practicing the new skill. Elicit ideas from staff members about when the skill can be used in the clients' environment. If indicated, role play how staff can prompt clients to use the specific skill and provide positive feedback when the clients use the skill.

5. Hand out homework for staff to complete with clients during the next week.

6. Discuss general problems that staff have experienced during the past week with clients. With the assistance of the staff, identify ways that the problems can be addressed using the social skills model.

7. Elicit suggestions for further social skills needed by the clients to be used in future groups.

---

the social skills training approach and, therefore, should be awarded as much time and energy as planning and conducting the group itself.

Summary

In this chapter we discussed issues related to starting a social skills group. We addressed practical considerations that are necessary when planning a group, detailed important characteristics to seek out when selecting group leaders, and presented guidelines for selecting clients and preparing them for group participation. We concluded the chapter with a discussion centering on the importance of developing collaborative relationships with other mental health professionals.

6

Using Curricula for Social Skills Training Groups

In this chapter we address curriculum planning for social skills groups. In contrast to other group psychotherapy approaches, social skills training groups employ preplanned curricula and teaching aides (such as posters and blackboards). Therefore, the selection of a curriculum and development of new curricula are central to the success of skills training groups. In this chapter, we first focus on the content of skills training curricula by identifying the basic skills that serve as building blocks for other skills. Guidelines for developing short- and long-term lesson plans based on these skills are provided, as well as examples of curriculum menus. Although we have provided a wide range of curricula for skills training in Part II, leaders often need to develop additional skills to address specific problems and achieve goals. To facilitate this process, we describe procedures for the development of a new curriculum for skills training groups. In addition, we discuss the importance of problem solving training and how to implement it in a group setting. Finally, we address a variety of issues related to teaching curricula including sensitivity to sociocultural differences, balancing training in verbal and nonverbal/paralinguistic skills, and training in social perception skills.

Using an Existing Curriculum

The curricula provided in Part II are grouped into seven broad skill areas: Conversation Skills, Conflict Management Skills, Assertiveness Skills, Community Living Skills, Friendship and Dating Skills, Medication Management Skills, and Vocational/Work Skills. These skills areas do not need to be taught in a particular order. Leaders are encouraged to teach the skills that are most relevant to the goals and skill level of the clients with whom they are working. There are a few skills, however, that we considered to be "basic social skills" that all clients can benefit from, regardless of their personal goals. These basic skills are Expressing Positive Feelings, Making Requests, Listening to Others, and Expressing Unpleasant Feelings. The skills are usually taught in this order, with the most difficult skill, Expressing Unpleasant Feelings, being taught after the clients have learned other skills and have more experience with the group process. These four skills serve as the building blocks for the other skills because they provide clients with the practice and tools necessary to master some of the more complicated skills. For example, the skill of Listening to Others is essential for the successful mastery of more complex skills such as Compromise and Negotiation, and Disagreeing with Another's Opinion without Arguing. Similarly, mastery of the skill Making Requests helps clients to learn skills such as Asking for Information and Asking Someone for a Date. In addition, leaders can use these basic skills to help clients become familiar with the process of social skills training. Table 6.1 contains the four basic skills and their steps.

TABLE 6.1. The Four Basic Social Skills

Listening to Others

Steps of the skill:
1. Maintain eye contact.
2. Nod your head.
3. Say "Uh-huh" or "Okay" or "I see."
4. Repeat what the other person said.

Making Requests

Steps of the skill:
1. Look at the person.
2. Say *exactly* what you would like the person to do.
3. Tell the person how it would make you feel.

Expressing Positive Feelings

Steps of the skill:
1. Look at the person.
2. Tell the person *exactly* what it was that pleased you.
3. Tell the person how it made you feel.

Expressing Unpleasant Feelings

Steps of the skill:
1. Look at the person. Speak calmly and firmly.
2. Say *exactly* what the person did that upset you.
3. Tell the person how it made you feel.
4. Suggest how the person might prevent this from happening in the future.

Guidelines for Using Skill Sheets

Each social skill that is included in Part II has its own individual skill sheet that serves as a guide for teaching that skill. As no two groups are the same, the skill sheets are intended to provide a framework for teaching those skills that leaders can tailor to meet the specific needs of the participants. Table 6.2 provides an example of one of the "skill sheets" located in Part II.

As illustrated by Table 6.2, the skill sheets are divided into six sections. The first section, located at the top center of the sheet, provides the gener-

TABLE 6.2. Sample Skill Sheet

CONFLICT MANAGEMENT SKILLS

SKILL: Compromise and Negotiation

RATIONALE: Often, people find that they disagree with each other, even when they want to do something together. At these times, it is helpful to work out a compromise. In a compromise, each person usually gets some of what he or she wants, but usually has to give up something. The goal is to reach a solution that is acceptable to all involved.

STEPS OF THE SKILL:
1. Explain your viewpoint briefly.
2. Listen to the other person's viewpoint.
3. Repeat the other person's viewpoint.
4. Suggest a compromise.

SCENES TO USE IN ROLE PLAYS:
1. You want to go to lunch with your friend at the pizza parlor. He or she does not want pizza that day.
2. Your case manager asks you to schedule an appointment for 2:00 P.M. on Wednesday. You have plans to go on a day program outing at that time.
3. You and your friend want to go see a movie. You want to see an action movie, and your friend wants to see a comedy.
4. In planning an outing for the Community Residence, the counselors suggest bowling. You would rather go out for ice cream.
5. You want to visit your family next weekend. They have other plans.

SPECIAL CONSIDERATIONS WHEN TEACHING THIS SKILL:
Not all clients will understand what it means to negotiate and come to a compromise. Therefore, it is important that the group leaders spend time explaining these concepts before beginning a role play. For example, to negotiate something, both parties have to state what it is that they want to get out of the interaction. Once all the wishes have been listed, both parties must review the list and decide upon a compromise. A compromise usually occurs when both parties get *some* of what they wanted.

al subject heading of the skill. The subject heading in Table 6.2 is Conflict Management Skills. The second section identifies the specific social skill being addressed (Compromise and Negotiation). The third section contains a rationale for teaching the skill. Based on this rationale, the leaders can generate discussion about the importance of the skill so that group members can appreciate why learning the skill will help them achieve their personal goals. Group leaders should use this section to help clients understand the personal relevance of the skills for dealing with situations and events that occur in their own lives. For example, questions that may be asked when discussing the rationale for the skill Compromise and Negotiation include "Why might it be helpful to be able to negotiate and compromise?"; "Can you think of a recent situation where using this skill would have been useful?"; and "Have you ever had a disagreement with someone that you weren't able to resolve? What happened?" Clients are motivated to work actively on learning new skills when they can understand how the skills are related to current issues or events affecting their lives. It should be noted, however, that the length of time spent on this section depends on the level of functioning of the group members. Less time should be devoted to the rationale for a skill in groups with lower-functioning clients who often have difficulty sustaining attention compared to groups with higher-functioning clients, who may benefit from a more involved discussion that emphasizes their personal goals.

The fourth section of the skills sheet provides the steps of the skill. Group leaders are encouraged to review each step with the members and elicit comments from the participants about the importance of each step. For example, the first step of the skill Compromise and Negotiation (Table 6.2) directs the person to "Explain your viewpoint briefly." Leaders can ask group members questions such as "Why is it important to explain your viewpoint?" and "Why it is helpful to be brief when doing so?" After having elicited reasonable answers for the first step of the skill, leaders then move on to each of the other steps and do the same thing. The fifth section includes examples of scenes that the leaders can use when modeling or setting up role plays. It is not necessary to use the particular scenes provided on the skill sheet when leading the group. These examples are provided to give leaders ideas for role plays and to provide a starting point for practicing the skill through the use of role plays. As group members become more proficient in using the skill, leaders can tailor the scenes so that they are directly relevant to situations experienced by the group members (see Chapters 3 and 7). The last section of the skill sheet includes special considerations for teaching the skill including suggestions for how to deal with issues that may arise in the group when teaching the skill. It is important for leaders to familiarize themselves with the information provided on the skill sheets before beginning a new skill. This will allow them the opportunity to anticipate questions or issues that may arise during the group so that they can feel more prepared when teaching the skill.

Developing Curriculum Menus and Lesson Plans

Developing curriculum menus and lesson plans is an important component of skills training. Both menus and lesson plans aid leaders in the process of mapping out strategies to address long- and short-term group goals. A "curriculum menu" is a list of specific skills related to a general topic area that will be the focus of the skills training group. Curriculum menus are useful when planning long-term group goals such as Anger Management, Coping with Substance Use, Managing Symptoms, and Vocational Maintenance. Table 6.3 provides examples of these and other menus for social skills training groups. Leaders may choose to develop other social skills menus by combining different skills, putting more than one menu together (e.g., Making Friends and Developing Romantic/Intimate Relationships), or developing additional skills for a particular menu (addressed later in this chapter).

Leaders are encouraged to develop lesson plans before beginning a social skills group in order to construct a tentative timetable for accomplishing the specific tasks of the group. These lesson plans may include suggestions for conducting the group, such as the order in which the skills will be taught, the approximate length of time that will be spent on each skill, and examples of possible role plays to conduct. Lesson plans assist leaders in modifying the skills identified in the curriculum menus according to the level of functioning of the group, providing a framework for monitoring the groups' progress in achieving its goal. For example, a lesson plan designed for a group of higher-functioning clients with goals related to improving anger management skills will differ from the plan for a group of lower-functioning clients with similar goals. Lesson plans may differ in the number of sessions each group spends on a skill, as well as in the level of difficulty of the role-play situations. Tables 6.4 and 6.5 provide sample lesson plans for a group with goals related to Anger Management. As can be seen, more sessions are allocated for each individual skill in the lower-functioning groups (Table 6.4) than in the higher-functioning groups (Table 6.5). In addition, leaders working with the lower-functioning group may decide that, before working on the skills in the lesson plan, it is necessary to review of some more basic skills such as Listening to Others and Getting Your Point Across.

Although it is important to be flexible, the leaders are advised to plan the group's curriculum 1 to 3 months in advance, depending on how well the leaders know the group and how well they function in the group. If clients are highly symptomatic or vary widely in their functioning, it is more difficult to predict how long it will take to teach a specific skill as well as

TABLE 6.3. Examples of Curriculum Menus

Anger Management

    Coping with Unpleasant Feelings
    Leaving Stressful Situations
    Responding to Untrue Accusations
    Expressing Angry Feelings
    Responding to Criticism
    Taking a Time-Out
    Disagreeing with Another's Opinion without Arguing
    Waiting for Your Request to Be Granted

Coping with Substance Use

    Coping with Negative Feelings
    Employing Alternatives to Drugs and Alcohol Use
    Refusing Alcohol or Street Drugs
    Leaving Stressful Situations
    Utilizing Social Supports
    Compromise and Negotiation
    Responding to Criticism
    Solving Problems

Using Leisure and Recreation Time

    Finding Common Interests
    Making Requests
    Refusing Requests
    Compromise and Negotiation
    Asking for Information
    Listening to Others
    Starting Conversations
    Getting Your Point Across

Managing Positive Symptoms

    Listening to Others
    Checking Out Your Beliefs
    Leaving Stressful Situations
    Letting Someone Know That You Are Afraid
    Making a Doctor's Appointment on the Phone
    Asking Questions about Medication
    Describing Medication Side Effects
    Describing Your Symptoms to a Medical Professional
    Taking a Time-Out
    Responding to Untrue Accusations

Vocational Maintenance

    Listening to Others
    Following Verbal Instructions
    Responding to Criticism
    Asking for Feedback about Job Performance
    Joining Ongoing Conversations at Work
    Disagreeing with Another's Opinion without Arguing
    Asking for Information
    Solving Problems
    Providing Reassurance to Others   *(continued)*

TABLE 6.3. *Continued*

Developing Romantic/Intimate Relationships

Giving Compliments
Accepting Compliments
Expressing Positive Feelings
Asking Someone for a Date
Expressing Affection
Refusing Unwanted Sexual Advances
Compromise and Negotiation
Requesting That Your Partner Use a Condom

TABLE 6.4. Partial Lesson Plans for Anger Management in a Low-Functioning Group

Session 1:	Generate a list of early warning signs of anger that people commonly experience (e.g., heart racing, muscles tense, jaw is clenched, desire to punch something, etc.). Have the group members discuss the items listed.
Session 2:	Generate a list of situations that commonly induce angry feelings in most people. Have the group members discuss the items listed.
Session 3:	Generate a list of coping strategies for dealing with angry feelings. Have group members discuss the items listed.
Session 4:	Introduce the skill Leaving Stressful Situations. Leaders model an example of using the skill and then practice the skill with each group member using the same role-play scene.
Session 5:	Continue with the skill Leaving Stressful Situations. Leaders practice the skill with each group member and begin to tailor the role play scenes to specific situations that the group members have experienced.
Session 6:	Continue with the skill Leaving Stressful Situations. Group members can begin to practice the skill with each other using role-play scenes.
Session 7:	Finish with the skill Leaving Stressful Situations. Group members can practice the skill with each other using role-play scenes that are relevant to their experiences.
Session 8:	Introduce the skill Expressing Angry Feelings. Leaders model an example of using the skill and then practice with each group member using the same role-play scenes.
Session 9:	Continue with the skill Expressing Angry Feelings. Leaders should practice the skill with each group member and begin to tailor the role-play scenes to specific situations that the group members have experienced.
Session 10:	Continue with the skill Expressing Angry Feelings. Group members can begin to practice the skill with each other using the same role-play scenes.
Session 11:	Finish with the skill Expressing Angry Feelings. Group members can practice the skill with each other using role-play scenes that are relevant to their experiences.

Note. Leaders continue to proceed at similar pace with the remaining skills listed on the curriculum menu for Anger Management.

TABLE 6.5. Partial Lesson Plans for Anger Management in a High-Functioning Group

Session 1:	Generate a list of early warning signs of anger that group members have experienced as well as a list of situations that commonly induce angry feelings. Have the group members discuss the items on both lists.
Session 2:	Generate a list of coping strategies for dealing with angry feelings (encourage group members to list strategies that they have personally used). Have group members discuss the items listed.
Session 3:	Introduce the skill Leaving Stressful Situations. Leaders model an example of using the skill and then practice with each group member tailoring the scenes to specific experiences.
Session 4:	Continue with the skill Leaving Stressful Situations. Group members practice the skill with each other using role-play scenes that are relevant to their experiences.
Session 5:	Finish with the skill Leaving Stressful Situations. Leaders practice the skill with each member while increasing the difficulty of the role-play scene.
Session 6:	Introduce the skill Expressing Angry Feelings. Leaders model an example of using the skill and then practice with each group member tailoring the role play scenes to specific experiences.
Session 7:	Continue with the skill Expressing Angry Feelings. Group members can begin to practice the skill with each other using role-play scenes that are relevant to their experiences.
Session 8:	Finish with the skill Expressing Angry Feelings. Leaders practice the skill with each member while they increase the difficulty of the role-play scene.
Session 9:	Introduce the skill Responding to Criticism. Leaders model an example of using the skill and then practice with each group member tailoring the scenes to specific experiences.
Session 10:	Continue with the skill Responding to Criticism. Group members can begin to practice the skill with each other using role-play scenes that are relevant to their experiences.
Session 11:	Finish with the skill Responding to Criticism. Leaders should practice the skill with each member while they increase the difficulty of the role-play scene.
Session 12:	Introduce the skill Responding to Untrue Accusations. Leaders should model an example of using the skill and then practice with each group member tailoring the scenes to each member's specific experiences.

Note. Leaders would continue to proceed at the same pace with the remaining skills listed on the curriculum menu for Anger Management.

which skill will be needed next. Planning the specific curriculum 1 month in advance is usually sufficient in these cases. If the group is higher functioning or if the leaders are well acquainted with the clients' abilities to master new skills, a 3-month lesson plan is feasible. Of course, all curriculum plans must be flexible; it is preferable to shift to a skill that is more relevant to the clients than to stick with one just because it is on the schedule.

Adding Skills to Existing Lesson Plans

Leaders need to be ever vigilant in monitoring how well the clients are responding to the specific lesson plan designed for the group and must be ready to modify it whenever necessary. By observing clients' behavior in and out of group meetings, and getting feedback regularly from significant others (e.g., staff members, relatives) who know about the clients' social behavior outside the group, leaders can add skills that will meet the ongoing needs of the group members. Often an interaction that occurs in group will indicate that the members need to learn a specific skill in order to deal with a problem. For example, if clients repeatedly argue with each other in group, teaching Disagreeing with Another's Opinion without Arguing or Compromise and Negotiation might be beneficial. If the leaders note that clients have difficulty conversing with each other beyond a simple greeting, they can teach skills related to maintaining conversations. If clients are observed making demands of each other, the leaders might consider reviewing Making Requests.

Self-reports by clients are also useful in choosing relevant skills to teach. A client may report that he or she is upset by a roommate who is very messy, which may be addressed by reviewing Expressing Unpleasant Feelings in the group. If relevant information does not come spontaneously, the leaders can elicit feedback from the group members, asking them about what problems they are currently experiencing. For example, if several clients report that a new resident at their community residence is demanding that they loan him their personal belongings, the leaders might decide to include Refusing Requests as a skill to be taught in the near future.

Staff members who are involved in the clients' treatment or living situation are also a good source of information. They may describe problem behaviors such as smoking cigarettes in a nondesignated area or refusing to keep medical appointments. If staff members do not spontaneously provide information, however, the leader can probe by asking about specific problem areas. For example, staff members might report situations such as clients accusing each other of stealing things, in which case the leaders could teach the skills How to Find Your Missing Things and What to Do If You Think Somebody Has Something of Yours.

Problem-Solving Training

There are some situations when clients cannot adequately deal with a problem by using a social skill or a combination of social skills. For example, many clients need to make decisions about complicated issues such as where they will live, how they will resolve legal problems, or how they can reestablish relationships with family members. At such times, it is helpful to use a step-by-step method of solving problems. Teaching the skills of solving problems is more complicated than most of the other skills in the curriculum. The skill has six steps: (1) define the problem (2) use brainstorming to generate possible solutions for the problem, (3) identify the advantages and disadvantages of each possible solution, (4) select the "best" solution or combination of solutions, (5) plan how to carry out the solution(s), and (6) follow up on the plan at a later time. Learning to complete these steps requires significant concentration, sequential thinking, and the ability to speak objectively about problem situations. However, it is worth the extra effort of the group leaders to teach this skill, because clients who improve their problem-solving ability may experience significant benefits with far-reaching effects on their ability to manage daily life challenges and with achieving personal goals. Even clients who have difficulty generalizing this skill outside the group may benefit from using problem solving in the group to address specific conflicts or goals.

Because of the complexity of the skill, problem solving is best taught after group members have covered the basic social skills and have experience with some of the more complicated skills, such as Compromise and Negotiation. Although formal teaching of the skill takes place later in the course of the social skill training group, group leaders can use this method from the beginning of training, both with clients and with other staff members. For example, group leaders can use problem solving to help clients overcome obstacles to attending the group (e.g., figuring out the mode of transportation, how to fit the group into their schedule, etc.) and to deal with crises that occur in the group (e.g., how to restore confidence in group safety after two members have had a heated argument).

Leaders model problem-solving skills during groups, engaging clients as much as possible in the process and pointing out that they will be learning this skill at a later date. By demonstrating that a step-by-step approach can successfully resolve a problem or deal with a crisis, group leaders serve as powerful models and help motivate clients to learn the steps of the skill. Using the same rationale, the group leaders can begin early on to model the use of the skill with other staff members. For example, the leaders can use the problem-solving skill to help staff members develop stategies to increase group attendance of a particular client.

When teaching problem solving, leaders follow the same format as in teaching other skills, beginning with a discussion of how this skill might be relevant in the lives of the clients. Throughout the teaching of problem solving, the leaders choose to work on problems that are important to the group members, beginning with ones that are relatively easy to solve. The leaders begin by modeling the steps of problem solving in one session so that clients can see how the overall skill works. Subsequently, several sessions are spent teaching the clients the six steps of the skill. For lower-functioning clients, leaders may want to spend some entire sessions focusing on some of the more difficult steps of the skill. As the clients become more familiar with problem solving, they can work together to solve a problem in a single session.

In higher-functioning groups, it is helpful to have a chairperson who assumes the task of systematically guiding the clients through the completion of the steps. The chairperson accomplishes this by reading aloud to the group the instructions for each step, eliciting input from group members and keeping the discussion focused on the task. It is also helpful to have a secretary or recorder, who writes down the results of each step and keeps a record to which other group members can refer. When conducting problem-solving training, group leaders will find it helpful to use a preprinted problem-solving worksheet such as the one provided in Appendix A. A sample skill sheet for solving job-related problems is presented in Part II (p. 239).

It is very helpful to teach problem solving to staff members simultaneously while teaching it to the clients. Staff members can be valuable role models to clients by responding to their problems using this step-by-step, solution-oriented approach. Problem solving is an especiallly useful skill for staff members because its emphasis is on helping clients develop their own solutions to problems, giving clients more responsibility for solving their problems and achieving personal goals. This relieves the pressure on staff members to always "come up with the answers" at the same time it provides clients with some much-needed experience in determining how to handle problems.

Developing a New Curriculum

In some instances, the leaders may identify a problem that is not addressed by the existing curriculum. When this occurs, leaders can design new skills to address the particular problem. We have found that the following steps are useful for developing a curriculum for new social skills. The first step involves talking about and defining the problem that is not being addressed. Once the problem has been identified and defined to everyone's satisfaction, the leaders move to the second step, which involves deciding what general skill might be able to resolve the problem situation. The third step requires leaders to develop a rationale for learning the skill. The fourth step involves brainstorming possible steps for the skill. When selecting the steps, it is important to remember that it is best if the skill has three to four steps, each of which is relatively brief. The fifth step involves developing role-play scenes for practicing the skill. Once these steps are completed, leaders move on to the sixth step, which involves trying out the new skill in their group. After piloting the skill(s), leaders can make any revisions needed (the seventh step). Leaders then devise a skill sheet that can be added to the curriculum that is taught (the eighth step).

We illustrate the process of developing new skills with an example from a community residence. Staff reported that the residents were getting into arguments and fights because they were falsely accusing one another of stealing their belongings. Staff members at the residence explained to the leaders that in most of the cases the accusing resident had simply misplaced the belonging in question. After reviewing their social skills curriculum, the leaders decided that this problem was not adequately addressed in the current curriculum and that new skills were needed to help residents deal with the problem of missing belongings. To address this need, the leaders developed two new skills: How to Locate Your Missing Belongings and What to Do If You Think Somebody Has Something of Yours. Steps for each of the skills were developed as well as the corresponding role-play scenes. Once leaders felt comfortable with what they had developed, they tried the skills out in their groups and then asked staff members for feedback regarding whether the skills were addressing the identified problems. Feedback from the staff members indicated that both of the skills were successful at addressing the issues. If the staff members had informed leaders that the new skills were not addressing the problem at hand, the group leaders would have needed to analyze the problems further and make modifications to the skills or to develop alternative skills that might be more successful. Table

---

TABLE 6.6. Summary of Steps Involved in Developing a New Curriculum

Step 1: Define the need that is not being addressed.

Step 2: Identify a skill that would address the need.

Step 3: Develop a rationale for the skill.

Step 4: Decide how best to break down the skill into clear and concise steps.

Step 5: Devise role play scenes conducive to the skill.

Step 6: Pilot the skill in the group.

Step 7: Revise the skill as necessary.

Step 8: Make a record of the new skill using the same format as the other skills and add it to the existing curriculum.

6.6 provides a summary of the steps involved in developing new curriculum.

Special Considerations

Sociocultural Issues

Social skills are the interpersonal behaviors that are socially sanctioned in a given community, and are therefore influenced by the specific sociocultural features of that community. For the purpose of this section, sociocultural factors refer to the social norms, roles, values, and beliefs that identify membership in a specific racial or ethnic group, subculture, or socioeconomic class. These factors may affect such skills as how a person uses or does not use eye contact, the distance a person stands from another, how assertive a person is, and how much affect is contained in one's voice.

As we have emphasized throughout this book, the ability to perceive and conform to specific social norms in a given community is a crucial component of social competence. A major error that leaders can make when conducting social skills groups is to operate under the assumption that different cultural groups employ the same verbal and nonverbal patterns of communication. Problems often arise when the communication styles of the leaders do not match the styles of the clients with whom they are working. What is appropriate or adaptive for one group or in one setting, may be inappropriate, or even maladaptive, for another group or setting. Clients who learn from models that are out of touch with the nuances of their particular sociocultural group or who are reinforced for behaviors that are maladaptive are unlikely to develop the social skills that are necessary for effective living within their community. Leaders need to be sensitive to the sociocultural factors relevant to the clients they are working with and be able to modify the skills taught so that they accommodate the differences in lifestyles, values, norms, and preferences. Being sensitive to sociocultural factors will increase the likelihood that clients will use the skills being taught and that they will have successful experiences with these skills.

There are several ways that leaders can enhance their understanding of the sociocultural factors that affect the groups with whom they work. They can elicit information about social values and norms from group members through discussions centering on what life was like growing up in their neighborhoods and communities. Leaders can also seek out resources that will aid them in their ability to identify the specific sociocultural needs of their clients. Seeking out individuals who have frequent contact with clients such as staff members and family can be helpful, as can having frank discussions with co-workers who share the same background as the clients. In addition, attending training sessions or workshops on multicultural issues, or seeking consultation with knowledgeable individuals can be helpful.

Social Perception Training

Difficulties with social perception are common among individuals with schizophrenia (Bellack et al., 1996; Mueser et al., 1996). These individuals often misread the verbal, and nonverbal, cues in their social environment. Leaders need to be aware of their clients' ability to accurately perceive another person's feelings through reading his or her facial expression, body language, or voice tone. Because accurate social perception is such an important component of being socially skilled, leaders should weave training in social perception throughout each group session.

Social perception training involves teaching individuals how to identify the behavioral components that accompany different emotions. Behaviors such as eye contact, voice quality, facial expressions, and body language provide important clues to how a person is feeling. By pointing out nonverbal and paralinguistic behaviors that occur during role plays in the group, and by discussing the role of these behaviors in interactions, leaders use "real-life" models that illustrate the wide range of behavioral cues that people provide. For example, when teaching the skill of Expressing Angry Feelings, leaders can elicit from the group the many behaviors that can indicate a person is feeling angry or upset. Leaders can ask questions such as "What might a person's face look like if he or she were angry?"; "What sorts of things would you notice about his or her body language?"; "How would his or her voice sound?"; and "What different type of behaviors might he or she show?" Depending on the level of functioning of the clients, leaders may then want to ask every member what behavior changes they notice in themselves when they are feeling angry (e.g., speaking in a louder or more angry voice tone). It is helpful if group leaders write the clients' responses to these questions on a board or flipchart so that they can be displayed and referred to throughout the lesson. Leaders and group members can then use the lists to provide helpful feedback to individuals who are practicing the skill through the use of role plays.

Group members who have very poor social perception skills can benefit from training in the group that helps them focus on one nonverbal or paralinguistic component at a time. For example, before conducting a role play, the leader may instruct one member to listen closely to another member's voice tone during the role play to determine whether it conveys a negative feeling. Then, immediately after the role play, the leader can ask the group member whether the voice tone of the person in the role play conveyed a negative feeling. If the client's observation is consistent with other group members, then praise is given for accurate social perception. If the group member's observation is significantly different than that of other group members, corrective feedback is given, and the client is instructed to watch for the same behavior in another role play. By giving individual clients specific assignments to attend to particular social perception behaviors, leaders are able to provide more focused training in social perception skills for those clients who most need it, while continuing to teach other skills to the group at large.

Summary

In this chapter we discussed how to plan the curriculum for a social skills training group. We reviewed the organization of skill sheets provided in Part II and described how different skills can be combined into "menus" to address general topic areas such as managing conflict, dealing with substance abuse, and friendship and dating skills. We addressed how to develop specific lesson plans tailored to the functional level of the group participants. Steps for developing new social skills not covered in Part II were provided. We also provided strategies for conducting training in problem solving. We concluded the chapter with a discussion of how to integrate training and social perception skills into social skills training groups.

7

Tailoring Skills for Individual Needs

Individuals with schizophrenia differ greatly in the specific problems they experience and in their personal goals for treatment. Likewise, they exhibit a wide range of social skill assets and deficits. Some clients have limited social skills deficits and may need to improve their skills in only a few areas, whereas others are more severely affected and require extensive training in many skills over long periods of time. Although social skills training is provided following a standardized structure of modeling, role play, feedback, and homework, the content and format of groups are flexible and can be tailored to respond to the specific needs of the individual.

Using the assessment techniques described in Chapter 2, the leaders can identify the specific abilities and deficits of each client in the social skills training group. Once the primary deficits are identified, the most effective way to tailor an individual's program is to work directly with him or her to set specific goals that have personal relevance. If clients feel that skills training is irrelevant or uninteresting, they will not be motivated to participate actively and may even stop attending groups altogether. Bearing in mind the individual assets, deficits, and goals of each client, however, the leaders can adapt skills training procedures to meet the needs of each person. In this chapter, we describe how to tailor social skills training to address a variety of problems common in clients with schizophrenia.

The Role of Assessment in Setting Individual Client Goals

In Chapter 2 we described the assessment of social skills, beginning with general questions about the client's activities and moving to more specific probes concerning his or her social functioning. If it is determined that the client has an interpersonal problem that is due to a social dysfunction, specific deficits in social skills must be identified. Understanding the nature of the skills deficit, including such factors as the circumstances under which the deficit occurs, will help the leaders target specific behaviors to modify.

Table 7.1 contains some examples of social skills deficits that are frequently identified by leaders during the assessment process and some possible goals related to addressing the deficits. In some examples, these goals could be broken down into smaller, more specific steps based on the individual client and his or her circumstances.

Setting goals for social skills training is a collaborative process; clients must be involved in setting all goals, although many will need group leaders to assist them. It is important for clients to identify goals that they would like to achieve and that have meaning for them. Clients' goals vary considerably, from staying out of the hospital to taking college-level courses. If group leaders can help clients understand that social skills training can assist them in achieving their own goals, they will participate more actively in the group and be more likely to practice the skills they are learning outside of the group. The process of skills training must feel relevant to clients in order for them to put forth the effort required to participate in the group. When clients are assisted in articulating their goals and when leaders keep those goals in mind in designing and conducting the group, the clients are far more likely to be engaged, to participate actively, and to benefit from the social skills training intervention. The clients' progress in achieving their goals should be regularly assessed throughout the treatment process, as described at the end of this chapter.

Table 7.2 provides examples of how important goals can be broken down into specific, attainable steps. Of course, the specific steps and time frame for goal attainment will vary depending on the individual client's capabilities and levels of functioning. Also, it is very important to define goals that can be achieved. Clients with schizophrenia often have had multiple experi-

TABLE 7.1. Goals Related to Specific Social Skills Deficits

Problems in social functioning	Possible goals for social skills training
No friends, socially isolated	To start conversations on a regular basis (e.g., daily)
Lack of interest in leisure activities	To participate in at least one form of recreation
Gives into unreasonable demands	To refuse inappropriate requests
Becomes physically aggressive when angry	To express anger appropriately (i.e., verbally)
Speaks in a monotone	To vary voice tone and expression
Speech is delusional and tangential	To stay on the conversational topic
Makes frequent demands	To make positive requests of others

TABLE 7.2. Breaking Down Goals into Smaller Steps

Goal	Possible steps to achieve goal
Make friends	Start a conversation with one person at the day treatment program. Attend the next social event at the drop-in center. Introduce self to one person.
Shop for clothes independently	Choose one item of clothing to purchase. Shop with the assistance of a relative. Establish size needed, approximate price. Select item for purchase.
Respond effectively to criticism from employer	Use reflective listening when receiving supervisory feedback. Ask clarifying questions to obtain more information. Request suggestion for improvement.
Use public transportation to all locations	Obtain schedule for buses stopping nearby. Choose a relatively close destination that does not require transferring buses. Ask friend to accompany on first trip.

ences in failing to achieve personal goals and may give up altogether in pursuing their ambitions; it is crucial that skills training reverses this pattern of failure, helping clients to realize that progress toward goals and an improved quality of life are possible.

Using Client Goals to Design Social Skills Training Groups

At every stage of a social skills training group, the leaders need to keep in mind the abilities and goals of the clients. The specific goals of each client are especially important when designing a group, which involves decisions about specific skills to teach, role plays to assign, and expectations about homework.

Choosing Appropriate Skills to Teach

As much as possible, it is important for the leader to choose the curriculum of a social skills group based on the needs and goals of its members. However, almost all clients who are entering social skills training can benefit from first learning certain very basic skills that can serve as a core curriculum to which other skills can be added. As described in Chapter 6, the four basic skills are Expressing Positive Feelings, Making Requests, Listening to Others, and Expressing Unpleasant Feelings.

Teaching this core curriculum in the beginning phase of the group serves at least three purposes. First, it is easier to orient the clients to the group format by teaching skills that are basic and not too complex. Many group members have participated in groups in the past where the format is quite different and need time to adjust to the expectations of a skills group. The process of learning basic skills is also more likely to give clients an opportunity to have a successful experience in the group. Second, the core skills are excellent "building blocks" for later, more complex skills. For example, Expressing Positive Feelings is very useful in skills related to conducting conversations, making friends, and living in the community. The skill of Expressing Unpleasant Feelings is helpful as a basis for teaching Conflict Resolution, Assertiveness, and Responding to Untrue Accusations. Third, teaching these basic skills provides the leaders and the group members with a common "vocabulary," a way of referring to fundamental aspects of social skills.

In some instances, such as conducting a group with clients with severe impairments, it may be most effective to focus primarily on the four basic skills without adding many others. For a severely impaired group, the leaders might spend a month on each of these skills and then teach them again in rotation. Even though the skills are being repeated, the leaders can vary the subject matter and complexity of role plays and homework to keep the group members engaged. Overlearning skills by repeatedly practicing them beyond the first few successes is advantageous since it promotes durability of the skills and their transfer to real-life situations, which is especially critical for lower-functioning clients.

In most groups, the leaders can build upon the skills of the core curriculum by adding skills that relate to the goals of the individuals in the group. The key to the process of selecting relevant skills is being able to link individual goals to specific social skills. With experience, the leaders learn to "translate" problems into goals and to relate goals to specific skills. For example, if a client is having difficulty getting along with his or her roommate, the leaders might help him or her to establish a goal of decreasing arguments. Achieving this goal could be facilitated by learning the four basic skills (Expressing Positive Feelings, Expressing Unpleasant Feelings, Making Requests, and Listening to Others) plus the following: Giving Compliments, Compromise and Negotiation, Disagreeing without Arguing, and Finding Common Interests.

Table 7.3 provides several examples of skills that might be chosen to help clients achieve specific goals. As can be seen in this table, many types of goals can be matched with learning the four basic skills. Also, different goals can be matched with the same social skills. Thus, the leaders can often include clients with different goals in the same group because their goals are all furthered by learning the same skills. The actual steps of the skills would

TABLE 7.3. Matching Individual Goals with Social Skills

Goal	Skills
Make a friend	Expressing Positive Feelings Giving Compliments Accepting Compliments Starting Conversations Finding Common Interests Maintaining Conversations by Asking Questions Maintaining Conversations by Giving Factual Information Listening to Others Ending Conversations
Talk to physician about reducing medication	Asking Questions about Health-Related Concerns Listening to Others Making Complaints Making Requests Disagreeing with Another's Opinion without Arguing
Apply for a volunteer position	Interviewing for a Job Listening to Others Staying on the Topic Set by Another Person Asking for Information
Improve assertiveness	Making Requests Making Complaints Asking for Information Refusing Requests Expressing Unpleasant Feelings Expressing Angry Feelings Making Apologies Leaving Stressful Situations

be taught in the same way, but the role plays and homework assignments would be tailored differently.

Structuring Role Plays

One of the major considerations in planning role plays is the level of functioning of the group members. If the clients are high-functioning, with good concentration and ability to attend to details, they can benefit from complex role plays that might involve a relatively detailed description of a specific scene and might require the client to modify some aspect of the skill he or she has been learning. For example, to practice the skill of Refusing Requests, the leaders might ask a high-functioning client to role play by saying:

"I'd like you to show me how you would refuse a request from your friend Humberto who is asking to borrow your new blue sweater to wear to a mixer at the drop-in center. Keep in mind that although you like Humberto and would like to help him out, you don't really want to loan your sweater."

If the group members are relatively low-functioning, it is best to keep role plays more basic, with simple descriptions of the scene and uncomplicated instructions regarding using the steps of the skill. For example, the leaders might ask a low-functioning client to role play Refusing Requests by instructing him or her as follows: "I'd like you practice saying 'No' to me when I ask you to borrow a whole pack of cigarettes; remember to look at me and to use a firm, clear voice."

In general, the leaders plan role plays to introduce and model a new skill, to demonstrate how to do a homework assignment, and to model how the skill can be varied in different situations. The subject matter selected for role plays must be relevant to the real-life situations of the clients in the group. For example, if the group is composed of clients who are all working at least part-time, the subject of the role plays might be related to an on-the-job situation, such as how to start conversations with new co-workers or how to ask for feedback about job performance. If the group members are in-patients in a psychiatric hospital, the role plays would be more relevant if they involved a situation that might occur on the ward, such as how to respond to another client who demands cigarettes or how to make a request of a busy nurse.

In addition to planning variety in role plays, the leaders must always be alert for opportunities to use role plays that are specific to the goals of an individual client. For example, if the leaders are aware that a client has had difficulties in planning an activity with a friend, when teaching Compromise and Negotiation, they can suggest a role play such as the following: "Let's say that you are talking to Sally about where you want to go on Saturday night. She wants to go to a movie and you want to go for pizza. I'd like you to use the steps of this skill to work out a compromise." The client would be more motivated to participate in this role play than in one that seems unrelated to his or her goal.

The leaders can also get ideas for role plays from the group members themselves. Asking members questions such as "What kind of situations have come up in the last few days when you needed to ask someone for help?" can yield a wealth of relevant subject matter for role plays. Family members and staff members can also provide examples of situations that clients have encountered that would lend themselves to role plays. Leaders' observations of problems in the group meetings can also lead to relevant role plays. For example, if a group is learning Expressing Unpleasant Feelings and the leaders observe two members arguing about one sitting too close to the other, that situation can be suggested for a role play. The leader could give instructions such as "Humberto, I just noticed that you seemed upset with Joe for moving his chair closer to you. I'd like you to use the skill of Expressing Unpleasant Feelings to let him know how you feel about what he did."

Table 7.4 contains examples of role plays that a leader might suggest to make skills more relevant to the individuals in the group.

Assigning Homework

The ultimate goal of social skills training is to enable clients to communicate more effectively in their naturally occurring interactions. For a skill to help clients achieve their goals, they must be able to practice that skill outside of the group. Homework assignments to practice targeted skills are most effective when they are designed to help clients progress toward their goals. Although all clients in a group may be working on the same skill, each of them can receive a different homework assignment, tailored to his or her individual abilities and goals.

TABLE 7.4. Choosing Role Plays Relevant To Individual Goals

Skills being taught	Individual goals	Role plays
Making Complaints	Shop independently	The woman at the clothing store gives you the wrong size.
	Increase self-assertion	The person at the fast food restaurant gives you the wrong order.
Listening to Others	Improve relationship with roommate	Ask roommate to tell you about his or her day.
	Increase ward privileges	Ask counselor about requirements for next level of privileges.
Expressing Positive Feelings	Develop an intimate relationship	Give your date a compliment about something he or she does well.
	Increase leisure opportunities at community residence	Tell staff member how much you enjoyed the last bingo game.
Eating and Drinking Politely	Achieve a promotion at work	You get catsup on your face while eating with supervisor.
	Feel comfortable going out for coffee with friends	When out with a new friend, you find your coffee is very hot, but you want to drink it.

The leaders can vary the setting and complexity of the homework assigned. For lower-functioning clients who are just beginning to learn a skill, it is preferable to start with assignments in familiar environments with people they already know. As clients show the ability to perform the simpler assignments, the leaders can make these assignments more complicated, including directing clients to less familiar environments and asking them to interact with people that they do not know as well. For example, in teaching the skill of Expressing Compliments, the assignments might start by asking clients to give compliments to staff members, then progress to giving compliments to other clients, then to a sales clerk in a store where the client shops often.

For higher-functioning clients who have demonstrated proficiency in a certain skill in the group, the leaders can assign homework that involves an unfamiliar setting or engaging with strangers. Gradually increasing the complexity of homework assignments will keep higher-functioning clients feeling challenged and will maintain their engagement in the social skills training process. For example, with high-functioning clients learning the skill of Making Requests, the homework assignments might progress from requesting a staff member to make a change in an appointment time, to requesting a roommate to turn down the stereo, to requesting an employee of a fast food restaurant to supply more napkins and catsup packets for customers.

Examples of homework assignments are included in Table 7.5.

TABLE 7.5. Homework Assignments Related to Client Goals

Skills	Goals	Homework assignments
Making Requests	Improve relationship with staff	Ask staff member to help with budget.
	Make friends	Ask person at drop-in center to sit with him or her at lunch table.
	Get a promotion at work	Ask boss for a more difficult assignment.
	Shop at local store	Ask clerk for cost of item.
Expressing Angry Feelings	Improve marital relationship	Tell spouse that you are angry that he or she forgot to pick you up.
	Avoid explosive anger	Tell roommate about anger due to unequal housekeeping chores.
Compromise and Negotiation	Improve enjoyment of living at home	Suggest compromise regarding how late you can play the radio.
	Increase self-assertion	Suggest compromise about where to go on group outing.
	Avoid unpleasant tasks on job	Suggest compromise about task assignments.

Managing the Range of Skill Levels

It is usually advantageous to have groups composed of clients with similar levels of concentration, symptomatology, and ability to follow role-play instructions. In most circumstances, however, a range of skill levels, goals, and motivation exists among the clients in the group. By keeping in mind the individual differences, the leaders can nevertheless overcome major obstacles by planning curricula, role plays, and homework assignments that will be appropriate to each group member's level of functioning, as described earlier in this chapter. In addition, it is helpful for leaders to devise strategies for dividing tasks of running the group and for responding to the needs of both the lower-functioning clients and higher-functioning clients in a social skills group.

Dividing Tasks between Co-Leaders

A common problem exists when some group members function at a fairly high level, and others are having difficulty with poor concentration or intrusive symptoms. Leaders can take this into consideration when dividing responsibilities for running the group, which is described in Chapter 5. One leader can focus on teaching the skill and setting up role plays, while the other leader can focus on redirecting the distractible client(s). The redirecting leader can use coaching (see Chapter 4) to help focus the client's attention on what is happening in the group. Sitting next to the client and speaking quietly, the leader can say something like, "Alice is doing a role play of Expressing Positive Feelings; let's watch how she does it."

Responding to Needs of Lower-Functioning Clients in the Group

Lower-functioning clients usually have more difficulty in concentrating, focusing on the group, and carrying out instructions regarding role plays. These clients can nonetheless benefit from learning the same skills as the higher-functioning ones, if the instructions and role plays are simplified. The leader can review all steps of the skill when addressing the group as a whole, but he or she can direct the lower-functioning clients to focus on only one or two steps at a time. The leader can also choose simple role plays that will allow the lower-functioning clients to practice the skill without being overwhelmed by detail.

Coaching is also helpful in assisting lower-functioning clients in performing specific steps of the skill. This enables the lower-functioning clients to practice successfully along with the rest of the group. More strategies for working with low-functioning clients are provided in Chapter 8.

Responding to Needs of Higher-Functioning Clients in the Group

Clients with a higher level of functioning may complain that the group is not challenging enough or not relevant to their needs. In spite of their protests, they often can benefit from mastering the social skills being taught. The leaders can remind the higher-functioning clients of the rationale for learning the skill and how it relates directly to their goals. The leaders can also design more challenging role plays that call for more complex responses and that relate more directly to their specific goals. Homework can be made more challenging, so that the higher-functioning clients are expected to use the skill in more difficult real-life situations. As mentioned in Chapter 5, many higher-functioning clients enjoy participating in a group with mixed abilities by serving as models and as confederates in the role plays with other clients because it provides an opportunity to feel pride in their abilities.

Keeping All Members Involved in the Group Process

Although the focus of the group is usually on the person performing the role play, it is important to keep the non-role-playing group members engaged in some aspect of the group throughout the session. Because of attentional deficits and distraction by symptoms, many clients tend to "tune out" when they are not directly involved in a role play. When this happens, they are no longer benefiting from the group process and may, in fact, become increasingly distracted and out of touch with what's going on around them. To prevent this "tuning out" process, the leaders must be aware of the level of involvement of each group member. When a member is uninvolved for a significant period of time, the leaders can try one of the following strategies.

Assigning Specific Tasks

The leaders can directly assign tasks to individuals in the group. For example, the leaders can ask a client to read the steps of the skill or to act as the confederate in a role play. They can also give specific assignments to individual clients regarding what to watch for or listen for during the role play. An example might be, "Jack, I would like you to watch during this role play to see if Jennifer looks at Paul while she's talking to him." After the role play is completed, the leaders can ask, "Jack, did you see if Jennifer was looking at Paul?"

Checking for Understanding

For a variety of reasons, such as attentional impairment, there are times when clients may not understand what is happening in the group. To increase the comprehension of such clients, it is helpful for the leaders to periodically check on the clients' understanding by asking questions. This is especially important when clients are participating in role plays or are observing others' role plays.

Leaders can check whether clients understand their own role plays by first asking them to repeat the instructions (e.g., "Please tell me what I just said about what I'd like you to do in this role play.") Leaders can also ask questions about the role play, such as "What is the skill we are working on in this role play?"; "Whom will you be doing the role play with?"; "What happens first in the role play?"; "What happens next?" Good questions to check for comprehension are: "What is your goal in this role play?" and "What do you want to accomplish?" The answer to these questions will reveal a great deal about what the client understands.

Leaders should also check whether clients understand what they are expected to do when observing others' role plays. They can ask clients to repeat back the instructions and can ask questions such as "Who is doing the role play?"; "What is the role play about?"; "What will you be watching for while Samuel and Tamika are participating in the role play?"; "What is Samuel's goal in this role play?"

Making Role Plays Lively

Sometimes the leaders might observe members of the group who are uninvolved, looking off into space, not watching the role plays, maybe even dozing. When assigning specific tasks and checking for understanding does not improve the situation, the leaders can try making the role plays more engaging. Some additional techniques to make the role plays more fun include introducing humor, adding movement, using theatrical techniques, and using current events or popular culture.

To introduce humor to a role play of Disagreeing without Arguing, the leaders can set up role plays where the confederate is instructed to mix up important facts, such as praising a famous football team for its skills in batting and home runs or insisting that W. C. Fields was the best president America has ever had. In groups where the members are aware of current events, the leaders can use topical examples in their role plays, such as asking the members to tell each other something they read in the newspaper recently as a way of practicing Listening to Others or thinking of compliments they might give the star of a currently popular television show to practice Expressing Positive Feelings.

To add movement to a role play of Starting a Conversation, the leader might suggest that the client stand up, walk out of the room, and pretend to be entering a party where he or she will strike up a conversation with someone standing near the food table. To loosen things up when introducing the skill of Eating and Drinking Politely, the leaders can use discrimination modeling (see Chapter 4) by first presenting a humorous example of not following the steps of the skill, perhaps gobbling their food or talking with their mouths full. When practicing the skill of Finding Common Interests, the leaders can suggest that clients ask each other about television shows they enjoyed when they were children or teenagers, perhaps even asking if they remember the "theme songs" from their favorite shows. When leaders make the role plays fun and engaging, even the members distracted by symptoms are more likely to pay attention and become involved.

Ongoing Assessment of Progress Made in Group

Chapter 2 contains information about assessing social functioning and social skills in clients with schizophrenia. It is also helpful for group leaders to regularly assess the progress made by individuals in social skills groups. Even when the leaders do not have the resources available for doing extensive assessments, a broad measure of progress every 3 to 6 months helps the leaders to evalute whether the skills are being learned, whether the clients are using them outside the group, and whether the skills are helping clients to achieve their goals. The answers to such questions aid leaders in planning how long to spend on specific skills, choosing skills to teach, and determining what efforts need to be made to increase participation in role plays and homework assignments. Information gleaned from regular assessments can also help the leaders give feedback to other treatment staff. For example, if the clients in a community residence are not using the skills outside of the group, the leaders might use this information to encourage staff to spend more time actively assisting the residents to practice the skills.

Are the Clients Learning the Skills?

As skills are being taught, it is important to assess whether the clients are actually learning them. When group members cannot perform the steps of the skill in the group session without being prompted, it indicates that they have not adequately learned the skill and require further assistance. The leaders must first evaluate if there have been sufficient opportunities for clients to practice; perhaps the group needs more sessions focusing on the skill in order to learn it. If the leaders spend more time on the skill but find that learning is not taking place in spite of sufficient opportunity to practice, they can try other strategies, such as actively coaching individual group members, modifying the role plays to make them more relevant, giving some group members extra opportunities to do role plays in the group, or adding more homework assignments.

In some instances, the clients have difficulty learning a skill because it is too complex. The skill may need to be broken down into more manageable segments. For example, if low-functioning clients have difficulty learning Compromise and Negotiation, the leaders can try separating the steps and practicing them in three different group sessions as follows: Step 1 (explain your viewpoint briefly); Step 2 and 3 together (listen to the other person's viewpoint and repeat the other person's viewpoint); Step 4 (suggest a compromise). After the group members have shown the ability to perform the steps separately, the leaders can ask them to practice the whole skill. If the clients are still unable to perform the skill without prompting, the leaders can return to a more basic skill, such as Listening to Others.

Are the Clients Using the Skills Outside of Group?

The success of social skills training hinges on the transfer of skills from the group setting to the outside world. Leaders can determine whether clients are using the skill outside of group in several ways: by asking the clients directly for examples of instances when they used the skill, by reviewing their homework assignments, and by asking others who have opportunities to observe the client, such as family members, day treatment staff or community residence staff. If the clients have learned to perform the steps of the skills while in the group but are not able to use them elsewhere, the leaders can try modifying both the role plays and the homework assignments to more accurately reflect the kinds of situations that occur in the clients' environment.

It is especially important to role play situations that occur frequently and that matter to the clients. "Real-life" examples are more likely to result in practice outside of the sessions. For example, while teaching the skill of Making Requests, group leaders in a community residence discovered that residents were not using the skill outside of the group; in fact, they were getting into frequent arguments with staff members because of the unpleasant manner in which they demanded their daily spending money. The residents were becoming discouraged by these arguments and reported feeling under increased stress. The leaders decided to implement a role play of clients politely requesting their spending money, which they practiced repeatedly in the group. The assignment was then given to practice this skill in the actual situation in the community residence. After this, staff members reported that the clients improved greatly in their ability to make requests outside of the group.

Are the Skills Helping the Clients to Achieve Goals?

If the clients are learning specific skills and using them outside of the group, the question remains as to whether these skills are helping them to achieve their personal goals. Because the achievement of goals is one of the strongest motivations for clients to participate in the group, if the skills are not helping clients to progress, they will often lose interest. To determine whether the skills are furthering the clients' goals, it is important to review the goals that were established during the initial assessment (see Chapter 5) and to determine whether any steps have been accomplished that would lead to the eventual achievement of those goals.

Sometimes it is necessary to ask whether the skill is helpful on its own or whether additional skills are needed to make it effective. For example, Richard, a client with the goal of being able to ask his physician to change his medication regimen, found it very difficult to use the skill of Making Requests when it came time to actually talk to his doctor. When the leaders taught the skill of Asking Questions about Health-Related Concerns, however, Richard was able to use it as a way of effectively introducing his request about medication.

In situations where using the skill is leading to little or no progress on achieving goals, the leaders may also need to evaluate whether the client may be engaging in other behaviors that are interfering with his or her ability to achieve the desired goal. For example, if a client with the goal of making friends is correctly using the skill of Starting Conversations but is very poorly groomed, he or she will have little success in getting people to talk. Working on improving the client's grooming may lead to more success in using the conversation skills to achieve his or her friendship goals.

In other situations, it may be that the skill itself needs to be modified to be even more specific to the client's goal. This might mean the addition of a step or a key phrase. For example, one client living in an inner-city environment who had established the goal of refusing money to panhandlers found that simply using the skill of Refusing Requests was not working. However, adding a phrase such as "I don't have any money to spare" or "I can't give anyone money" improved her effectiveness.

Summary

Although social skills training is a very structured approach, the procedures can be adapted to meet the needs of individual clients. Once the clients' goals have been established, the group leaders can help them break down the goals into smaller steps and identify which social skills would be helpful in accomplishing those steps. In designing a group, the leaders can choose a curriculum based on the skills the clients need to learn, and they can structure role plays and assign homework using situations that are relevant to the clients' individual circumstances. The leaders can also make the role plays and homework more or less challenging based on the clients' levels of functioning.

In some situations, the leaders can design a group for clients with similar needs and levels of functioning (for example, a group for high-functioning clients who need to improve their vocational skills). However, many times a range of skill levels, goals, and motivation exists among the clients in the group. Individualizing the role plays and homework assignments helps overcome some difficulties related to different levels of functioning in clients. In addition, the leaders can assign specific tasks to different members of the group, such as reading the steps of the skill or watching for a particular step in a role play, in order to keep them engaged.

Tailoring social skills training to individual needs is an ongoing process. Leaders need to set aside time regularly to review clients' progress and ask questions such as "Are the clients learning the skills?"; "Are they using the skills outside the group?"; "Are the skills helping them achieve their goals?" The answers to these questions will help the leaders know how to help each client meet his or her own personal goals.

8

Troubleshooting I:
Common Problems and
Problems with Highly
Symptomatic Clients

As with any clinical intervention, practitioners of social skills training need to know special strategies to prevent or deal with problems that occasionally occur. Many difficulties can be anticipated and prevented by carefully planning the group and tailoring the treatment to individual needs. Efforts made at the planning stage serve to build a firm foundation for the training process and pay off countless times throughout the intervention.

However, even with optimal planning, problems may arise. Some problems may occur in any group, such as reluctance to role play or noncompliance with homework; other problems, such as withdrawal or distraction by substance abuse issues, are more specific to groups with particular themes. In this and the next chapter, we address common problems and problems specific to three different types of clients: severely impaired, high-functioning, and dually diagnosed. By applying the strategies provided in these two chapters, social skills leaders will be able to keep their groups running smoothly and effectively.

Common Problems in Conducting Social Skills Training Groups

Following the Group Format

Prior to participating in social skills training, most clients will have experienced other group therapy approaches that were less structured, more insight-oriented, and where members were encouraged to "let their feelings out." When first attending a social skills training group, clients might be surprised at its structure and at its approach to teaching. Because of their previous experiences, some clients think that the goals of a skills training group are to express feelings and to discuss whatever is on their minds. Consequently, they may have difficulties following the group format at first.

To counteract the tendency to see the social skills group as an insight-oriented therapy group, the leaders should provide a clear description and explanation for the format of social skills training groups in their initial interviews with the clients (see Chapter 5). The leaders can be specific about how social skills groups are different from other types of group therapy. For example, the leaders can explain how clients who practice expressing unpleasant feelings (such as anger) in the skills group often find it easier to express these feelings when they experience them in real-life situations. Many leaders find it useful to provide a brief description of the skills training format in a handout provided during the initial orentation (see Appendix A).

Even with good preparation, however, some clients find it difficult to follow the group format. In such instances, it is helpful for the leaders to remind group members of the format at the beginning of each session. They might say something such as "Today we will be focusing on the skill of Giving Compliments. First we'll talk about why it's important to be able to give compliments, and then we'll discuss the steps of the skill. We will then show you an example of how to give a compliment, and then everyone in the group will have a chance to practice giving compliments themselves." Throughout the session, the leaders can point out each phase of the format as the group progresses. For example, the leaders might say, "Now it's time for each person to have a chance to practice Giving Compliments. Steve, I would like you to start."

When clients deviate from the format, the leaders can gently but firmly redirect them to the task at hand ("Right now I'd like you to hold your comments while you watch Steve do a role play"). Praising group members who make progress in following the format is also beneficial. For example, to a client who previously interrupted role plays and has now begun to observe them quietly, the leaders could say, "I liked the way you waited until Steve finished his role play before you gave feedback."

Usually clients are able to follow the group format after several sessions. If difficulties persist, however, it might be helpful to make a brief handout, listing the steps of the format that the leaders can use in the group. Table 8.1 contains an example of a handout that can be used with group members. A brief discussion of the steps in a group meeting and the rationale for each step can be quite helpful. A copy of the format can also be posted in the group room, and the group leaders can refer to it as necessary.

TABLE 8.1. Steps of a Social Skills Training Group Meeting

1. Review the last homework assignment.
2. Identify the skill that will be worked on in the group and talk about the reasons for using the skill.
3. Discuss the steps of the skill.
4. Watch a role play of the group leader using the skill.
5. Give feedback to the leader about how he or she used the steps of the skill.
6. Each group member does a role play using the skill.
7. Each group member receives feedback about how he or she used the steps of the skill.
8. Each group member has a chance to improve his or her performance in another role play.
9. Homework is assigned.

Reluctance to Role Play

Like many people in the general population, some clients feel uncomfortable or awkward speaking in front of a group. This may make them reluctant to role play. First, it is important for the leaders to acknowledge the client's feelings and that his or her discomfort is understandable. It is helpful to let the client know that many people feel shy when they first try role playing, but that they gradually get used to it and may even start to enjoy it. The client can be reminded that role plays are very brief and that everyone in the group will be doing them. Some clients are concerned that they will be criticized or teased. The leaders can point out that the emphasis of skills training is on providing positive feedback and suggestions for helping clients be even more effective at using the skills and that negative comments and criticism are avoided.

Second, reviewing the rationale for role playing is important. The most common rationale is that "People need to practice the skills they are learning so that they can really know how to do them. It's like learning to play the piano or tennis. You have to practice to get skillful." The leaders can add that, by role playing, people usually feel more comfortable when a situation comes up in real life where they need to use the skill.

Third, it often helps clients to observe other group members role playing, so that they can see that role plays are in fact brief and that criticism is avoided. If a client is adamant about refusing to do role plays, he or she can build up to it by first giving feedback to other clients. Or, some clients may feel more comfortable serving as confederates in role plays first. These stages of participation can continue until the client is comfortable attempting a brief role play. After letting the client observe others role playing, the leaders encourage the client to "give it a try," usually asking the client to first do a shortened version of a role play, perhaps just the initial step. Whatever effort the client makes should be followed by praise, such as "I really liked the way you looked at Bernice" or "You used a calm voice; that was good." The leaders can keep the interaction brief, moving on to the next client, first saying something like "Thanks for giving it a try; you did a good job on that first step of looking at the person." In later role plays, the leaders can gradually increase the number of steps that they ask the client to do.

Difficulty Providing Appropriate Feedback

When clients are first involved in a social skills training group, they sometimes give feedback to each other that is either critical or vague. This is not surprising, as this is the kind of "feedback" most clients have received in the past. Also, many people find it is easier to find fault than to praise, and learning how to give specific feedback takes time. With practice, however, clients can learn to give feedback that is both positive and specific. There are many ways that the leaders can facilitate this.

In explaining the group format in the initial sessions, the leaders can describe how feedback will be given in the social skills group, being sure to include that feedback is specific about the steps of the skill, starts with positive comments, and gives suggestions (one at a time) for improvement. The leaders can provide brief examples of appropriate feedback, as described in Chapter 3. After explaining the desired format for feedback, the leaders serve as important models. In giving feedback, therefore, the leaders must be conscious of always starting with positive feedback after a role play. The clients in the group will learn to expect that kind of feedback and can "imitate" the leaders. The leaders can also remind group members to give positive feedback by saying something such as "Jose, I'd like you to give some feedback to Robin about how she did in that role play about Accepting Compliments. Remember to start with what she did well."

If a client starts to severely criticize another client, the leaders need to interrupt the criticism as soon as possible. Since clients with schizophrenia may be very sensitive to criticism (Bellack et al., 1992), it is better to "nip criticism in the bud." The leaders can say something such as "Let's stop there, Jose. First I'd like you to tell me what Robin did well. Later we can offer a suggestion for improvement." If a mild criticism occurs after some positive feedback, the leaders can try reframing the critical feedback into a constructive suggestion immediately, such as "Would you suggest that Robin try to use a friendlier tone of voice?" It is also important to praise clients who begin to make positive comments after having been critical in their previous feedback. For example, the leaders might say, "Thanks, that was very helpful feedback. You really noticed what Robin did well."

The leaders also serve as role models in providing specific feedback. Starting with general comments such as "Good job," "Nice work," or "Fine" is a good start, but the leaders need to follow with more specific feedback. For example, the leaders might say, "Good job, Robin. I especially liked the way you did Step 2. You said thank you in a very sincere way." The leaders can also directly guide or instruct the group members to be more specific. This can be done by asking questions. For example, when it is Jose's turn to give feedback, the leaders might ask him, "How did Robin do on Step 1, 'looking at the person'?" If Jose is vaguely positive about Step 1, the leaders can prompt him by saying, "Yes, I think Robin did well, too, but can you be more specific? Did she look directly at the person she was talking to?" When a client gives specific feedback, the leaders can praise his or her efforts by pointing it out, saying something such as "Telling Robin that she looked right at Joe is very specific. That's very helpful feedback."

After the group has met for several weeks, a sense of cohesion usually develops, and clients become more supportive of each other's efforts. They may begin to offer positive feedback spontaneously and might even applaud group members who accomplish something that was very difficult for them in the past. If appropriate feedback does not occur after several weeks, it might be helpful to review what is meant by constructive feedback and to provide a written handout to group members and to post a copy in the group room. See Guidelines for Giving Constructive Feedback in Appendix A for an example of such a handout.

Noncompliance with Homework

For clients to get the most benefit from social skills training, they must practice the skills outside the group. Because practice does not usually occur spontaneously, it is important to assign homework for using the skill in real-life situations. Chapters 3 and 4 include descriptions of how homework is assigned and reviewed and how role plays in the group can be structured based on the homework. An example of a homework assignment sheet can be found in Appendix A.

Even when clients understand the rationale for doing homework and the assignment is written down, they often have difficulty following through. The leaders need to be persistent, however, in giving the clear message that homework is important and will be pursued. Each group starts with a review of the homework assigned in the previous session. The leaders praise any efforts at completing the homework, even if the clients were not totally successful. When clients report that they encountered difficulties, the leaders can ask for more details, helping the group members to problem solve how specific obstacles can be overcome.

It is best to start by assigning relatively simple tasks for homework, so that group members have a good chance of being successful. As they demonstrate that they can accomplish homework at the basic level, the difficulty of the assignments can gradually be increased. Clients are also more likely to put in effort on their homework assignments when they are interesting and related to their personal goals. The leaders can tailor assignments with this in mind, as described in Chapter 7. For example, if a client has a goal of increasing his spending money, his assignment for the skill of Making a Request might be to ask a counselor at the community residence if there are any jobs that can be done for extra money. Group members can also be actively involved in deciding the details of their own assignments. For the skill of Giving Compliments, for example, the leaders can ask the client, "Is there someone in your family whom you would like to give a compliment to?"

Clients who have difficulty with their memory and/or who have low motivation can benefit from someone actively helping them to complete their assignments. For example, if a client lives at home, a family member might be asked to prompt the client about homework by saying something such as "It's 2:00, time to do your homework. Let's look at the assignment sheet together." The family member can also participate in completing the assignment by being the person with whom the client practices the skill. For example, the client could be assigned to give a compliment to a specific sibling who has agreed to the assignment. In residential settings for highly impaired clients, it is usually more effective for the leader to assign the homework task to a specific staff member to prompt the resident to practice the skill. The staff member then takes responsibility for initiating the completion of the assignment and for recording the results. This method of assigning homework to staff members is most effective when they receive training about how to prompt and reinforce the clients' use of social skills. When a staff member or family member is involved in completing the homework assignment, they should praise the client on the spot for his or her efforts. Immediate, specific praise is very reinforcing for the client. Staff members and family members also have the advantage of being able to use a variety of *in vivo* situations and outings to the community as opportunities to help clients practice the skills of the homework assignments.

The word "homework" has a negative connotation for some clients for a variety of reasons. For some, homework brings back memories of doing poorly at school; for others, doing homework is experienced as demeaning because it is something "just for kids to do." For clients who do not feel comfortable with the term "homework," the leaders can substitute another term, such as "practice" or "assignment." For example, the leaders might say, "I'd like you to practice this skill before our next group; I've written down your assignment on this sheet to help you remember."

Table 8.2 provides a summary of strategies for the common problems encountered in conducting social skills training groups.

TABLE 8.2. Strategies for Common Problems in Social Skills Training Groups

General principles

1. Encourage participation from each client according to his or her ability.
2. Set clear expectations.
3. Praise small steps toward improvement.

Specific problems	Strategies
Difficulty following group format	At the beginning of group, remind members of format. As group progresses, point out each phase. Consistently redirect clients when they go off the topic or interrupt others. Provide written handout or poster of format if problems persist.
Reluctance to role play	Acknowledge shy feelings. Engage client in observing others role play. Engage client in providing feedback. Start with a shortened version of role play. Gradually increase the number of steps to perform in a role play.
Providing vague or critical feedback	Consistently model appropriate feedback. Guide clients by asking questions about specific steps. Stop critical comments. Reframe criticisms into constructive suggestions. Provide written handout or poster if problems persist.
Noncompliance with homework	Write down assignments. Start with simple tasks. Help plan where, when, and with whom assignments will be completed. Review previous assignment at beginning of each session. Problem-solve about obstacles encountered in completing assignments. Consistently assign and follow up homework. Request assistance in completion from family or staff members. Tailor assignment to the individual.

Problems Related to Highly Symptomatic Clients

Poor Attendance

One of the most fundamental problems leaders encounter when they conduct social skills training groups with highly symptomatic clients is getting them to attend and/or to stay the entire length of the session. This problem is not unique to social skills training; most professionals working with the severely mentally ill report that getting them to attend programs of any kind is an ongoing struggle. There are several reasons for this problem. Many of the positive symptoms, such as persistent auditory hallucinations and delusions, are often persecutory in nature and lead clients to be suspicious of any new person or activity. Symptoms also cause substantial stimulation, and attending a group or an activity makes some clients feel overstimulated. The negative symptoms of schizophrenia, such as apathy and anhedonia (difficulty experiencing pleasure), also interfere with attendance. Finally, clients may be reluctant to attend social skills training groups because of past experiences with group approaches that were less structured and more affectively charged and, therefore, not suitable for people with schizophrenia.

From the very first contacts with the clients, it is helpful for the leaders to express warmth and enthusiasm about participation in social skills training. The leaders need to convey the expectation that the group will help clients to achieve personal goals and that they will enjoy attending. For clients who express extreme reluctance, have poor attentional capacity, or have a very poor attendance record with other programs, it is desirable to set small goals for initial attendance. For example, the leaders might ask the client to "Give it a try for 10 minutes" and make very few demands during those 10 minutes. Clients who observe the process of the group are usually reassured by what they see and become more receptive to attending the group. As the client becomes more comfortable during short periods in the group, the leaders can gradually increase their expectations for how long the client will attend.

It is important to provide positive reinforcement to clients for all efforts at attending the group. Even when a client attends for only a few minutes, it helps for the leaders to praise him or her, saying something such as "Thanks for coming today; I hope you come back on Thursday." Most clients respond well to sincere praise and encouragement, which can come from a variety of sources, including the leaders, other treatment staff, family members, and friends. Other reinforcers, such as food, increased privileges, special outings, or time with a favorite staff member also help provide motivation for increasing attendance. In settings in which a token economy is in place, attendance can be rewarded with tokens. Some community residences develop a reward system where goals for attendance and participation are set each month, and clients who achieve their monthly goals are invited to a party. Progress toward these goals is recorded on a chart in the room where the social skills group is held. The party includes pizza and games.

At times the leaders might feel discouraged when a particular client does not attend the group. However, it is important not to give up. With encouragement, even clients who do not attend any other treatment programs may attend social skills groups. We have seen several cases where clients who had vigorously resisted attending a social skills group for months finally tried attending. This kind of breakthrough can occur for different reasons. One reason is that, even for the severely ill, the symptoms of schizophrenia fluctuate. Clients who have even a brief reduction of symptoms may experience a "window of opportunity" when they are able to think more clearly or feel less suspicious; at that time, they are more willing to try coming to a social skills training group. Once they try attending, the chances are good that they will return.

Another reason clients might begin attending after a long period is that it takes time to develop a trusting relationship with the group leaders. Therefore, it is important for leaders, especially those who are not regular staff members or who come from another agency, to establish relationships with clients whom they want to join the group. For example, the leaders can regularly greet nonattending clients, saying that they are glad to see them, and develop topics of conversation, such as favorite foods, television shows seen recently, outings, pets, and so forth. It is also important to conduct the group consistently on the same days and at the same time; keeping the same routine helps the client to "count on" the fact that the group will continue to occur. Leaders should avoid scheduling social skills groups that conflict with other activities scheduled at the same time, especially leisure and recreational activities.

In residential settings where social skills training groups are conducted by regular staff members, the staff members can use their existing relationships with clients to encourage them to attend groups and can enlist the help of their co-workers. It is also beneficial to have an additional staff member assigned to assist with each social skills group. The assisting staff member can remind clients in advance of the scheduled group time and can gather or direct clients into the group room. The reminders and requests for attendance should be very positive and convey an expectation of attendance. When reminding the client about group, it is preferable to make a direct request saying something like "It's 5 minutes until social skills group; I'd like you to go to the living room now," or "I'd like you to go to social skills group; it would be great to have you attend today." On the other hand, making the request in the form of a question such as "Do you want to come to social skills group?" leaves the client the option of merely answering "No," which is difficult to counter. In addition to gathering clients for groups, staff members can also help by attending the group, because some clients feel more secure when there is a trusted staff member in the room. In the group, staff members can also serve as confederates in role plays and can assist the leaders in designing role plays that relate to the clients' natural environment.

Difficulties in Comprehension

Because of the cognitive impairments that are common to schizophrenia, some clients have difficulty understanding what is happening in the group and what is being said to them. Many clients also experience symptoms such as delusions or auditory hallucinations on a continual basis. For some clients, voices may be a low background noise, for others they may be loud and commanding. Regardless of the level of voices, however, many clients experience voices as being "in competition" with the speech of real people and find it difficult to fully attend to what others are saying and doing.

To help improve clients' comprehension, the leaders can begin by keeping the group relatively short, from 30 to 40 minutes, to better match the clients' limited ability to concentrate. It is also helpful to make sure that communication is brief and to the point. Excessive detail or digression makes it difficult for the client to pick out the main points. When the client looks puzzled and asks, "What am I supposed to do?" after listening to the instructions for a role play, it is usually a sign that the leaders need to be more brief and to speak in shorter sentences. They may also need to simplify what the client is being asked to do. The leaders need to check regularly whether the clients are comprehending by asking questions such as "Could you please repeat back what I said?" or "Tell me what you're going to do in this role play."

Clearly delineating the different stages of the group also helps to keep the client focused on what is happening in the session. Announcing, "Now it's time to give feedback about the role play that Mary and Clinton just did," or "Now it's Alice's turn to practice making a request for a cigarette" can be helpful. Gradually even highly symptomatic clients who attend the group can understand the format of the group and what is expected of them. In addition to clearly identifying the stage of the group, leaders will benefit by judiciously shortening certain stages of social skills groups that contain severely impaired clients. For example, spending less time on the rationale allows leaders to move directly to the more active stages of modeling and role playing, which hold the clients' attention better.

There may also be times when the leaders have difficulty comprehending what a client is saying. For example, when one client, Lyle, became excited or agitated about certain subjects, he would hurry his words and not pronounce them clearly, making it very difficult to understand him. Leaders found it helpful to ask Lyle to slow down and to speak in short sentences.

The leaders also need to check whether they are understanding a client correctly by asking questions and repeating back what they heard. An example of checking for comprehension would be, "Let me see if I'm understanding you correctly; you're saying that you are upset because you think someone took your seat?" It is important to show an interest in what clients say, even if they don't make sense immediately. However, the leaders must guard against spending too much time on one-to-one interactions that exclude the rest of the group. Individual conversations can be pursued after the group.

Distractibility

It is difficult for many clients to focus their attention and to concentrate for significant periods of time, especially when symptoms are competing for their attention. To help clients maintain their concentration, it is important to keep other distractions to a minimum, such as street noise, people walking in and out of the room, telephones ringing, and people being called out of group. It is also important to keep communication brief and clear in the group; the leaders themselves must avoid long explanations and must redirect other group members who speak for long periods or in vague terms. Because "a picture is worth a thousand words," especially to clients who are already distracted by symptoms, it is often preferable for leaders to give a simple example by demonstrating what they mean rather than giving a lengthy explanation.

To help keep the client's attention during the group, the leaders can design role plays that are brief, lively, and contain scenes that reflect the client's real-life situation. The leaders can also stand up in front of the group like teachers to explain the steps of the skills, provide rationales and model the skills. They can also ask clients to stand up during their role plays. This helps clients to recognize whom to watch and to listen to during the group. To gain attention, the leaders also need to speak in a voice that is pleasant, animated, and sufficiently loud. Speaking too softly or without authority will lose group members' attention.

Some clients can remain focused while they are participating in a role play themselves but become distracted when others are speaking or role playing. It is useful, therefore, for the leaders to assign tasks to group members observing role plays. These tasks of observation can vary from requiring a small amount of concentration (listening for the tone of voice) to a large amount (listening for the specific suggestion made in Step 3 of Expressing Unpleasant Feelings). When clients are not engaged in specific tasks, the pull of competing stimuli becomes more powerful and their distractibility increases.

Disruptions

When clients are particularly troubled by symptoms, they may respond with behavior that is highly disruptive to the rest of the group. For example, if a client is hearing voices that say that an alien force is trying to harm him, he might call out, "I need help—someone is trying to hurt me!" Or a client who has visual hallucinations might report seeing fire coming in the window. Someone with active delusions might accuse the leaders of being members of the Mafia. The leaders should be understanding and empathetic about these symptom-based interruptions, but nonetheless they are disorienting to both the clients and leaders and must be addressed.

When clients have symptom-related outbursts, they are often afraid or alarmed by what they're experiencing. In situations where a client is obviously distraught, the leaders' first goal is to reassure him or her. Many clients feel reassured when the leaders remind them that the group is a safe place. It is also reassuring when the leaders say something to show that the client is welcome in the group, such as "We're glad you're here with us today." The next goal is to redirect the client in a kind but firm manner, reminding him or her of the focus of the group and assigning the client a specific task to perform. For example, the leaders might say, "What we're doing in the group right now is focusing on how to Give Compliments. I'd like you to listen to Dorothea practice giving a compliment to Alice. Notice if she looks at Alice when she speaks."

In some situations, the leaders can suggest that the client take his or her mind off the disturbing symptom by paying close attention to the group. The leaders might say something like "I'm sorry you feel that someone wants to steal your jewelry; I don't think that is going to happen here. It would be a good idea to take your mind off the subject by concentrating on what we're doing in the group. Today we're talking about Making Requests." In other situations the leaders can omit the reference to "taking your mind off the subject" and simply suggest focusing on the topic of the group. In still other situations the outburst can actually be linked to the group topic, and the client can practice expressing his or her concern by using the skill being practiced. For example, in a group where Barbara shouted at Joe to get away from her, the leaders could say something such as "It sounds like you're worried about Joe's intentions toward you, and you would like him to move his chair away from you. Since we're working on the skill of Making Requests today, I'd like you to practice using the steps of the skill to ask Joe to move his chair. Remember to use a calm voice."

If the client persists in talking about hallucinations or delusions, a leader can suggest that they could talk about it together after the group, giving a specific time for the conversation. It is important, however, for leaders to follow up by initiating a conversation after the group, or the client will lose faith that the leaders are really interested in his or her concerns.

In rare circumstances, some clients may have such severe symptoms that it is impossible to reassure or redirect them. For example, after the leaders make two or more unsuccessful attempts to get the client to concentrate on the topic of the group, they might consider asking the client to "take a break" from the group until he or she is better able to concentrate and/or follow the rules of the group. There are three questions that the leader can ask him- or herself to guide the decision about whether to ask a disruptive client to leave: (1) Can I continue to conduct the group if the client stays? (2) Can other group members concentrate if the client stays? (3) From what I know of the client's history, does this level of disruption usually escalate?

If the decision is made to ask the client to leave, it is important to refer to the specific behavior that was disruptive and to "leave the door open" for the client to attend the next group. The leaders should not ask the client to leave the group as a punishment, but rather as an acknowledgment that the client is currently having difficulties that prevent effective group participation. It is also important to express the expectations that the situation can improve. For example, the leaders might say, "Since it's very hard for you not to shout during the group today, I'd like you to take a break from the rest of this session. But I'll look forward to seeing you on Wednesday; you can give it another try then."

Finally, there are social skills that the clients can learn that are specifically designed to address symptomatic behavior. After several disruptions, the leaders might choose to introduce one of these skills, such as Responding to Untrue Accusations, Checking Out Your Beliefs, Letting Someone Know That You Are Afraid, Staying on the Topic Set by Another Person, and What to Do When You Do Not Understand What a Person Is Saying (see curriculum in Part II).

Social Withdrawal/Lack of Engagement

In constrast to clients who are disruptive, there are those who are withdrawn and uncommunicative during the group. Some are withdrawn because of negative symptoms such as poverty of speech, apathy, and anhedonia. For these clients, it is very difficult to become involved in any activity, including a social skills group. Other clients are withdrawn as a response to positive symptoms. For example, if someone is hallucinating, hearing several voices at once, he or she might withdraw in order to cut down on the amount of stimulation experienced. In addition, some clients are slow to become involved in social skills groups because they are apprehensive that they will make a mistake or will be criticized. This last group of clients usually increase their participation over time as they see that the group environment is supportive rather than critical.

Some clients are so withdrawn that they may not respond to questions or refuse to participate. This "negativism" can be misinterpreted as "rudeness" or "hostility" when it is not. It is helpful for the leaders to remind themselves that the behavior is due to the negative symptoms of schizophrenia and differs from willful rudeness. The leaders must avoid seeing the client's lack of involvement as a criticism of the group or of their leadership. The most effective way to improve rapport with severely withdrawn clients is to reward them for even the smallest efforts at involvement. The leaders' goal is for the clients to develop a positive association with the group; this process may be very gradual and often requires a great deal of persistence on the part of leaders.

To maximize positive interactions with very withdrawn clients, the leaders must keep their communication pleasant and brief. It is also helpful to communicate initially by making statements that do not require the clients to respond. For example, the leaders might give a client a compliment ("I like your shirt today, David; purple is one of my favorite colors") or praise the client's attendance ("I'm really glad you are in group today"). Asking questions that require an answer, such as "What kind of situations do you encounter where you have to make requests?" are often too demanding at first for the withdrawn client. When some kind of rapport has been established, the leaders can begin asking very simple questions that can be answered with "Yes" or "No" (such as "Did you hear Jose asking Robin a question in the role play?") and should positively reinforce any responses given. Gradually the leaders can begin to ask questions that are more open-ended.

Although the leaders may be very curious about the reason for clients being withdrawn, it is often ineffective to persist in asking such individuals why they feel this way. Although some clients can tell why they feel a certain way, it is more common for withdrawn clients not to know why and to feel embarrassed that they cannot respond. Leaders should avoid offering interpretations about the reason behind the client's withdrawal because it is extremely difficult to know what is going on in a client's mind. For example, a leader once suggested to a client that perhaps he was uncomfortable because the group was too large. The client heatedly denied this, saying he was not participating in group because "everyone is speaking pornography, and I don't want any part of that." Another client, who regularly attended group but remained silent and appeared distracted during the sessions, once surprised group leaders by responding to a general question with a very detailed answer, which showed that he had indeed been attending closely.

Table 8.3 provides a summary of strategies for responding to problems related to conducting social skills groups with highly symptomatic clients.

TABLE 8.3. Strategies for Problems Related to Highly Symptomatic Clients

General principles

1. Keep communication brief and to the point.
2. Be consistent in maintaining structure and holding group in same time and place.
3. Praise efforts and small steps toward improvement.
4. Teach and review basic skills frequently.

Specific problems	Strategies
Poor attendance	Build rapport by communicating warmth and enthusiasm. Set small goals. Use reinforcers such as praise, food, increased privileges, time with a favorite person. Enlist help of other staff members or family members. Identify obstacles to attendance. Consistently request client to attend.
Difficulties in comprehension	Keep group time relatively short; Check frequently whether clients are understanding. Simplify language and instructions. Allow members ample opportunity to observe and practice skills.
Distractibility	Keep other distractions to a minimum. Avoid lengthy explanations. Use examples, role plays to illustrate points. Redirect promptly to topic of group. Design engaging role plays which are relevant to real-life situations. Use a pleasant, sufficiently loud voice. Assign specific tasks to group members observing role plays.
Disruptions related to symptoms	Reassure clients of safety of group. Redirect kindly and firmly to topic of group. When appropriate, link content of disruption to skill being taught. Suggest discussing clients' concerns after group. Teach social skills designed to manage symptoms.
Withdrawal	Understand that withdrawal is not a criticism of leaders or group. Build rapport by communicating in a warm, low-key manner. Avoid excessive questioning. Avoid interpretations of why the client is withdrawn.

Summary

In this chapter we described clinical strategies for managing problems encountered during social skills training. In any skills training group, it is important to set clear expectations, praise small steps toward improvement, and encourage participation from each client according to his or her ability. The leaders need to follow the structured format of the group as much as possible and model appropriate social skills in their interactions with group members, especially when making requests and redirecting clients.

In groups with highly symptomatic clients, the leaders need to keep their communication brief and to the point, be consistent in holding group sessions at the same time and place, and teach and review basic skills frequently. The leaders will benefit from building individual rapport with the clients, communicating warmth and enthusiasm, and praising them for their efforts and progress made in small steps. The leaders also should be prepared to respond to disruptions related to symptoms, by redirecting clients to the topic, reassuring them of the safety of the group, and teaching social skills designed to help clients manage their own symptoms.

9

Troubleshooting II: Problems with High-Functioning Clients and Dually Diagnosed Clients

In this chapter we address clinical strategies for common problems of two more specific types of client: the high-functioning client and the dually diagnosed client.

Problems Related to Higher-Functioning Clients

Difficulty Accepting the Need for Social Skills

Clients who function at a relatively high level may protest that they don't need the training provided in social skills group. They may say that they are bored or that they "know all about socializing." In fact, a minority of clients with schizophrenia need little or no social skills training (Mueser, Bellack, Douglas, & Morrison, 1991). For the most part, however, the high-functioning clients who protest the loudest are the ones who need the skills the most.

There are several reasons that high-functioning clients have difficulty acknowledging that they need social skills training. Because they are functioning well compared to others with the illness, some clients feel that they do not need treatment. They may differentiate themselves from lower-functioning clients by saying, "Those other people need social skills training, not me." They may also express that a social skills group is "too easy" or "too repetitive." Others feel that a social skills group reminds them of the losses they have suffered because of schizophrenia, such as the ability to form close friendships and interact easily with others, and they find it painful to be reminded of these losses. Still others fail to see any connection between the problems they have experienced and the need for improved social skills.

139

In responding to higher-functioning clients who object to social skills training, it is important for the leaders to avoid confrontation and to focus instead on how skills training will contribute to achieving personal goals. Most high-functioning clients find working on goals to be a positive experience. Once goals are established, breaking them down into smaller steps will provide opportunities for the leaders to suggest how accomplishing the steps would be facilitated by developing specific social skills (see Chapter 7). For example, a high-functioning client with the goal of earning a college degree might see the advantage of starting off by taking one course at a time. In thinking about what is needed to do well in the course, the client might see the advantage of using the skill of Listening to Others to make sure that he or she is understanding what the professor is saying. Once social skills have been linked to a goal, the client is usually more receptive to hearing about the benefits of social skills training.

For clients who feel that the group is "too easy," it can be helpful for the leaders to use the analogy of learning to play the piano—one needs to start with basic pieces before playing complicated ones. The leaders can explain the process of starting with the basic skills first, then building up to the more complicated skills involved in accomplishing more complicated goals. For clients who protest that the group is "too repetitive," the leaders can explain that practicing social skills is like practicing a musical piece over and over to make it sound smooth and automatic. It may be useful to give a title to the social skills group that reflects the learning component, such as "Social Skills Class," or "Communication Skills Group," or "Problem-Solving Workshop."

After high-functioning clients have started attending group sessions and show the ability to perform the basic skills, the leaders can reduce the chances of boredom by making role plays successively more challenging. The leaders can also provide opportunities for the clients to practice situations that are specific to their goals. For example, when teaching Starting Conversations, the leaders can assign Jack, whose goal is to improve his relationships with coworkers, the role play of making brief small talk with the person at the desk next to him in the office. The leaders can encourage high-functioning clients to tailor their own role plays, by asking such questions as "What kinds of situations do you encounter when you need to use this skill?" and "With whom would you like to practice this skill?"

Discomfort Interacting with Lower-Functioning Clients

Some higher-functioning clients say that they feel uncomfortable in groups where the other members are more impaired than they are. Some high-functioning group members find it difficult to be patient with others who move at a slower pace, taking longer to perform role plays and provide feedback. They may also feel that they don't have much in common with the goals of the lower-functioning clients. Other high-functioning clients feel that it "brings them down" to associate with clients who have the same illness as they do and who are more visibly impaired by it. Clients who feel this way often do not want to reveal having difficulties of any type, including problems in social situations. Being in the same group as clients who have more obvious needs for better social skills may be perceived as an unpleasant reminder of their own illness.

The leaders can respond to high-functioning clients who are reluctant to be in a group of clients with mixed abilities by first reminding them of their goals and how social skills training will help them achieve those goals. If the client objects to the group format, the leaders can point out that people learn social skills best in a group because they can practice with others and get feedback from others. It is especially helpful to be able to practice social skills with a variety of people. The leaders can remind clients that it is important to be able to get along with other people, even those with whom they feel uncomfortable.

With some higher-functioning clients, it is helpful to acknowledge that they are more socially skilled than others in the group and to engage them in helping the other group members learn the skills through modeling or acting as the confederate in role-play rehearsals. Once the higher-functioning clients are engaged in the group, the leaders must be alert to opportunities to conduct skills training directly with them, tailoring the role plays and homework to their ability. Higher-functioning clients will appreciate receiving more challenging assignments in the group. As mentioned earlier, the clients can also be involved in choosing their own role plays and homework, which is stimulating and keeps them engaged.

Most high-functioning clients can be persuaded to attend groups. In rare instances, however, it may be necessary to consider one-to-one training as a preparation for joining the group. When the goal of individual training is for the client to participate in sessions of an ongoing group, the individual client and the group members should be simultaneously taught the same skills, so that they will all be familiar with the same skills. When there are several higher-functioning clients, the leaders might consider forming a group tailored for them, with a curriculum addressing more challenging skill areas, such as forming intimate relationships, dealing with conflicts on the job, or improving family relationships.

Tendency to Engage in Excessive Discussion

Instead of following the format of the social skills training group, some higher-functioning clients attempt to engage the leaders or other group members in extended discussion. Even when discussion is related in some way to the skill being taught in the group, it usually distracts other clients from the task of learning and practicing the skill. For example, a client may want to discuss at length his or her opinion that it is more difficult for men to compromise than it is for women. This might be an interesting discussion point, but it takes considerable time away from teaching group members actual skills that they can use to compromise.

There are a variety of reasons for engaging in discussion during social skills group. Some clients seem to have a strong need for expressing themselves and have few outlets for doing so. Other clients are accustomed to process-oriented groups where lengthy discussion is encouraged, and they return to that format out of habit. Still others are uncomfortable with the idea that they need social skills training and turn to conversation and discussion as a way of avoiding the tasks of the group.

When clients get "side-tracked" into discussion, the leaders can first acknowledge that the topic is interesting or that a good point is being made. However, it is important to quickly redirect the group members to the task at hand. The leaders might say, "That's an interesting example of how your father had difficulty compromising. What we're doing in this group is emphasizing the practical considerations of how we can go about compromising and negotiating." If possible, the leaders can then engage the client in an active role within the group format, such as reading the steps of the skill, role playing, or giving specific feedback.

Many leaders find it useful to schedule time at the end of every group for unstructured socializing and discussion. For example, the group might last 45 minutes with 15 minutes at the end for conversation and snacks. Many clients find it reinforcing to spend unstructured time after group socializing with the leaders and/or other clients. Also, when clients attempt to carry on extended conversation during the training portion of the group, leaders can direct them to continue their discussion during the scheduled socialization time. For example, if a group member wants to engage in conversation during the group, the leaders might say, "We need to focus on learning how to make compromises now, but I'd like to talk about the subject you just raised after 2:00, when we have snacks."

Table 9.1 provides a summary of strategies leaders can use for responding to problems commonly encountered when conducting social skills training groups with clients who are high-functioning.

Problems Related to Clients Who Abuse Drugs or Alcohol

Need for Integrated Models of Treatment

There is now widespread evidence that people with severe mental illness are at increased risk to develop substance use disorders (Drake & Mueser, 1996).

TABLE 9.1. Strategies for Problems Related to High-Functioning Clients

General principles

1. Make a connection between group participation and achieving goals.
2. Engage in challenging role plays.
3. Encourage clients to help other group members learn targeted skills.

Specific problems	Strategies
Difficulty accepting need for training	Avoid confrontation. Focus on goals. Provide rationale comparing social skills training to learning to play piano.
Discomfort interacting with lower-functioning clients	Remind clients of the need to get along with a variety of people. Praise their ability to act as role models.
Engaging in excessive discussion	Acknowledge that client's topic is interesting. Redirect to the task at hand. Reserve time at the end of group for discussion.

Substance abuse has significant negative consequences for clients with the diagnosis of schizophrenia, including increased vulnerability to relapses and rehospitalizations, interference with the therapeutic effect of medications, noncompliance with medications, increased vulnerability to HIV infection, and greater incidence of depression, suicide, violence, housing instability, and homelessness.

Although research on the efficacy of specific interventions for this population is in the preliminary stage, there is growing evidence to indicate that an integrated treatment approach that provides interventions for both mental health and substance abuse problems simultaneously can be effective in reducing substance abuse in this population. An important aspect of integrated treatment is that treatment for both substance abuse and mental illness are provided by the same clinicians, with the responsibility of integrating different aspects of treatment falling on the clinicians rather than the clients. There are many indications that social skills training groups can be a very useful component in comprehensive programs for treating clients dually diagnosed with schizophrenia and substance abuse, especially when combined with proper medication, intensive case management, psychoeducation, teaching symptom-coping techniques, and relapse prevention training.

One of the most useful models for understanding the process of recovering from substance use disorders is that clients go through a progression of stages (Prochaska, DiClemente, & Norcross, 1992). Drake, Bartels, Teague, Noordsy, and Clark (1993) describe a four-stage model that clinicians have found quite helpful in treating the dually diagnosed. In this model, the first stage is *engagement* (the client becomes engaged in treatment for substance abuse), followed by *persuasion* (the client agrees that substance abuse is a problem), then *active treatment* (the client begins to work on reducing substance use), and finally *relapse prevention* (the client achieves abstinence or nonharmful use and works toward preventing relapses of substance abuse).

It is important for leaders to keep in mind the stages of recovery when designing social skills training groups for dually diagnosed clients. In some settings, it is posible to form groups for clients who are at similar stages; that is, clients in the engagement and persuasion stage would be in one group, while clients in the active treatment and relapse prevention stages would be in another. When conducting groups composed of clients who are at different stages, however, leaders need to keep in mind the differences in clients' levels of motivation and their commitment to change substance abuse behavior. Because of these differences, clients will have different goals concerning treatment and abstinence and will be more or less receptive to learning social skills that are particularly focused on changing substance abuse.

Substance abuse is a chronic, relapsing disorder, and clients often progress in a nonlinear fashion, going back and forth between different stages. It is important for social skills leaders to be sensitive to the individual's stage in the recovery process, to teach skills that are consistent with the client's stage, and to avoid the kind of confrontation (sometimes called "tough love") that is often used in treating substance abusers who do not have schizophrenia. Such confrontation can be very stressful to clients with schizophrenia and even drive them away from treatment.

From the perspective of social learning theory, abusing substances can serve a variety of functions for clients, such as facilitating socialization, reducing anxiety, dealing with boredom, and reducing depression. Even though substance abuse may appear to produce short-term benefits, it frequently causes long-term negative consequences, such as increased risk of relapse of schizophrenic symptoms, legal problems, poor social relationships, and financial calamities. Until clients can be taught more adaptive skills for satisfying the needs met by substance abuse, they will continue to abuse substances and experience the negative consequences. Therefore, the goal of social skills training is to teach clients more adaptive strategies for achieving needs currently met by abusing substances and for resisting offers to use substances in social situations.

There are several models for using social skills training to help the dually diagnosed develop more adaptive behavior. One approach is The Better Living Skills Group (Mueser, Fox, Kenison, & Geltz, 1995), which is designed to be conducted in either an inpatient or outpatient setting with acutely ill or moderately ill dually diagnosed clients. The program is conducted for 6 weeks, meeting three times per week for 1-hour sessions. The leaders require that clients have sufficient cognitive functioning to participate in group discussions and skills training and that their symptoms be stable enough to allow them to attend at least 30 minutes of the group. However, leaders do not require that clients acknowledge they have a substance use disorder.

There are six skill areas covered in the group: conversation, dealing with angry feelings, stress management, drink/drug refusal skills, coping with unpleasant thoughts and feelings, and increasing recreational and leisure activities. Education about substance abuse is interspersed in short segments in the process of conducting skills training. For example, in teaching Expressing Unpleasant Feelings, the leaders might explain that some people resort to drugs or alcohol use when they feel angry, which often leads to negative consequences.

If group leaders have several months to work with a group of dually diagnosed individuals, additional skill areas can be addressed. Learning skills related to relationships, self-care, money management, relapse prevention, sleep hygiene, avoiding high-risk situations, communicating with medical personnel, participating in self-help groups or peer counseling, using transportation, and participating in vocational/educational endeavors can be extremely useful to dually diagnosed clients (Nikkel, 1994).

In some settings it may be impractical to form a group of all dually diagnosed clients. Groups can be conducted with a mix of clients with and without substance abuse, using the principles of the Better Living Skills group and expanding its curriculum as necessary. In a mixed group, the leaders will need to be alert to opportunities to incorporate education about substance abuse into the process of skills training. Role plays related to substance abuse can be designed for the substance-abusing clients. A list of social skills that are useful in a group containing at least some substance-abusing clients can be found in Chapter 6.

Range of Motivation to Change Substance Abuse

One of the main problems reported by leaders involved in treating dually diagnosed clients is that clients often lack motivation to change their substance abuse behavior. Clients who abuse drugs or alcohol may be in a treatment program even though they are still at the engagement or persuasion stage of the recovery process and are quite ambivalent about changing their substance abuse. Although they may have experienced multiple problems, they may deny even the most obvious consequences or have difficulty giving up drugs or alcohol because of positive effects associated with their use. Furthermore, many clients have developed a social network of people who also abuse substances, which is difficult to relinquish. Many substance-abusing clients in treatment remain preoccupied with thinking about acquiring alcohol or drugs and getting intoxicated or high. It can be difficult to motivate such clients to attend and participate in social skills training.

Group leaders must continuously evaluate each group member's severity of substance abuse and his or her motivational stage (Mueser, Drake, et al., 1995) and attempt to match the social skills intervention with the client's stage. There are several therapeutic models that provide suggestions and techniques for helping group leaders assist clients in progressing to the next stage in the process of recovery, including Motivational Enhancement Therapy (Miller & Rollnick, 1991), Dual Diagnosis Relapse Prevention (Ziedonis, 1992), and Motivation-Based Dual Diagnosis Treatment (Ziedonis & Fisher, 1994). These models emphasize the importance of a positive collaboration between client and clinician, and stress that change is a gradual process. Because the process of change in substance abuse behavior is often slow and subject to setbacks, leaders must be prepared to be particularly patient and persistent.

One important way leaders can keep clients invested in social skills training during the various phases of the recovery process is to assist them in developing goals that are specific to their stage of substance abuse treatment. For example, clients in the active treatment stage may have goals related to reducing substance abuse, whereas those in the engagement or persuasion stage have other goals, such as improving interpersonal relationships or finding employment. Although the leaders can see clear advantages of abstinence as a goal, they must resist pressuring clients to embrace this goal too soon. The client is more likely to respond positively to goals that are short-term; confrontations over whether the client wants to give up substances "totally and forever" are best avoided.

Since the dually diagnosed members of a group may not be at the same stage, the leaders can vary the role plays so that clients whose goals are to reduce substances will be engaged in scenes that involve this subject matter. For example, in a group that is learning the skill of Refusing Requests, clients in the engagement or persuasion stage might initially be given a role play of refusing the requests of friends asking for money or cigarettes, whereas clients in the active treatment stage might be given the role play of saying "No" to friends who offer to share marijuana.

Some clients may resist participating in role plays to practice skills that are directly related to substance abuse, such as Refusing Alcohol or Street Drugs. If they are at the persuasion stage, they should be encouraged to engage in role plays despite their initial reservations. One strategy is for the leaders to suggest that even though the client is not interested in reducing his or her drug or alcohol use now, there may still be situations when he or she would prefer not to use substances. Examples of reasons for refusing substances at certain times include not feeling well, not trusting that the substance offered is safe, not wanting to be in the company of the person offering the substance, fear of the police, and so forth. The client can also be reminded that trying out the skill in the group does not *obligate* him or her to use the skill outside of the group. If the client still will not practice the skill in a role play, the leaders can ask him or her to be the "confederate" in the role play; that is, the person offering the drugs or alcohol to the client practicing the skill of refusal. The client can also be asked to provide feedback to others practicing the skill, including making suggestions about how they could be more effective at resisting offers to use drugs or alcohol.

Clients at all levels of motivation benefit from liberal praise and encouragement for their efforts. Substance abuse is a very complex and difficult problem, and clients need ample positive reinforcement for trying to deal with it. Attendance and participation should be praised as much as possible without overdoing it. Absences need to be followed up immediately. When calling a client in the community about an absence, the leaders can say something like, "We really missed you in group today. What happened?" The leaders can then help the client in problem solving how he or she will be able to attend the next group. In addition, the leaders can enlist the help of staff members and family members in encouraging the client to attend and participate in the group.

Distraction by Problems Related to Substance Abuse

As mentioned earlier, many clients who abuse substances have legal and financial problems related to the abuse. In addition, they may also have impaired relationships with family members, no steady address, and poor physical health. These problems can be very distracting to clients and can make it difficult for them to concentrate on social skills training. Also, crises related to domestic problems may interfere with group attendance, especially for clients living in the community.

Obviously, social skills training cannot address all the problems of the substance abuse client. Leaders working with this population will find it advantageous to work closely with other agencies and professionals who can address the multiple problems involved. Appropriate agencies include community mental health centers, health clinics, emergency housing agencies, detox centers, legal assistance offices, supported employment programs, "job clubs," Alcoholics Anonymous (AA), and Narcotics Anonymous (NA). It is important to note that although some dually diagnosed clients benefit from AA and NA, they may need some help to develop skills to participate in these meetings. Social skills training can include communication skills about how to participate in meetings and how to use the language common to such meetings. Conducting a "mock meeting" is also helpful to give clients a chance to practice what they might say in an actual meeting. Clients should be encouraged to investigate different meetings to determine which ones feel more comfortable.

It is also important to be aware of how different professionals contribute to the treatment of the dually diagnosed client. For example, social workers can determine which services the client is entitled to, and intensive case managers can coordinate appointments and services and, in some cases, arrange transporation. It is important for all involved professionals to plan treatment together, to address as many of the client's problems as possible, to communicate frequently, and to avoid duplication of effort. If the client's problems are being addressed, he or she will be less distracted by them, more likely to attend group regularly, and better able to concentrate on social skills training while in the group.

Because many clients have unstable living situations, it is a good idea for the leaders to identify a "contact person" in case there is a need to communicate concerning absences or changes in the schedule of the group. The contact person may be a relative, friend, or a professional whom the client trusts and sees frequently. The contact person can also be helpful in providing encouragement to the client to attend the group.

There are several social skills in the curriculum that can be used to help clients solve problems related to substance abuse. Examples of these skills include Making Requests, Refusing Requests, How to Disagree without Arguing, Getting Your Point Across, Compromise and Negotiation, Listening to Others, and Problem Solving. When clients feel they are learning skills that help them improve their situation, they are both more motivated and more focused on the group.

Attending Group While Intoxicated or High

The course of reducing substance abuse is not a smooth one. Clients go back and forth in the stages of commitment to change and fluctuate in their ability to follow through on their resolve to curb substance abuse. And even when progress has been made in both commitment and ability to follow through, there are frequent setbacks when clients resume abusing substances. Inpatients usually do not have access to substances. However, clients living in the community continue to have access and may even attend group intoxicated or high. Although this situation is actually rare, it can be very frustrating to leaders, since such clients may concentrate poorly, behave inappropriately, and set a negative example to other group members.

It is helpful for the leaders to keep in mind that difficulty avoiding substance use is one of the major reasons that clients cannot treat the problem themselves and that setbacks are inevitable in treating substance abuse. However, because it is nearly impossible to conduct social skills groups with clients who are intoxicated or high, precautions must be taken to reduce the incidence of such occurrences. When the leaders are orienting the clients to the group, they must clearly state that group members may not attend the group if they have used substances before coming into the group that day. This rule can be included in written orientation materials and may also be included in the list of basic rules that is posted in the group room.

Leaders must be aware of the signs of substance abuse and be able to assess its severity. Signs vary by the specific drug being used, although common signs of drug abuse include dilated pupils (sometimes disguised by dark glasses), agitation, drowsiness, euphoria, nervousness, and slowed reflexes. Alcohol abuse tends to result in drowsiness, slurred speech, loss of motor coordination, slowed reaction time, and feelings of depression. The leaders need to become familiar with the signs for the specific substances abused by the clients in their social skills group.

There is a range of severity of the effects of the abuse. In some situations the client may have abused a small amount of alcohol that morning and be only mildly impaired and able to behave appropriately in the group. In other situations, the client may have abused cocaine just prior to attending group and may be hyperalert, highly energetic, more symptomatic, and unable to concentrate on the group. Different responses would of course be used in these different situations and would depend on the policy of the facility housing the group.

Leaders need to plan in advance what they will do if a client arrives at the group showing signs of using drugs or alcohol. It is important not to wait until the situation actually occurs. Having a clear plan of action will minimize confusion and cause the least disruption to the group. Leaders must, however, first determine their policy concerning substance use and the presence of intoxicated people on the premises. Some facilities forbid substance use on their property but allow a nondisruptive person to remain if he or she used the substance before arriving. Other facilities require immediate expulsion of anyone with evidence of substance abuse. There are also different policies concerning how people who are expelled from the group may be transported away from the premises. For example, agencies would be at risk for liability if their staff members allowed an intoxicated person to drive. The leaders need to be prepared with lists of relatives who could transport the client, taxi companies to call and funding sources for paying for transportation. Also, the leaders must decide where the client can go if he or she is expelled from group: home?; the community?; a detox center?; another treatment facility? Information should be obtained concerning security personnel available to the leaders if a client refuses to cooperate.

In making policies about how to handle group members who use substances prior to attendance, it is important to keep in mind that these clients are often the ones who need the treatment the most. If the client's behavior is manageable, it is preferable to keep him or her in the group. Also, it is important *not* to tell these clients to "come back when you've dealt with your substance use." The goal of integrated treatment programs is to avoid fragmentation of services to the dually diagnosed clients; therefore integrated programs should provide easily available treatment resources for clients to turn to when they need help returning to sobriety. The decision to exclude clients who use substances from group sessions or from the treatment facility should be made reluctantly.

When a client attends the group high or intoxicated, the leaders should respond to the situation immediately, by using the following kinds of planned actions. Depending on the severity of the situation, the leaders can gently but firmly inform the client that they are aware of the substance abuse and repeat the rule forbidding this behavior. The leaders may prefer to speak to the client outside of the group room, especially if he or she is likely to become agitated. If the leaders determine that the situation is severe enough to warrant expelling the client from the session, the client must be informed that he or she cannot continue in the session, although he or she is welcome to return to the next session if sober. Depending on the action plan, the leaders then direct the client to the appropriate type of transportation and destination. In addition, the leaders should refer the client to a specific member of the treatment team (preferably available on site) to talk about the current substance abuse to help him or her return to sobriety before the next group meeting. It is best if the client can meet with the appropriate staff member immediately or within a few hours. When the leaders of the social skills training group are members of the client's integrated treatment team and have time available after the group session, they may be the most appropriate ones to work with the client.

Before the next scheduled session of the group, the leaders can call the client to encourage sobriety for the next group meeting and to express that both leaders and group members look forward to seeing him or her again soon. The leaders can also engage the client in problem solving how to resist the pressure to drink or use substances and how to find alternative activities. The next time the client attends a group meeting and is not intoxicated, the leaders need to praise him or her for this accomplishment.

Table 9.2 summarizes the strategies that can be used to respond to problems that arise in conducting social skills groups with dually diagnosed clients.

Summary

In groups with high-functioning clients, strategies for increasing their engagement include using more challenging role plays, encouraging them to

TABLE 9.2. Strategies for Problems Related to Clients Who Abuse Drugs or Alcohol

General principles

1. Be aware of stages in the recovery process.
2. Avoid confrontation and "tough love" approach.
3. Encourage a supportive environment.
4. Teach more effective skills for coping with situations

Specific problems	Strategies
Lack of motivation to change substance abuse	Help clients set goals that relate to solving their individual problems. Provide education about substance abuse as opportunities arise. Avoid initial goals for abstinence. Liberally praise efforts.
Distraction by problems related to abuse	Coordinate with other professionals and agencies to work on problems. Establish a contact person. Enlist support of family members and friends.
Attending group while intoxicated or high	Become familiar with signs of substance abuse. Develop action plan for responding to intoxicated or high clients. Respond based on the severity of the situation. Immediately address problem when it occurs. Include group rules about sobriety. Welcome client back when he or she attends sober; praise efforts.

help other group members learn targeted skills, and helping them make a connection between their participation in the group and achieving personal goals. Higher-functioning clients benefit when leaders engage them actively in the process of the group by asking for their ideas for role-play scenarios and homework assignments, requesting their assistance in modeling a skill, and asking them to serve as the confederate in a role play with another client.

In groups that include clients who abuse drugs or alcohol, the leader needs to provide a supportive atmosphere, to avoid confrontational approaches, to teach skills to cope with situations that are related to substance abuse, and to be aware of each client's stage in the recovery process. It is especially helpful if the social skills training group is part of an integrated treatment approach, in which interventions are provided simultaneously for both schizophrenia and substance abuse.

10

Reducing Relapse by Creating a Supportive Environment

Stress is major factor in precipitating relapse in clients with schizophrenia. Even when it does not lead to relapse, stress can interfere significantly with clients' ability to learn or practice new skills. Stress exists in many different forms, including life events, daily hassles, boredom, conflict, overly demanding environments, and critical, negative communication. One way to reduce stress for clients is to increase the usual support and structure available in their immediate environment. This chapter focuses on specific strategies for creating a supportive environment that will both facilitate the learning of social skills and reduce the risk for symptom relapse. The strategies are applicable to family members as well as staff members.

Recognizing a Stressful Environment

What determines whether an environment is stressful to someone with schizophrenia? First, the way people communicate is very important. Clients find yelling and arguments to be stressful, even when they are not directly involved. It is particularly distressing, however, when staff members or family members criticize them (e.g., "You're too lazy to get out of bed") or order them around (e.g., "Get over here right now for your medication"). Second, the atmosphere of the physical setting is significant. Clients find it stressful when the setting is crowded and noisy and there are no comfortable places to sit quietly. Third, the level of structure affects the clients' stress level. Clients experience stress if the environment is overly demanding (e.g., if clients are required to be involved in highly organized activities all day). Stress also results when the environment does not provide meaningful structure (e.g., if clients are not expected to do chores or be involved in any activities). A setting that is unpredictable or confusing may be upsetting to clients, for example, if there are several competing activities going on at the same time or if meals are served at widely different times each day. Table 10.1 contains a summary of factors that contribute to a stressful environment.

Clients, like everyone else, are faced with daily stressors, which are often referred to as "hassles." These stressors are usually minor, but they can add up if they occur regularly. For example, messy roommates, unpleasant chores, frequent criticism, and being around arguments or conflicts are all "hassles" that can wear people down. The negative effects of ongoing daily hassles can be as stressful as major life events, and they should be recognized as such.

In addition, research shows that most people experience life events (major life occurrences, such as moving, losing a job, being ill, and experiencing a loss) as stressful. Even events that are the source of happiness, such as getting married or starting a new job, can be the source of stress. Recognizing that a client's life event is likely to be stressful is helpful for staff members and family members. For example, when a client living in a community residence gets a new roommate or experiences a death in the family, staff members can anticipate that this might be stressful and can prepare themselves to provide more support.

TABLE 10.1. Elements of a Stressful Environment

Patterns of communication

- Loud voices
- Giving orders/making demands
- Frequent criticism and expression of anger
- Heated arguments
- Name calling

Physical setting

- Distracting amount of noise
- Crowded
- Poor housing conditions
- Unsafe neighborhood
- Poor access to public transportation
- Lack of privacy
- Unappetizing food

Level of structure

- Demanding, rigid schedule
- Unpredictable schedule
- Lack of stimulation and meaningful activities

The Importance of Family Members and Staff Members in Creating a Supportive Environment

As stated in earlier chapters, the leaders need to create an environment conducive to learning inside the group. This includes providing a comfortable setting, avoiding criticism and negativity, encouraging the efforts of the group members, and giving generous positive feedback. However, the group takes place for only a few hours per week. The clients' remaining time involves contact with people who are not group leaders. The total amount of time the clients spend in skills training group is minimal compared with that spent outside of group. Thus, although the group leaders are important, family members and other staff members often have far more contact with clients and provide more ongoing support. If family members and staff members are not supportive, and if they contribute to a high-stress environment, it works *against* the progress made in the social skills group. A critical or demanding environment provides few opportunities for clients to practice skills and receive positive feedback. Even if the group leaders conduct an effective social skills group, their work can be undone by the environment. On the other hand, a supportive environment both inside and outside the group contributes to optimal acquisition and generalization of skills.

Characteristics of Supportive Staff Members, and Family Members

Knowledge of Schizophrenia, Behavioral Management, and Social Skills Training

It is very important for family members and staff members to be well informed about the illness of schizophrenia, especially regarding symptoms and how they affect behavior. Understanding the illness-related reasons for clients' difficulties can help staff members and family members respond more empathically and equip them to develop more effective strategies for overcoming the difficulties. For example, recognizing that the cognitive deficits of the illness can make it difficult for the client to understand complex language gives family members the necessary insight to reword requests more simply and repeat important information. Understanding that the positive symptoms of the illness (such as auditory hallucinations) can be very distracting helps staff members think of strategies for increasing clients' concentration in groups. Finally, knowing that the negative symptoms of schizophrenia include decreased motivation helps family members be more patient and supportive to their relative who is starting a new activity.

The supplemental reading list in Appendix A contains several publications that staff members and family members can read to learn about the illness. It is useful to keep some basic texts such as *Understanding Schizophrenia* (Keefe & Harvey, 1994), *Coping with Schizophrenia: A Guide for Families* (Mueser & Gingerich, 1994), and *Surviving Schizophrenia* (Torrey, 1995) easily available as references. Chapter 1 of this book also contains specific information that would be helpful to staff members and family members about how schizophrenia contributes to difficulties in social skills.

It is also helpful when all staff members are well informed about the basic principles of behavioral management and the philosophy of social skills training. *Behavior Modification: What It Is and How To Do It* (Martin & Pear, 1996) contains useful chapters about defining behavior, getting a behavior to occur more often with positive reinforcement, decreasing a behavior with extinction, and getting a new behavior to occur by shaping. Chapter 3 of this book contains definitions and examples of social learning principles, including modeling, reinforcement, shaping, overlearning, and generalization, as well as the techniques for conducting social skills training. *Behavioral Family Therapy for Psychiatric Disorders* (Mueser & Glynn, 1995) describes the methods for using the social skills training model with families that contain a mentally ill member and provides educational handouts about several mental illnesses, including schizophrenia and schizoaffective disorder. "Social Skills Orientation for Professionals," a handout in Appendix A, provides a short overview of social skills training. In addition to reading about the above topics, staff should be kept informed about the specific social skills training that is being conducted at their facility by attending ongoing staff training meetings (addressed in more detail later in this chapter).

Use of Good Communication Skills

It is important for staff members to use good communication and problem-solving skills themselves. There are two main reasons for this. First, staff members and family members who use good communication skills serve as positive role models for clients. The more opportunities clients have to observe effective social skills in others, the better they can learn the skills. Second, using good social skills helps staff members and family members communicate with clients in a clear, direct manner, with less probability of misunderstanding or causing conflict. When staff members and family members use good communication skills with each other, it contributes to better working relationships and promotes teamwork. Part II contains an extensive curriculum of social skills that can be used to improve communication. In addition, Table 10.2 provides suggestions for skills that are especially useful in communicating with clients: Getting to the Point, Expressing Positive and

TABLE 10.2. Guidelines for Communicating with Clients

Get to the point.

- Clearly state your topic or concern.
- Use direct, simple language.
- Keep it brief.

Express feelings directly.

- Use "I" statements.
- Make verbal feeling statements.
- Speak in a calm voice.
- Don't assume the client will know how you feel if you don't tell him or her.

Use praise effectively.

- Make eye contact.
- Tell the client specifically what he or she did that pleased you.
- Use an "I" statement to say how it makes you feel.

Check out what the client thinks or feels.

- Listen carefully; don't rush the client.
- Ask questions when you don't understand.
- Repeat back what you heard and ask if that is what the client meant.
- Ask more questions, if necessary.

Be clear and specific.

- Avoid long sentences and "introductions" to topics.
- Make direct requests that specify exactly what you would like the client to do.
- Concentrate on one topic at a time.

Unpleasant Feelings, Using Praise, Checking Out What the Client Feels or Thinks, and Being Clear and Specific.

It is also important to avoid certain types of communication that commonly lead to stress and tension with clients who have schizophrenia. Table 10.3 lists some examples of "pitfalls" to supportive communication; staff members and family members who avoid these pitfalls will be rewarded by fewer arguments and a calmer atmosphere for all concerned.

Staff members and family members who can manage conflict effectively contribute greatly to a less stressful environment. Conflicts that stem from disagreements and misunderstandings are frequent sources of stress to clients with schizophrenia. Using the communication skills provided in Table 10.2 and avoiding the pitfalls in Table 10.3 can help prevent some conflicts. To resolve a conflict, however, it is usually best to address it as soon as possible, staying calm, speaking clearly, and paying attention to both sides of the conflict. In addition, it is helpful to avoid blame or criticism, to use short, clear statements, to highlight the main points, and to focus on specific behaviors rather than on personality or attitudes. Using the skills of Making Requests,

TABLE 10.3. Pitfalls to Supportive Communication

Communication problem	Example of nonsupportive statement	Alternative statement
Coercive statements ("shoulds")	"You *should* know when lunch is served"	"I would appreciate it if you would come to lunch at 12:30."
Mind reading	"You're angry because your friends forgot to visit."	"You look angry. Are you feeling that way?"
Making "always" or "never" statements	"You never take your medicine like you're supposed to."	"I'm concerned that you did not take your medication this morning."
Giving orders	"Pick up your clothes right this minute."	"I would appreciate it if you could pick your clothes up off the floor before breakfast."
Put-downs or sarcasm	"You're so lazy."	"I was disappointed that you did not take out the garbage last night."
Mixing positive and negative	"You're dressed okay, but your hair is a mess."	"I like your new outfit today."

Note. Adapted from Mueser and Gingerich (1994, p. 132). Copyright 1994 by New Harbinger Publications. Adapted by permission.

Compromise and Negotiation, Leaving Stressful Situations, and Solving Problems (see curriculum in Part II) can help staff and family members resolve conflicts in some instances. Informal problem solving, using the basic principles but not necessarily the specific steps of the problem-solving skill, can also be helpful.

Ability to Prompt and Reinforce Use of Skills

Group members are better able to generalize skills they have learned in the social skills group to other settings when they receive support and encouragement from people outside the group. The most important support is provided by staff members or family members who prompt clients to use specific social skills in situations that arise in their natural surroundings and who praise them for using a skill or attempting to use one. One example of prompting occurs when a staff member notices a client who is starting to get into an argument and reminds him, "This would be a good time to practice Expressing Angry Feelings the way you've been learning in social skills group." If the client does not remember the details of expressing angry feelings, the staff member can review the steps of that skill. If the client attempts to use the skill, the staff member can reinforce the effort by saying something such as "I liked the way you stayed calm in expressing your feelings, and how you were specific about what Sam did that upset you." The more often the clients are encouraged to practice the skills they are learning in group, the more likely they will be able to use them spontaneously in real-life situations. Helping clients complete their homework assignment is a structured way of helping them use their skills in situations outside the group.

Working as a Team

Teamwork and sharing responsibility are very important in minimizing stress in the environment. Schizophrenia is a very complex and confusing illness, whose symptoms can lead to unpredictable and even alarming behavior. If the bulk of responsibility for managing clients falls on too few people, it will become burdensome and stressful for those few. When family members or staff members are under significant stress, the clients are aware of it and find it distressing. However, when the responsibility is shared and when people know that they can count on each other's help, it is less burdensome and less stressful. In community residences, inpatient programs, and day treatment centers, it is helpful to explicitly divide the tasks among staff members in each shift and rotate tasks that are particularly difficult (for example, waking up clients who are reluctant to be wakened). In promoting teamwork, it is also useful to have clear guidelines to follow in certain key situations, such as responding to aggressive behavior. When guidelines are well-known in the residential or treatment setting, staff members can minimize confusion about what to do and can concentrate instead on dealing with the situation. In the home setting, it is also useful for family members to divide responsibilities and to have a plan of action about what to do in situations such as symptom exacerbation (Falloon et al., 1984; Mueser & Glynn, 1995).

Characteristics of a Supportive Living Situation

Structured But Not Overtaxing Routine

Since the symptoms of schizophrenia may result in a client's internal experience of the world being quite confusing, it is helpful if the client's external environment is organized and predictable. A daily routine that strikes a balance between understimulation and overstimulation is important in preventing excessive withdrawal on one hand and overexcitement on the other hand. Therefore, it is beneficial to have periods of organized activities interspersed with unstructured time for clients to relax and unwind. The amount of time spent on organized activities needs to be adapted to clients' cognitive capacities to avoid overtaxing them. For example, many clients are able to work several hours per week, but not more than 2 hours at a stretch. It is also critical to monitor the clients' fluctuating symptomatology and capabilities so that scheduled or structured activities can be flexible and responsive to clinical changes. For example, if a client who usually enjoys trips to the zoo has an increase in hallucinations one day, it would be important to explore with the client whether a trip to the zoo might be helpful or might exacerbate this symptom.

Reasonable House Rules

The presence of realistic "house rules" at home or at a residential setting contributes to reducing stress in the environment. Research has shown that people with schizophrenia often lack an understanding of the unwritten rules that govern much social behavior. Explicit household rules can help compensate for clients' lack of social judgment by making clear what is expected and what is not allowed. If there is a lack of clarity about expectations, it can result in unpredictable behavior, frequent arguments, and high levels of stress. Because all settings are different, the "house rules" need to be tailored to individual needs and requirements, and should be kept at a minimum, so that it is not an effort for clients to remember them. However, there are certain fundamental rules related to ensuring the safety of people and property and preventing disruptive, socially unacceptable or illegal behavior. An example of six basic house rules are included in Table 10.4.

Improving Stress Management in the Client's Environment

Recognizing the Signs of Stress

Recognizing the sources of stress, as described earlier, helps staff members and family members to take preventive action. However, it is also important

TABLE 10.4. Basic House Rules

- No violence to people or property.
- No inappropriate touching.
- Smoking is permitted only in designated areas.
- Bathe and shower regularly.
- No illegal drug use.
- Everyone must do some chore(s) to help in the running of the house.

Note. Adapted from Mueser and Gingerich (1994, p. 172). Copyright 1994 by New Harbinger Publications. Adapted by permission.

to recognize the signs that stress is already affecting the client. These can include changes in physical state (headaches, muscular tension, indigestion), thinking (difficulty concentrating, paying attention), mood (irritability, anxiety) and behavior (pacing, nail-biting). In addition, clients with schizophrenia may experience an increase in the symptoms of their illness, such as more hallucinations or delusions, when they are under stress. Most clients show a combination of signs in response to stress. When staff members and family members recognize the stress–response pattern of the individual client, they can begin to help him or her to manage the stress. Many clients are unaware of their own patterns and benefit greatly from the feedback of others.

Reducing the Sources of Stress

When staff members and family members are familiar with what clients find stressful and the signs of stress, they can help the clients to reduce the stress to which they are exposed. To help clients avoid unnecessary stress, it may be useful to consider situations that have been stressful in the past. Although it is undesirable to avoid *all* stress, since this would interfere with taking on new roles and activities, some situations that have caused excessive stress in the past can be avoided or modified. For example, if a client became tense and agitated when he or she went home for 4 days during Thanksgiving, staff and family members might consider suggesting abbreviating the next holiday visit to make it more manageable. Or if living with a messy roommate consistently irritates an orderly client, a change of roommates might be advised.

A common source of stress that can often be reduced is the stress of unreasonable expectations. If a client finds volunteering 5 mornings a week to be too much of a strain, perhaps the activity could be reduced to two or three mornings per week. Another common source of tension that can be addressed is an understimulating environment. An increase in activites that are scheduled often reduces a client's experience of stress. Attending a day program, taking a class, or scheduling regular physical exercise (such as taking a walk, swimming, or bowling) can decrease stress, increase a sense of well-being, and give the client something to look forward to. Some clients also enjoy activities such as going to the movies, taking a van ride, doing arts and crafts, or eating out.

Communicating Directly

As mentioned earlier in this chapter, it is very important for staff members and family members to communicate clearly and directly with clients. This is especially important when the client is under stress. For example, if a client is experienceing stress from beginning a new job, it is helpful for a staff member to express direct interest in the responsibilities of the job, to ask questions about which aspects the client finds stressful, and to help the client engage in problem solving to reduce any stress he or she may experience.

In addition, it is helpful to encourage clients to communicate directly about stressful situations, which often provides some immediate relief. The longer clients keep feelings to themselves, the more likely it is that their emotions will be released in an inappropriate way, such as in arguments, aggressive behavior, or self-destructive behavior. When clients talk about their feelings as they arise, the process itself can prevent stress from building up. Direct discussions also give staff members and family members an opportunity to suggest ideas for dealing with a stressful situation. For example, if a client is able to express that he or she is experiencing stress from increased auditory hallucinations, a staff member or family member can suggest some coping strategies, such as increasing distraction from the voices and consulting with the physician regarding a medication evaluation. Not all clients voluntarily share information about their feelings; it is important to inquire gently about what they are experiencing. For example, a staff member might say, "I noticed that you missed 3 days of your program this week; how have you been feeling?" However, if the client prefers not to talk about feelings, he or she should not be pressured to do so.

Sometimes talking to a single staff member or family member is not sufficient to help a client reduce his or her stress level. If the client is experiencing a severe amount of stress, it may be helpful to get together with others who are familiar with the client to discuss the situation and explore possible solutions to the problem that is causing the stress. This meeting should include the client when possible as well as family members and staff members from other agencies who are well acquainted with the client and/or may have the resources to implement certain solutions. For example, residential staff members often find it useful to include a client's case manager in such meetings because he or she coordinates several aspects of the client's care and knows what resources might be available. It is important that meetings use the basic principles of problem solving (see Appendix A) and focus on solutions. Family members often benefit from holding family meetings where they and the client work together on solving problems (Falloon et al., 1984; Mueser & Glynn, 1995).

Helping Clients Reframe Their Thoughts

Some clients are able to reduce stress by reframing their thoughts about the situation. The more negatively clients view particular situations, the more stress they experience. When they respond with negative, self-defeating thoughts such as "This is awful," "I can't stand it," or "I"m going to crack under this pressure," it tends to make the situation worse. However, they may be better able to deal effectively with the situation when they can replace self-defeating thoughts with more "positive self-talk," which includes making coping-oriented statements to themselves such as "I'll do my best," "I can deal with this," and "I am strong enough to handle this." Staff members and family members can coach clients explicitly on using positive self-talk and can help develop simple phrases that work well for them. They can then remind the clients of the phrases when they note that clients are showing signs of stress. For example, a family member might tell a client, "It seems like the voices are bothering you more today; try saying, 'These voices are annoying, but I can ignore them,' like we talked about last week."

Using Relaxation Techniques

Learning simple relaxation techniques such as deep breathing exercises and progressive muscle relaxation is helpful to some clients. These methods of stress reduction require a staff member or family member to teach the steps of the skill to the client and to encourage him or her to practice the technique regularly. Relaxation techniques are best taught when the client is relatively calm; they are generally not effective if they are introduced in the middle of a crisis. Although there are many books and classes available for learning relaxation techniques, some are too complicated to use with clients. It is preferable to choose techniques that have clear instructions, are not too time consuming to practice, and that can be used in a variety of settings (Davis, Eshelman, & McKay, 1995; McKay & Fanning, 1987). Clients are often receptive to learning a deep breathing exercise, such as the one in Table 10.5.

Clients may also be encouraged to develop their own approach to relaxation, including choosing images to relax to, or selecting music or recordings of nature sounds to accompany their imagery. The specific technique used to relax is not important. Rather, the point of relaxation is for the client to set aside time to calm down and relax in a way that works best for him or her.

Managing the Stress Level of Staff Members and Family Members

Finally, it is important for staff members and family members to be aware of their own stress levels. Working with people with schizophrenia can be quite stressful; it is very common for staff members and family members to feel overwhelmed. Stress in staff or family members may be reflected by negative

TABLE 10.5. Deep Breathing Exercise

1. Make yourself comfortable, sitting in a chair or on a couch with good back support.
2. Breathe deeply through your nose and out from your mouth, approximately 10 times.
3. Notice the way your chest fills with air as you inhale, then empties when you exhale.
4. As you breathe deeply, silently repeat a calming word or short phrase such as "Relax," "Unwind," or "At ease" as you exhale. Do this about 30 times, but do not worry about exact counting.
5. Think of standing under a waterfall or shower; imagine the water washing away feelings of tension.
6. Begin to breathe normally again. Concentrate on your breathing.
7. Sit quietly for a minute or two before returning to activity.

Note. Adapted from Mueser and Gingerich (1994, p. 164). Copyright 1994 by New Harbinger Publications. Adapted by permission.

communication patterns, such as criticism, hostility, speaking in a loud voice, or in other ways, such as tenseness, body language, facial expression or frequent worrying. The experience of tension or stress in staff or family members can be passed on to clients, either directly (via communication) or indirectly. The techniques described above for clients (communicating directly, reframing thoughts, using relaxation techniques) can also help others in contact with the client cope more effectively with tension and stress. In addition, it is helpful to give each other a break when the pressure gets to be too high. Taking a little time away from the situation can be relaxing and give people new perspectives and renewed energy for dealing with their responsibilities.

Developing a Social Learning Milieu in a Residential or Inpatient Program

Rationale

Some inpatient and residential settings have succeeded in creating a milieu where social learning and skills training are strong components of the philosophy of treatment and are woven into nearly every aspect of the staff members' interaction with clients. Two factors are vital to the success of such a milieu.

First, support from the administrative, departmental, and supervisory levels of the setting is critical (Corrigan, 1995). Without the backing of professionals at the upper levels, it is very difficult to schedule social skills groups, to encourage the cooperation of staff members, and to free up time for staff members to attend social skills groups and training sessions. However, if the administrators and supervisors provide strong backing to a social skills program, there is a high likelihood of success. One of the best ways to assure such backing is for group leaders to arrange regular meetings with administrators and supervisors to discuss clients' progress in skills training and to report any problems that have been encountered. Some form of written monthly or bimonthly report containing information about number of groups held, attendance, homework compliance, and skills acquisition can help staff members and administrators to appreciate the scope of the skills training groups and to track clients' progress in these groups.

Second, the participation of all staff members is crucial. The social skills training group sessions provide a good beginning for clients to learn skills, but, as we have previously emphasized, most of the work of putting those skills into practice goes on outside of the group. On-line staff members, who usually have the most contact with clients, need to be familiar with the skills being taught, to recognize opportunities for clients to use the skills, and to help clients with their homework assignments. Social skills programs without the support of on-line staff members are unlikely to succeed.

Training On-Line Staff Members

One of the first steps for bringing a social learning focus into the general milieu is to teach all staff members the general principles of social skills training: social learning theory, modeling, practice, positive and corrective feedback, and generalization to the natural environment. It is helpful for the group leaders to conduct a workshop (or series of workshops) explaining and demonstrating social skills training for all staff members who have client contact. After the introductory training, group leaders should continue staff training on a regular basis. One effective model of ongoing training involves weekly meetings with staff members who represent each shift. Each representative staff member is expected to report back to his or her shift about what was discussed at the meeting and to return with feedback and questions from co-workers. In this model of staff training, each meeting follows a similar format, as shown in Table 10.6.

At staff training meetings, it is important for staff members to feel that they are learning something that will help them do their job more effectively and with less stress. The agenda must be flexible enough to respond to staff concerns about other clinical issues related to their work with clients. Staff members often have questions about how to respond effectively when clients are delusional, noncompliant, verbally abusive, or difficult to motivate. The group leaders who conduct staff training can give suggestions about which

TABLE 10.6. Format of Staff Training Meetings

---

1. Review last week's homework assignment.
   - Thank staff members for their assistance.
   - Engage in problem solving to help clients who did not complete their assignments.

2. Discuss the social skill that was taught at the last group.
   - Hand out copies of the steps of the skill.
   - If it is a new skill, model an example of how it can be used.
   - Ask staff members to engage in brief role plays of the skill.

3. Hand out homework assignments for practicing the current skill in the clients' environment.
   - Review instructions.
   - Answer questions about assignment.

4. Discuss opportunities for clients to practice the new skill.
   - Elicit ideas from staff members about situations when the clients could use the skill.
   - Suggest how staff can prompt clients.
   - Remind staff members of the importance of providing positive feedback for any efforts.
   - If necessary, role play examples of prompting and providing feedback.
   - Anticipate any difficulties in completing the homework.

5. Discuss general problems that staff members experience in managing clients.
   - Suggest ways that the social skills model can be used to address the problems.
   - Provide information about schizophrenia and other behavioral techniques as needed.

6. Elicit ideas for social skills that clients would benefit from learning in future groups, including skills not yet developed.

---

skills the staff members can encourage the clients to use and which skills staff themselves can use in specific problematic situations. For example, when staff members report that clients blame them for things they did not do, the staff could be directed to use the skill of Responding to False Accusations. When clients are reluctant to do their household chores, staff members can be advised to try Making a Request, followed by Expressing Positive Feelings when clients do even a portion of their tasks. When clients curse the staff members, they can be directed to use the skill of Expressing Unpleasant Feelings. When necessary, new skills can be designed specifically for staff members, using the principles described in Chapter 6.

When staff members attend training on a regular basis, they become familiar with the social skills perspective and terminology and begin to approach problems with the question "What skills would be most effective to use in this situation?" As staff members begin to "speak the same language" as the social skills leaders, the clients receive a consistent message and have multiple sources of prompting and positive feedback for using their social skills. Staff members also find, that by using social skills themselves and by prompting clients to use skills, they are better equipped to deal with difficult situations, which helps them do their jobs more effectively and with less stress.

Displaying Social Skill Materials

As part of creating a social learning milieu, it is helpful to post copies of the skills being taught in the group. For example, staff members can post copies of the current skill on the central bulletin board. Copies of skills that are relevant to ongoing issues (e.g., Eating and Drinking Politely) can be permanently posted in the appropriate area. Copies of all the social skills contained in the curriculum in Part II should also be available to all staff members. Some residences also find it useful to post attendance charts in the room where the group is held so that clients and staff members can see at a glance who has been attending.

Encouraging Client Attendance at Social Skills Training Groups

As mentioned in Chapters 5 and 8, it is important to schedule social skills training groups at a time when clients are most likely to attend. Having the social skills group be a fixed part of the week's schedule is very helpful. In addition, staff members need to reduce the chances that the group will conflict with another activity that the clients want to attend or are required to attend. For example, if outings, medical appointments or cigarette dispensing are scheduled at the same time as the social skills group, it may serve as a disincentive to attend the group. Clients benefit from regular attendance; missing even occasional groups causes them to lose momentum and to get out of the habit of attending.

To ensure the continuity of the skills training group, it is also important that groups are not cancelled when a leader is sick or on vacation. It is very useful to have a back-up leader or to have another staff member act as co-leader when one of the leaders is unable to attend.

Providing Consistent Positive Feedback and Constructive Suggestions in Day-to-Day Interactions

Positive feedback is one of the most powerful tools for shaping the behavior of clients. Sometimes staff members feel that praising the clients will "spoil" them or that it is unnecessary because "People should know when they've done something right." Some staff members think that their responsibility is to point out incorrect or inappropriate behavior rather than to help clients learn more appropriate alternatives. Helping staff members understand that positive feedback is more potent in changing behavior than negative feedback is an important goal for social skills leaders. When clients are praised for something they have done, it not only boosts their self-esteem, it also increases the probability that the behavior will be repeated. Staff members and family members need to be adept at the skills of Expressing Positive Feelings and Giving Compliments (see Part II). It is especially important to be specific, telling the client exactly what he or she did that was pleasing. For example, a staff member might tell a client, "I really liked the way you cleared the table without being asked. I was very pleased." Staff members need to be alert to instances when the client does something well and be generous with positive feedback.

Of course, clients may also behave in ways that are inappropriate or offensive. In such cases, staff members and family members need to provide constructive feedback (see guidelines in Appendix A). First, it is important to find something to praise, even if it is a small aspect of the client's behavior. For example, if a client loudly demands his or her hourly cigarette instead of requesting it politely, a staff member might still be able to give positive feedback for asking at the appropriate time. Clients appreciate hearing that they haven't "done *everything* wrong." Second, focus on only *one* aspect of the client's behavior that needs improving, even if he or she has done several things incorrectly. If more than one error is pointed out, clients often begin to "tune out" or have difficulty pinpointing what they did wrong. Be specific and brief about the actual behavior that was a problem. Third, avoid critical language (e.g., "You know that's the wrong way to ask for a cigarette"). Finally, make a brief suggestion for how the client can improve his or her behavior. For example, a staff member might say, "I liked the way you asked for your cigarette at the time we agreed on; I would appreciate it if you could ask me for your cigarette in a quiet voice, though." The most effective suggestions for improvement avoid the word "should" and use simple, direct language that does not require the client to guess what he or she is expected to do.

Special Considerations for Family Members

Research has shown that family members can be especially helpful in creating a supportive environment for their ill relative (Gingerich & Bellack, 1995; Falloon et al., 1984; McFarlane et al., 1995; Anderson, Reiss, & Hogarty, 1986), especially if they receive support and accurate education about the illness. Family members often have a special rapport and strong relationship with the client that professionals cannot hope to duplicate. However, family members also experience additional pressures. For example, family members who provide care for an ill relative cannot "leave at the end of their shift," unlike the staff of a residential program. Schizophrenia is an illness that is poorly understood by the general public. Because of this, many family members often feel isolated and stigmatized by having an ill relative. It may be hard to find people who understand their situation and the problems they are dealing with. Family members often feel that they have little time for friends or other activities because all their time is taken up with managing the illness (Hatfield & Lefley, 1987, 1993; Lefley & Johnson, 1990). It is difficult to provide a supportive environment for the client when they are under such stress.

Before family members can provide support to their ill relative, they must take care of their own needs and get adequate support for themselves. One way for family members to receive more support is to share responsibilities for caring for their ill relative. One family member cannot do everything; teamwork is very important. When several family members are involved, it is easier to take breaks and to pursue friendships and hobbies that they all enjoyed before their relative developed schizophrenia. Another way for families to get support is to seek out community resources and services, such as psychosocial clubhouses, consumer-run drop-in centers, vocational programs, or day programs for their ill relative. Clients may need to be encouraged to attend community programs, both for their own socialization needs and for their family members' needs.

Many family members benefit greatly from the support offered by organizations such as the National Alliance for the Mentally Ill (NAMI), which is the largest self-help and advocacy organization in the United States for relatives of persons with a psychiatric disorder (2101 Wilson Boulevard, Suite 302, Arlington, VA 22201, 703-524-7600; they also have a Help Line at 800-950-6264). Each state has a chapter, and many communities also have their own chapters. NAMI is an excellent source of up-to-date information about the illness of schizophrenia and current treatment strategies. It also provides a very good way to meet other family members who have similar experiences, both at the monthly meetings of the local chapters or at the annual conventions of the national organization. One of the greatest stresses that family members report is feeling that they are all alone, that they are isolated in their experience. Belonging to an organization such as NAMI helps people to realize that there are many others who are in a similar situation, who understand what they are going through, and who might be able to offer suggestions for each other's problems.

Summary

A supportive environment, both inside and outside the social skills training group, is essential for clients to learn and generalize new skills. The most important factors in a supportive environment are staff members and family members, the physical setting, the level of structure, and stress management.

The presence of supportive staff members and family members who are knowledgeable about schizophrenia and its treatment, who use good communication skills themselves, and who prompt and reinforce appropriate social skills is extremely beneficial to clients. The manner of communication is especially important; staff members and family members should avoid giving orders, making critical or hostile comments, and speaking in ways that are indirect or confusing to clients.

The physical setting also contributes to the climate of support; it should be safe, have adequate privacy, be relatively quiet, and be in good condition. In the setting, reasonable house rules, a structured but not overtaxing routine, and a predictable schedule help to reduce sources of stress for the client. When stressors do occur, they need to be handled in a supportive manner, using strategies such as empathic listening, problem solving, and encouraging clients to use relaxation techniques or participate in recreational activities.

In addition to helping clients deal with stress, residential settings can develop a social learning milieu where social skills training is a strong component of the rehabilitation philosophy of treatment and is woven into nearly all aspects of the staff members' interaction with clients. The milieu is most effective when all staff members receive ongoing training in the principles of social learning, when written materials about social skills are available and on display in the living environment, when clients are encouraged to attend the skills groups, and when staff members provide consistent positive feedback and constructive suggestions to clients regarding their use of social skills.

II

STEPS FOR TEACHING
48 SPECIFIC SOCIAL SKILLS:
CURRICULAR SKILL SHEETS

Introduction

In Part I of this book, we explained why we conduct social skills training with clients with schizophrenia and how the effects of training can be evaluated. We also described our teaching strategy, and provided guidelines for how to be successful. For example, we recommended a specific format that has been found to be most useful, including instructions, modeling, role play, and corrective feedback (see Chapters 3 and 4), and we offered strategies for managing commonly encountered problems (see Chapters 8 and 9). Even though armed with this background, many new skills trainers have difficulty determining precisely what to teach.

In Part II, we offer a ready-made curriculum that the reader can use to guide his or her efforts. The skills sheets that follow were developed from our own experience with diverse groups of clients. Most of the units are designed with relatively impaired participants in mind. We encourage clinicians to tailor the material to their own clients' needs and interests. We refer readers to Chapter 6 for further details on how to use the skill sheets that follow as well as how to develop new curricula.

The following curricula are grouped into seven broad skill areas. Within each of these broad areas, we offer a number of skill sheets for teaching specific skills. In essence, each skill sheet is a lesson plan, a handy guide to conducting groups sessions on the specific skill. Each skill sheet suggests a rationale, breaks the skill down into three to four smaller steps, suggests scenes to role play, and alerts you to special considerations. As indicated in Chapter 6, the steps of each skill should be transferred onto a poster, blackboard, or written, large-type handout to use with clients during a group session. The broader areas and the specific skills do not need to be taught in any particular order. Note, however, that there are four basic skills that serve as building blocks for the others (see Table 6.1). The following lists the specific skill sheets that follow.

OVERVIEW OF SOCIAL SKILLS CURRICULAR SKILL SHEETS

1. **Conversation Skills**   177
   Listening to Others   179
   Starting Conversations   180
   Maintaining Conversations by Asking Questions   181
   Maintaining Conversations by Giving Factual Information   182
   Maintaining Conversations by Expressing Feelings   183
   Ending Conversations   184
   Staying on the Topic Set by Another Person   185
   What to Do When Someone Goes Off the Topic   186
   Getting Your Point Across   187

2. **Conflict Management Skills**   189
   Compromise and Negotiation   191
   Disagreeing with Another's Opinion without Arguing   192
   Responding to Untrue Accusations   193
   Leaving Stressful Situations   194

3. **Assertiveness Skills**   195
   Making Requests   197
   Refusing Requests   198
   Making Complaints   199
   Responding to Complaints   200
   Expressing Unpleasant Feelings   201
   Expressing Angry Feelings   202
   Asking for Information   203
   Making Apologies   204
   Letting Someone Know That You Are Afraid   205
   Refusing Alcohol or Street Drugs   206

4. **Community Living Skills**   207
   Locating Your Missing Belongings   209
   What to Do If You Think Somebody Has Something of Yours   210
   What to Do When You Do Not Understand What a Person
      Is Saying   211
   Checking Out Your Beliefs   212
   Reminding Someone Not to Spread Germs   213
   Eating and Drinking Politely   214

5. **Friendship and Dating Skills**   215
   Expressing Positive Feelings   217
   Giving Compliments   218
   Accepting Compliments   219
   Finding Common Interests   220

Asking Someone for a Date   221
Ending a Date   222
Expressing Affection   223
Refusing Unwanted Sexual Advances   224
Requesting That Your Partner Use a Condom   225
Refusing Pressure to Engage in High-Risk Sexual Activity   226

6. **Medication Management Skills   227**
Making a Doctor's Appointment on the Phone   229
Asking Questions about Medications   230
Asking Questions about Health-Related Concerns   231

7. **Vocational/Work Skills   233**
Interviewing for a Job   235
Asking for Feedback about Job Performance   236
Responding to Criticism   237
Following Verbal Instructions   238
Solving Problems   239
Joining Ongoing Conversations at Work   240

Conversation Skills

CONVERSATION SKILLS

<u>SKILL:</u> Listening to Others

<u>RATIONALE:</u> Whenever you are in a conversation, it is important to show the other person that you are listening, that you are paying attention. When the other person can tell you are listening, he or she is more likely to want to continue talking to you. There are some specific things you can do to show your interest to the other person.

<u>STEPS OF THE SKILL:</u>

1. Maintain eye contact.
2. Nod your head.
3. Say, "Uh-huh," or "Okay," or "I see."
4. Repeat what the other person said.

<u>SCENES TO USE IN ROLE PLAYS:</u>

1. Listening to someone who is talking about a favorite hobby.
2. Listening to someone who is talking about a favorite TV show.
3. Listening to a staff member who is talking about the rules at the Community Residence.
4. Listening to your doctor telling you about your medication.
5. Listening to a friend talk about a recent outing.

<u>SPECIAL CONSIDERATIONS WHEN TEACHING THIS SKILL:</u>

1. Role plays should be set up using two people: One person talks about a topic, while the person who is practicing the skill follows the steps.
2. Clients often have difficulty paying attention when someone is speaking to them. It is important to keep the role plays short (30 seconds or less) and simple when first practicing the skill.

CONVERSATION SKILLS

SKILL: Starting Conversations

RATIONALE: There are many situations when you want to start a conversation with another person. This may be someone you know or someone you have never met but would like to get to know. Sometimes people feel shy about starting a conversation. We find that things go more smoothly when you keep specific steps in mind.

STEPS OF THE SKILL:

1. Choose the right time and place.
2. Introduce yourself or greet the person you wish to talk with.
3. Make small talk (e.g., talk about the weather or sports).
4. Judge if the other person is listening and wants to talk.

SCENES TO USE IN ROLE PLAYS:

1. A new person is starting at the day program.
2. People are waiting for an activity to begin at the Community Residence or the day program.
3. You are at a family gathering.
4. You are sitting with another person at lunch.
5. You are meeting your new case manager for the first time.

SPECIAL CONSIDERATIONS WHEN TEACHING THIS SKILL:

1. Steps 1 and 4 require the client to make judgments regarding what are the appropriate time and place to begin a discussion as well as whether the person being addressed is interested in participating. Therefore, it is important for group leaders to spend time assisting clients with the identification of social cues that they can look for when making such judgments.
2. Clients may not be familiar with what constitutes "small talk" (Step 3). Group leaders may want to generate a list of topics with the group that can be used for making small talk.

CONVERSATION SKILLS

SKILL: Maintaining Conversations by Asking Questions

RATIONALE: Sometimes you may want to go further than a brief conversation; you may want to talk longer with someone because you like the person or are interested in what is being said. Often, people don't know how to keep a conversation going, or they feel uncomfortable. One way to keep a conversation going is by asking questions.

STEPS OF THE SKILL:

1. Greet the person.
2. Ask a general question.
3. Follow up on what the person says with a specific question.
4. Judge if the person is listening and is interested in pursuing the conversation.

SCENES TO USE IN ROLE PLAYS:

1. Watching a TV program with another person who also seems to enjoy the program.
2. Seeing your roommate after he or she has spent a day with his or her family.
3. Having a cup of coffee with a friend at the day program.
4. Sharing a chore (such as cleaning up after dinner) with someone.
5. Talking to a counselor about a supported employment program.

SPECIAL CONSIDERATIONS WHEN TEACHING THIS SKILL:

1. Clients may have difficulty determining what kinds of questions are socially appropriate to ask in different situations. Group leaders can use the role play scenes to help clients identify socially appropriate questions to ask in various situations. For example, group leaders can ask clients to generate a list of questions that would be appropriate to ask a friend with whom they are having coffee *before* role playing the scene so that they have some options to choose from.
2. Group leaders need to distinguish "general" questions from those that are more specific. Providing the group with examples of the two types of questions will be useful.
3. Group leaders may need to assist members with the identification of social cues required in Step 4.

CONVERSATION SKILLS

<u>SKILL:</u> Maintaining Conversations by Giving Factual Information

<u>RATIONALE:</u> Asking questions is one way to keep a conversation going. Another way is to give factual information to the other person. This allows people to learn more about each other and the kinds of things they might have in common. Factual information is the kind of information that tells someone who, what, where, when, and how.

<u>STEPS OF THE SKILL:</u>

1. Greet the person.
2. Give some information to the other person.
3. Judge if the other person is listening and is interested in pursuing the conversation.

<u>SCENES TO USE IN ROLE PLAYS:</u>

1. Telling someone at the Community Residence about an outing planned for the weekend.
2. Telling a friend about a movie or TV show that you saw recently.
3. Telling someone at your day program about a current event that interests you.
4. Telling someone about a change in the local bus schedule.
5. Telling a counselor about some hobbies that interest you.

<u>SPECIAL CONSIDERATIONS WHEN TEACHING THIS SKILL:</u>

1. Group leaders should use the role play scenes to help members identify what information is appropriate to give in each situation used. Group leaders can discuss with members the importance of being discriminating with the type of information they provide in a given situation. For example, personal information that would be appropriate to provide to a counselor during a therapy session would not be appropriate to discuss with an acquaintance in a social setting.
2. Group leaders may need to assist members with the identification of social cues required in Step 3.

CONVERSATION SKILLS

SKILL: Maintaining Conversations by Expressing Feelings

RATIONALE: Giving factual information is one way to keep a conversation going. Another way is to tell someone how something makes you feel. This allows people to learn more about each other's feelings and whether they might have more in common to talk about. Examples of feelings that might be expressed are happy, sad, excited, disappointed, pleased, upset, and irritated.

STEPS OF THE SKILL:
1. Greet the person.
2. Make a brief statement about how something makes you feel.
3. Judge if the other person is listening and is interested in pursuing the conversation.

SCENES TO USE IN ROLE PLAYS:
1. Telling a staff member that you don't like your assigned chore at the Community Residence.
2. Telling your case manager that you enjoyed the last group.
3. Telling a family member that you are excited about going to the movie this weekend.
4. Telling a staff member that you are disappointed that a day program party was canceled.
5. Telling a friend that you liked a TV program last night.

SPECIAL CONSIDERATIONS WHEN TEACHING THIS SKILL:
1. Group leaders should assist members with generating a list of different feelings that people might want to express to each other.
2. Group leaders should also assist members with identifying situations that they are likely to encounter when expressing feelings would be appropriate.
3. Group leaders may need to assist members with the identification of social cues required in Step 3.

CONVERSATION SKILLS

SKILL: Ending Conversations

RATIONALE: Conversations don't go on forever. Sooner or later someone must end the conversation. Many times it may be up to you to end the conversation. There are many reasons for ending a conversation, including running out of time, needing to go somewhere else, or running out of things to say. You can end conversations more smoothly if you keep certain steps in mind.

STEPS OF THE SKILL:

1. Wait until the other person has finished speaking.
2. Use a nonverbal gesture such as glancing away or looking at your watch.
3. Make a closing comment such as "Well, I really must be going now."
4. Say, "Good-bye."

SCENES TO USE IN ROLE PLAYS:

1. Talking about a TV show with someone at the Community Residence, but it becomes time for the evening group.
2. Finishing lunch with another person at the day program, but it becomes time to meet with your counselor.
3. Talking with a friend before group starts.
4. Talking with a new person at your drop-in center, and you run out of things to say.
5. Talking with a friend during breakfast, and it's time to go to work.

SPECIAL CONSIDERATIONS WHEN TEACHING THIS SKILL:

Clients may not be aware of how the use of nonverbal gestures can either help make a social interaction run more smoothly or make it more awkward. A brief group discussion regarding how to utilize nonverbal gestures can be quite helpful.

CONVERSATION SKILLS

SKILL: Staying on the Topic Set by Another Person

RATIONALE: Whenever you are in a conversation with another person, it is important to show that you are paying attention to what is being said. Being able to stay focused on the topic being discussed demonstrates to the person that you are listening and are interested in what is being said.

STEPS OF THE SKILL:

1. Decide what the topic is by listening to the person who is speaking.
2. If you still do not understand what the topic is after listening, ask the person.
3. Say things related to the topic.

SCENES TO USE IN ROLE PLAYS:

1. A staff member at the Community Residence talks to you about the new chore list.
2. A counselor at the day program is talking to you about the new current events group that has started.
3. A friend talks to you about a movie he or she has seen.
4. Your roommate talks to you about painting your room a new color.
5. Your doctor is talking to you about eating healthy foods.

SPECIAL CONSIDERATIONS WHEN TEACHING THIS SKILL:

1. This skill has two specific tasks: identifying the topic and saying things related to the topic. Group leaders may need to focus on only one of the tasks per role play when working with clients who have difficulty concentrating.
2. Group leaders should begin each role play by clearly stating what the topic is. For example, they should begin by saying something like "I want to talk to you about _____," and then repeat key words throughout the role play.

CONVERSATION SKILLS

SKILL: What to Do When Someone Goes Off the Topic

RATIONALE: Having a conversation with another person requires that both people understand what the topic is. Understanding the topic allows both people to contribute to the discussion, which then makes it more meaningful for both people. Sometimes, however, we find ourselves in a situation where the other person suddenly has gone off the topic being discussed, leaving us feeling confused. When this occurs, it is best to immediately let the other person know that we are confused and then to try to get back to the original topic.

STEPS OF THE SKILL:

1. Politely tell the other person that you are feeling confused or do not understand how what is being said relates to the topic that you were discussing.
2. Tell the person what you think the topic is, *or* ask him or her what the topic is.
3. Suggest that you return to the original topic.

SCENES TO USE IN ROLE PLAYS:

1. You are in the middle of a discussion with a friend about a movie you both saw when your friend suddenly starts talking about the weather.
2. You are telling your mother about the new job you just started when your mother starts to tell you about your cousin who just enlisted in the army.
3. Your case manager is discussing with you the progress you have made at the supported employment program when she is interrupted by a phone call. After the call, she returns to the conversation with you and starts discussing when you and she can go shopping for a coat for you.
4. Your roommate asks you for directions to the museum. As you start to tell him the directions, he suddenly changes the topic to shopping.
5. You are having lunch with a friend who is telling you about a TV program that she saw last night when, in the middle of her description she starts to tell you about a new person she just met.

SPECIAL CONSIDERATIONS WHEN TEACHING THIS SKILL:

1. Some members may find it difficult to tell the other person that they do not understand because they feel as though they are being rude. Group leaders can help members practice polite ways to interrupt a conversation.
2. This skill is very useful when dealing with a person who is symptomatic and is having difficulty concentrating.

CONVERSATION SKILLS

SKILL: Getting Your Point Across

RATIONALE: There are times when we all have something that we want to talk about or explain to others. Being able to get your point across in a clear and concise manner is an important component of effective communication. It makes it easier for others to understand and respond to what you are saying.

STEPS OF THE SKILL:

1. Decide on the main point you want to get across.
2. Speak in short sentences and stay on the topic.
3. Pause to let the other person speak or ask questions.
4. Answer any questions.

SCENES TO USE IN ROLE PLAYS:

1. You tell a friend the best place to buy cigarettes.
2. You tell a staff member that you want to start to hold your own cigarettes.
3. You tell your new roommate at the Community Residence how the chore assignments work.
4. You suggest to a family member a place you would like to go on an outing.
5. You explain to your case manager that you are bored at the day program.

SPECIAL CONSIDERATIONS WHEN TEACHING THIS SKILL:

Group leaders can discuss with clients the importance of staying calm and speaking in a clear voice that is not too loud or too soft when trying to make a point. For example, group leaders can discuss how it is more likely that a person will not be listened to when he or she is yelling and agitated. Therefore in order to be understood, it is important to be in reasonable control of one's feelings.

Conflict Management Skills

CONFLICT MANAGEMENT SKILLS

SKILL: Compromise and Negotiation

RATIONALE: Often, people find that they disagree with each other, even when they want to do something together. At these times, it is helpful to work out a compromise. In a compromise, each person usually gets some of what he or she wants, but usually has to give up something. The goal is to reach a solution that is acceptable to all involved.

STEPS OF THE SKILL:
1. Explain your viewpoint briefly.
2. Listen to the other person's viewpoint.
3. Repeat the other person's viewpoint.
4. Suggest a compromise.

SCENES TO USE IN ROLE PLAYS:
1. You want to go to lunch with your friend at the pizza parlor. He or she does not want pizza that day.
2. Your case manager asks you to schedule an appointment for 2:00 P.M. on Wednesday. You have plans to go on a day program outing at that time.
3. You and your friend want to go see a movie. You want to see an action movie, and your friend wants to see a comedy.
4. In planning an outing for the Community Residence, the counselors suggest bowling. You would rather go out for ice cream.
5. You want to visit your family next weekend. They have other plans.

SPECIAL CONSIDERATIONS WHEN TEACHING THIS SKILL:

Not all clients will understand what it means to negotiate and come to a compromise. Therefore, it is important that the group leaders spend time explaining these concepts *before* beginning a role play. For example, to negotiate something, both parties have to state what it is that they want to get out of the interaction. Once all the wishes have been listed, both parties must review the list and decide upon a compromise. A compromise usually occurs when both parties get *some* of what they wanted.

CONFLICT MANAGEMENT SKILLS

SKILL: Disagreeing with Another's Opinion without Arguing

RATIONALE: Not everyone we come in contact with will agree with all of our ideas or opinions, just as we do not agree with all of theirs. Disagreeing with another person's opinion does not have to lead to bad feelings or an argument. In fact, life would be boring if everyone had the same ideas. When you disagree with another person's opinion, things often go more smoothly if you keep certain things in mind.

STEPS OF THE SKILL:

1. Briefly state your point of view.
2. Listen to the other person's opinion.
3. If you do not agree with the other person's opinion, simply state that it is okay to disagree.
4. End the conversation or move on to another topic.

SCENES TO USE IN ROLE PLAYS:

1. You and a friend have a different opinion about a movie you just saw.
2. You and your roommate have a different opinion about which musical group is better.
3. You and a staff member at the Community Residence have a different opinion about what type of clothing looks best on you.
4. You and a family member have a different opinion about a candidate in an upcoming election.
5. A counselor differs with you about what has been the most helpful thing in getting you a job.

SPECIAL CONSIDERATIONS WHEN TEACHING THIS SKILL:

It is important to emphasize that this skill is designed to be used in situations where there are no significant consequences for having a different opinion. In situations where there may be more serious consequences, such as disagreeing with a doctor's opinion about using medication, the skill Compromise and Negotiation should be employed. There may also be situations where any kind of disagreement may cause a strong or even violent reaction, such as encountering a political or religious extremist. In these situations, Leaving Stressful Situations may be a more appropriate skill to use.

CONFLICT MANAGEMENT SKILLS

SKILL: Responding to Untrue Accusations

RATIONALE: Most of us have found ourselves in situations where we have been accused of doing something that we have not done. Usually when this happens, the person making the accusation truly believes that we have committed the act and is not able to listen to reason. It is therefore important to remain calm and not get into a fight or argument when this occurs. We have found that there are some specific things you can do to help stay calm when you are falsely accused of something.

STEPS OF THE SKILL:

1. Using a *calm* voice, simply deny the accusation.
2. If the other person continues to accuse you, ask the person to stop.
3. If the person does not stop accusing you, tell him or her that you are going to get a staff member to assist with the situation.
4. Walk away and get assistance.

SCENES TO USE IN ROLE PLAYS:

1. A housemate accuses you of stealing his or her clothes from the communal dryer.
2. A housemate accuses you of not doing your assigned chores.
3. A person at the day program accuses you of listening in on his or her conversations.
4. A staff member at the Community Residence accuses you of starting a fight with another resident.
5. A relative accuses you of stealing money during your last visit.

SPECIAL CONSIDERATIONS WHEN TEACHING THIS SKILL:

1. Group leaders can point out that some untrue accusations occur when someone simply has made an error, while other accusations are the results of symptoms of an illness. In both instances, it is important to stay calm and not get into an argument.
2. It is important to note that clients may not have access to a staff member, as referred to in Step 3. Group leaders can work with clients to generate a list of other helpful people to turn to if no staff are available. The skill Leaving Stressful Situations may also be useful when staff are not around.

CONFLICT MANAGEMENT SKILLS

SKILL: Leaving Stressful Situations

RATIONALE: There are times when we find ourselves in situations that we consider stressful. For instance, when others criticize us or when we do something that another does not like. Often, remaining in situations that are stressful only makes us feel worse and at times may even aggravate the situation. Many times, leaving until you have calmed down and then dealing with it afterwards is the most productive way of managing the stressful situation.

STEPS OF THE SKILL:

1. Evaluate whether the situation is stressful (i.e., tune in to your thoughts, feelings, and physical sensations).
2. Tell the other person that the situation is stressful and that you must leave.
3. If there is a conflict, tell the person that you will discuss it with him or her at another time.
4. Leave the situation.

SCENES TO USE IN ROLE PLAYS:

1. A relative has falsely accused you of stealing $10.00.
2. A friend is angry because you won't go to a bar with him or her.
3. A relative is upset because he or she found drugs in your room.
4. A staff member at the Community Residence is upset because you came home late and forgot to call and let him or her know.
5. Your roommate is angry because you wore his shirt without asking to borrow it.

SPECIAL CONSIDERATIONS WHEN TEACHING THIS SKILL:

1. It is important to emphasize that this skill is only to be used with people whom the clients know and want to maintain a relationship with. This skill should not be used with "strangers out on the street" as it could have dangerous repercussions. For example, it would be very dangerous to use this skill if you have been approached on the street by someone who wants to rob you. In situations such as that, giving the person what they asked for and going for help after they leave is probably safer than using the skill.
2. Group leaders should assist the group in understanding Step 1 by generating a list of ways a person can tell if he or she is either feeling stressed. This is important because many clients are not in touch with what may be stressful to them.

Assertiveness Skills

ASSERTIVENESS SKILLS

<u>SKILL:</u> Making Requests

<u>RATIONALE:</u> In anyone's life, situations come up where it is necessary to ask another person to do something or to change his or her behavior. A request that is heard as a demand or as nagging usually does not make the other person want to follow through with the request. Making a request in a positive way, however, is usually less stressful and is more likely to lead to the request being met. There are no guarantees, of course, but a request usually goes better if you keep in mind the following points.

<u>STEPS OF THE SKILL:</u>

1. Look at the person.
2. Say exactly what you would like the person to do.
3. Tell the person how it would make you feel.

    In making your request, use phrases like:
    "I would like you to _____."
    "I would really appreciate it if you would do _____."
    "It's very important to me that you help me with _____."

<u>SCENES TO USE IN ROLE PLAYS:</u>

1. Ask someone to go to lunch with you.
2. Ask someone to help you with a chore or an errand.
3. Request a counselor to talk about a problem.
4. Ask your friend to borrow his or her music tape.
5. Ask someone at the day program to turn down his or her radio.

<u>SPECIAL CONSIDERATIONS WHEN TEACHING THIS SKILL:</u>

1. It is important to tailor this skill so that the higher-functioning clients do not get bored. Therefore, it is helpful to elicit specific situations where a client may have wanted to make a request but was unable to.
2. For lower-functioning clients, it is helpful to suggest just one phrase, such as "I would appreciate it if you would_____," to use when making a request.
3. Remind clients that although a request made in this manner is most likely to lead to receiving the request, it does not guarantee that the request will be granted.

ASSERTIVENESS SKILLS

SKILL: Refusing Requests

RATIONALE: We can't always do what other people ask us to do. We may be too busy, or not feel capable, or may not want to do what someone asks. If we refuse in a rude or gruff manner, it can make for hurt feelings or anger. On the other hand, if we are not clear about refusing or if we speak in a hesitant way, it might lead to a misunderstanding or argument.

STEPS OF THE SKILL:

1. Look at the person. Speak firmly and calmly.
2. Tell the person you cannot do what he or she asked. Use a phrase such as "I'm sorry but I cannot _____."
3. Give a reason if it seems necessary.

SCENES TO USE IN ROLE PLAYS:

1. Your case manager asks to meet with you at 3:00 P.M., but you already have an appointment.
2. A friend asks you to go to a basketball game, but you don't like basketball.
3. Your roommate asks you to pick up some groceries, but you're feeling tired.
4. A friend asks you to lend him or her money, but you are broke.
5. Your counselor asks you to help prepare dinner, but you have plans to watch a special TV show.

SPECIAL CONSIDERATIONS WHEN TEACHING THIS SKILL:

1. It is important for the group leaders to remind clients that there are some situations when a request is made of them where refusing would be inappropriate, such as when a staff person asks the client to complete his or her assigned chore or follow a safety rule.
2. There are also instances when refusing a request may result in some harm to the client. Situations such as the client refusing to take medication or go to the doctor need to be handled delicately because the consequences can be severe. In these instances, it may be helpful to encourage clients to use the skill Compromise and Negotiation instead of Refusing Requests.

ASSERTIVENESS SKILLS

SKILL: Making Complaints

RATIONALE: A number of unpleasant situations can be avoided by expressing yourself clearly and making requests in a positive way. However, situations often come up where something displeasing does happen. At those times you need to make a complaint. Making a complaint usually works best if you can also suggest a solution.

STEPS OF THE SKILL:

1. Look at the person. Speak firmly and calmly.
2. State your complaint. Be specific about what the situation is.
3. Tell the person how the problem might be solved.

SCENES TO USE IN ROLE PLAYS:

1. You lose money in the vending machine.
2. Someone interrupts you when you are speaking.
3. You order a cheeseburger, but the waitress brings a plain hamburger.
4. You buy a bus pass, and the clerk gives you the wrong change.
5. Someone in a nonsmoking area lights up a cigarette.

SPECIAL CONSIDERATIONS WHEN TEACHING THIS SKILL:

1. This skill requires that a group member be able to identify possible solutions *before* stating a complaint. Group leaders should encourage group members to brainstorm possible solutions before a role play is practiced so that the participants have an idea of what solution they will propose ahead of time.
2. Group leaders can remind members that this is the best way to make a complaint, but there are no guarantees that the solution they suggest will be carried out.

ASSERTIVENESS SKILLS

SKILL: Responding to Complaints

RATIONALE: As careful and considerate as you might try to be, there will be times when someone has to make a complaint to you. For instance, you accidentally bump into someone or you forget an appointment. If you get upset when someone complains to you, it only makes the situation worse. Following the steps of the skill will help you respond in a calm manner.

STEPS OF THE SKILL:
1. Look at the person and remain calm.
2. Listen to the complaint, keeping an open mind.
3. Repeat back what the person said.
4. Accept responsibility and apologize if necessary.

SCENES TO USE IN ROLE PLAYS:
1. Someone complains to you that you interrupted them.
2. Someone complains to you that you lit up a cigarette on the bus.
3. Your case manager complains that you are late for your appointment.
4. Your counselor at the Community Residence complains that you have not done your weekly chores.
5. Your roommate complains that your music is too loud.

SPECIAL CONSIDERATIONS WHEN TEACHING THIS SKILL:

There may be some group members who have a difficult time remaining calm while listening to a complaint being lodged against them. Therefore, it may be helpful for group leaders to discuss strategies for managing angry feelings. For example, taking a time-out or counting to 10 may be useful strategies to employ in certain situations.

ASSERTIVENESS SKILLS

<u>SKILL:</u> Expressing Unpleasant Feelings

<u>RATIONALE:</u> Even when people do their best to please each other, there will be times when things are displeasing or unpleasant. It is only natural in the course of living with other people and going to programs with other people that unpleasant feelings arise. Examples of unpleasant feelings are anger, sadness, anxiety, concern, or worry. How people express their feelings can help to prevent arguments and more bad feelings. It is helpful to keep certain things in mind when expressing an unpleasant feeling.

<u>STEPS OF THE SKILL:</u>
1. Look at the person. Speak calmly and firmly.
2. Say exactly what the other person did that upset you.
3. Tell the person how it made you feel.
4. Suggest how the person might prevent this from happening in the future.

<u>SCENES TO USE IN ROLE PLAYS:</u>
1. Your roommate left dirty clothes in the living room.
2. Your case manager missed an appointment with you.
3. You are worried when your roommate is out later than expected.
4. Your family canceled a weekend visit.
5. Your friend was late meeting you for lunch.

<u>SPECIAL CONSIDERATIONS WHEN TEACHING THIS SKILL:</u>

This skill requires that group members identify an unpleasant feeling (Step 3). However, not all members will be able to do this. It is helpful in the first session of teaching this skill to generate a list of unpleasant feelings. The list can be written on a flip chart and placed where it can be seen when group members are role playing.

ASSERTIVENESS SKILLS

SKILL: Expressing Angry Feelings

RATIONALE: One type of feeling that many people have special difficulty expressing is anger. At times everyone gets angry. This does not have to lead to shouting or hitting or cutting off friendships or relationships. It is usually helpful to relieve feelings of anger by expressing yourself in a direct, honest way. Sometimes you might want to wait until you have "cooled off" a little and are feeling calm.

STEPS OF THE SKILL:

1. Look at the person, speak firmly and *calmly*.
2. Tell the person specifically what he or she did that made you angry. Be brief.
3. Tell the person about your angry feelings. Be brief.
4. Suggest how the person might prevent the situation from happening in the future.

SCENES TO USE IN ROLE PLAYS:

1. Dinner is late every night for a week.
2. Your roommate smokes in the room, which is against house rules.
3. Your relative promises to cash your check by Friday but does not do so.
4. Someone spills coffee on your new white slacks without apologizing.
5. Someone borrows your radio without asking and breaks it.

SPECIAL CONSIDERATIONS WHEN TEACHING THIS SKILL:

1. Many members have a particularly difficult time expressing angry feelings, even in the context of a controlled role play. It is therefore important to devote some time "preparing" group members for this skill. Spending one or two sessions helping members identify common "early warning signs" of anger (such as feeling tense, heart racing, etc.) as well as strategies for managing angry feelings (one of those strategies being the skill at hand), will be extremely useful.
2. Depending on the composition of the group, it may be helpful to divide this skill into three parts and practice each part as a separate role play. The first part would encompass Steps 1 and 2; the second part would encompass Step 3; and the third part would encompass Step 4. Not all members will need the skill divided in this way, but for those who are having some difficulty, this allows them to have positive role-play experiences while practicing the skill.

ASSERTIVENESS SKILLS

SKILL: Asking for Information

RATIONALE: There are many times when people need to ask others for information. People ask for information about directions, how to do certain tasks, to explain something that they just read. The list of things to inquire about is endless. Often people feel awkward or apologetic about asking for information and therefore choose not to ask. It has been our experience that things go much better when we have all the information we need and that in most cases people are more than happy to share with you what they know.

STEPS OF THE SKILL:
1. Use a calm and clear voice.
2. Ask the person for the information you need. Be specific.
3. Listen carefully to what the person says.
4. Repeat back what he or she says.

SCENES TO USE IN ROLE PLAYS:
1. Asking a staff member about what public transportation to take downtown.
2. Asking your counselor about how to use the washing machine.
3. Asking a sales clerk at Sears about where the jeans are.
4. Asking your case manager about applying for a work training program.
5. Asking your doctor about side effects of your medication.

SPECIAL CONSIDERATIONS WHEN TEACHING THIS SKILL:
1. This skill requires that the client make a judgment about who might be an appropriate person to approach for help. Not all clients will be able to do this. Therefore, it may be helpful for the group leaders to get clients to identify an appropriate person to approach *before* they role play.
2. Group leaders can point out that this skill is especially useful when clients find themselves in situations where they need help or assistance.

ASSERTIVENESS SKILLS

SKILL: Making Apologies

RATIONALE: Even when people are very careful, they sometimes do things that bother or inconvenience others. Rather than ignore the situation or make light of it, we have found it generally makes things go more smoothly if the person apologizes for his or her behavior as soon as possible. This is true no matter whose fault it was.

STEPS OF THE SKILL:

1. Look at the person.
2. State your apology: "I'm sorry for _____."
3. If realistic, assure the person that it won't happen in the future.

SCENES TO USE IN ROLE PLAYS:

1. Being late to group because of talking to a friend.
2. Bumping into someone while using the vending machines.
3. Interrupting someone who is talking during dinner.
4. Borrowing a CD without asking the owner.
5. Shouting at someone when you're in a bad mood.

SPECIAL CONSIDERATIONS WHEN TEACHING THIS SKILL:

It is important to point out that apologies are appropriate even when the client did not intend to upset the other person ("I didn't know it was his CD") or when the situation was not his or her fault ("But I only bumped into him because Sandy pushed me"). Remind clients that the person who is upset will usually feel better because of receiving an apology.

ASSERTIVENESS SKILLS

<u>SKILL:</u> Letting Someone Know That You Are Afraid

<u>RATIONALE:</u> All of us at some time in our lives feel afraid. Sharing our fears with someone we trust usually makes things feel less scary. The person may have suggestions that will help you cope with feeling afraid or have suggestions that will help you change the situation that you are afraid of.

<u>STEPS OF THE SKILL:</u>
1. Choose a person you trust to speak to.
2. Tell that person what you are afraid of. Try to be *specific* about your fears.
3. Ask the person for advice.

<u>SCENES TO USE IN ROLE PLAYS:</u>
1. You tell your case manager that you are afraid to start at the day program.
2. You tell your case manager that you are afraid to go to the doctor for a physical examination.
3. You confide to your AA group that you are afraid to walk to the meeting because you pass one of the bars that you used to hang out in and are worried that you might go in.
4. You tell a staff member at your new Community Residence that you are afraid that your roommate will not like you.
5. You tell your case manager that you are afraid that your doctor is going to hurt you.

<u>SPECIAL CONSIDERATIONS WHEN TEACHING THIS SKILL:</u>

This skill requires that the client make a judgment about who might be an appropriate person to trust. Not all clients will be able to identify people with whom they trust. Therefore, it may be helpful for group leaders to get clients to identify people whom they might be able to trust in different situations *before* role playing.

ASSERTIVENESS SKILLS

SKILL: Refusing Alcohol or Street Drugs

RATIONALE: Many people have difficulty refusing offers of street drugs and alcohol. Because these substances are available in a wide array of settings, being approached by someone who invites you to use is inevitable. Therefore, it is important to prepare oneself for the possibility of being asked to use. The following steps have been found to be helpful when refusing someone's request.

STEPS OF THE SKILL:

1. Using a clear and firm voice, say "No" to the person.
2. If appropriate, suggest some alternative activity.
3. If the person persists, ask him or her to stop.
4. Walk away if necessary.

SCENES TO USE IN ROLE PLAYS:

1. A friend approaches you and pressures you to use drugs.
2. You agree to join some co-workers at a bar after work. You have had some trouble with alcohol in the past and are resolved to drink club soda. Once you arrive, one of your co-workers insists that you join him for a beer.
3. You are approached on the street by someone who wants to sell you some drugs.
4. You are attending a relative's birthday party, and the host wants you to join a toast and hands you a glass of wine.
5. You are at your day treatment program when a friend asks you if you want to get high out back.

SPECIAL CONSIDERATIONS WHEN TEACHING THIS SKILL:

It is important for leaders to remind the group that there are different issues involved in refusing drugs and alcohol and that those issues depend on the person who is offering the substances. For instance, if you are approached on the street by someone who wants to sell you drugs, it would be inappropriate and possibly dangerous to offer an alternative suggestion (Step 2). On the other hand, if a family member or friend pressures you to have a drink, you might want to explain why you are refusing before offering an alternative activity.

Community Living Skills

COMMUNITY LIVING SKILLS

<u>SKILL:</u> Locating Your Missing Belongings

<u>RATIONALE:</u> Everyone has times when he or she cannot locate something that belongs to him or her. Sometimes we have lost the item altogether either because of carelessness on our part or because someone else has taken it. Most of the time, however, when we cannot find an item of ours, it is because we have simply misplaced it. Following certain steps can help us to search for the missing item in a systematic way that hopefully will lead us to find it.

<u>STEPS OF THE SKILL:</u>

1. Ask yourself these questions:
   a. When did I have it last?
   b. Was there anyone around me at that time?
2. Take some time to look carefully for the item you cannot find.
3. If you still have not found the item, ask someone for help. Say something like "Have you seen my _____? I am looking for it."

<u>SCENES TO USE IN ROLE PLAYS:</u>

Refer to Step 2 under "Special Considerations When Teaching This Skill"

<u>SPECIAL CONSIDERATIONS WHEN TEACHING THIS SKILL:</u>

1. It is helpful if this skill is taught in conjuction with the skill What to Do If You Think Somebody Has Something of Yours since the two usually go hand in hand. Group leaders can explain that before a person decides that someone else has his or her belonging, it is important to first follow the steps of this skill to make sure it hasn't been misplaced.
2. Group leaders can have members practice this skill by having them tell another person how they are planning to go about looking for a particular missing item.

COMMUNITY LIVING SKILLS

SKILL: What to Do If You Think Somebody Has Something of Yours

RATIONALE: If you think that a person has something of yours and you would like to get it back, it is important to remain calm and talk to the person. It is not usually helpful to accuse someone, because the person will try to defend him- or herself, which makes it harder for you to get their cooperation. Besides, you may be mistaken about the person, and accusing him or her will undoubtedly cause bad feelings.

STEPS OF THE SKILL:

1. Using a calm voice, ask the person if he or she has the item. *Do not accuse the person.*
2. Listen to the person's answer.
3. If you are not satisfied with his or her answer, ask a staff person or someone you trust for help.

SCENES TO USE IN ROLE PLAYS:

1. Your favorite T-shirt is missing, and you think your roommate may have it because he has a habit of borrowing things without asking.
2. A friend has often told you that she loves your necklace. Recently you discover that it is missing and wonder if she has it.
3. You were sitting in the kitchen drinking a soda. You left the room briefly to use the bathroom. When you returned, you noticed that your soda was missing. There was only one other person in the room with you, so you decide to ask that person if he has the soda.
4. The wallet that you left on your dresser is missing. You think a certain person living in the house who has a reputation for stealing may have taken it, and you confront him about it.
5. You think that a staff member has been keeping your mail from you and ask about it.

SPECIAL CONSIDERATIONS WHEN TEACHING THIS SKILL:

1. This skill should be taught after clients have practiced the skill Locating Your Missing Belongings. Clients may need to be reminded about looking carefully for their items before asking people if they have them.
2. It may be helpful for group leaders to point out that it is better not to ask someone if he or she has your item while in front of other people.

COMMUNITY LIVING SKILLS

<u>SKILL:</u> What to Do When You Do Not Understand What a Person Is Saying

<u>RATIONALE:</u> Situations often come up where we do not understand what some-one has said to us. Maybe the person was speaking too quickly, or used words that we didn't understand, or even said too many things at once. Also, there are times when we may be distracted and find it hard to concentrate on what the person is saying. Whatever the reason, it is better not to pretend that we understand when we really don't understand. Using the steps of this skill will help you to clear up any misunderstandings that you may have about what has been said.

<u>STEPS OF THE SKILL:</u>

1. Tell the person that you are confused or that you did not understand what was said.
2. Ask the person to repeat or explain what was just said.
3. Ask further questions if you still do not understand.

<u>SCENES TO USE IN ROLE PLAYS:</u>

1. Your job coach has described some new tasks you will be expected to do. You are not sure you understand everything your job coach has said.
2. You have asked a staff member to give you directions to go downtown but had difficulty understanding the directions because the staff person talks very quickly.
3. Your doctor has prescribed new medication for you and explained how it will help to make you feel better. You are not sure you understand.
4. Your case manager at the day program has explained to you about a new group she will be conducting. She has an accent and speaks very quickly so you missed a lot of what she was saying.
5. Your teacher at the vocational rehabilitation center is giving a lecture on im-proving interviewing skills and is using words that you do not understand.

<u>SPECIAL CONSIDERATIONS WHEN TEACHING THIS SKILL:</u>

1. This skill can be used to help clients who are symptomatic and are finding it difficult to follow conversations.
2. Group leaders can help clients generate a list of strategies to improve under-standing, including asking the other person to slow down or to speak more loudly.

COMMUNITY LIVING SKILLS

SKILL: Checking Out Your Beliefs

RATIONALE: Sometimes we think something may be true, but others disagree. It helps to check out our beliefs by talking to someone we trust. Hearing that person's point of view can be helpful. We may not change our minds, but at least we know that there is another way people might see the situation.

STEPS OF THE SKILL:

1. Choose a person you trust to talk to.
2. Tell the person what your belief is.
3. Ask the person what his or her opinion is.
4. Repeat back the opinion, and thank the person for his or her point of view.

SCENES TO USE IN ROLE PLAYS:

1. You believe that the owner of the corner store mocks you every time you buy something from him.
2. You believe that a person from the day program wants to harm you.
3. You believe that your supervisor at work does not like you.
4. You believe that one of the staff members at the Community Residence is angry with you.
5. You believe that you are being followed everytime you leave the Community Mental Health Center.

SPECIAL CONSIDERATIONS WHEN TEACHING THIS SKILL:

1. This skill requires that the client makes a judgment about who might be an appropriate person to trust. Not all clients will be able to do this. Therefore, it may be helpful for the group leaders to get clients to identify people whom they trust *before* they role play.
2. This skill can be extremely helpful to clients who are symptomatic and are experiencing disturbing delusions. It is a skill that might be most appropriate to teach when a situation arises where a client is having delusions and is confronting other people with them.

COMMUNITY LIVING SKILLS

SKILL: Reminding Someone Not to Spread Germs

RATIONALE: When people live together, it is important to be careful not to spread germs. Although people usually try to be careful about not spreading germs, sometimes they forget or they don't realize that something they are doing is likely to spread germs. When you notice that someone is doing something that is spreading germs, you can point it out by using the steps of this skill.

STEPS OF THE SKILL:

1. Look at the person.
2. Tell the person how he or she is spreading germs: *Be specific.*
3. Suggest what the person can do differently.
4. Thank the person if he or she follows your suggestion. If your suggestion is not followed, tell someone in charge.

SCENES TO USE IN ROLE PLAYS:

1. You are talking to a friend who begins to cough without covering his or her mouth.
2. You notice that your roommate seems to be leaving his or her used tissues around the bedroom.
3. The last few times you have entered the bathroom at the Community Residence, you have noticed that the toilet has not been flushed. You decide to mention this during a house meeting.
4. You are having dinner at the Community Residence when another person uses your fork.

SPECIAL CONSIDERATIONS WHEN TEACHING THIS SKILL:

1. It is helpful for group leaders to spend a session having members generate a list of situations that promote the spread of germs and one that addresses how to prevent the spread of germs before beginning to role play.
2. Some members may be reticent to use this skill outside of the group because of a concern that they may cause an argument or fight. Group leaders need to emphasize that using this skill is to be done in a polite and calm manner. It is helpful when practicing this skill to frequently remind patients that "reminding" is not the same as "yelling" or "being angry."

COMMUNITY LIVING SKILLS

SKILL: Eating and Drinking Politely

RATIONALE: Many social situations involve eating and drinking. People will enjoy including us in these situations when we eat and drink politely. Many people know how to do this already, but it always helps to review the main points.

STEPS OF THE SKILL:

1. Take your time and check the temperature of the food or drink.
2. Take small bites or sips, and chew all food thoroughly.
3. Swallow what is in your mouth before speaking.
4. Use a napkin to wipe hands and mouth.

SCENES TO USE IN ROLE PLAYS:

Refer to Step 2 under "Special Considerations When Teaching This Skill."

SPECIAL CONSIDERATIONS WHEN TEACHING THIS SKILL:

1. Group leaders should remind group members that the steps listed in the skill are just "main points" and then should assist them in generating a list of other components that are involved in eating and drinking politely.
2. This skill needs to be practiced with actual food and drink. If the group already includes snacks, it is preferable to bring in special food (e.g., pie, pizza, or ice cream) to use when practicing. Group leaders will provide feedback on how well the group members followed the four steps of the skill as well as on any other component that the group identified as being important.

Friendship and Dating Skills

FRIENDSHIP AND DATING SKILLS

SKILL: Expressing Positive Feelings

RATIONALE: When people have encountered a series of difficulties, they tend to focus on the problems around them and forget to notice the positive things that other people do. Noticing positive things helps to increase a person's sense of belonging and sense of being able to do things well. Also, a person who knows he or she is doing something well is more likely to repeat what he or she has done to please others.

STEPS OF THE SKILL:
1. Look at the person.
2. Tell the person exactly what it was that pleased you.
3. Tell them how it made you feel.

SCENES TO USE IN ROLE PLAYS:
1. A staff member at the Community Residence cooked a meal you enjoyed.
2. A friend helped you out with a problem.
3. A counselor woke you up so that you would be on time for an appointment.
4. A family member gave you a ride to an outside appointment.
5. A co-worker at your new job ate lunch with you.

SPECIAL CONSIDERATIONS WHEN TEACHING THIS SKILL:

Sometimes clients may protest that it is not necessary to say positive things because people already know when they are doing something nice. Group leaders can remind clients that *everyone* likes it when someone has appreciated something that he or she has done.

FRIENDSHIP AND DATING SKILLS

SKILL: Giving Compliments

RATIONALE: Giving specific compliments is a good way to express positive feelings. Compliments are usually given about something that can be seen, such as an article of clothing, a haircut, or a pair of shoes. Giving and receiving compliments make people feel good about each other.

STEPS OF THE SKILL:
1. Look at the person.
2. Use a positive, sincere tone.
3. Be specific about what it is that you like.

SCENES TO USE IN ROLE PLAYS:
1. Liking someone's new pair of shoes.
2. Liking the color of someone's sweater or shirt.
3. Noticing someone's new pair of jeans.
4. Noticing someone's recent haircut.
5. Liking the way someone is combing his or her hair.

SPECIAL CONSIDERATIONS WHEN TEACHING THIS SKILL:

This is a good skill to review frequently. Clients usually enjoy it, and it can be a welcome break from more difficult skills, such as Expressing Angry Feelings and Compromise and Negotiation.

FRIENDSHIP AND DATING SKILLS

<u>SKILL:</u> Accepting Compliments

<u>RATIONALE:</u> In addition to being able to give compliments, it is also important to be able to receive or accept compliments from others. If you accept a compliment well, people are more likely to compliment you again in the future. It is important not to minimize or undo a compliment.

<u>STEPS OF THE SKILL:</u>

1. Look at the person.
2. Thank the person.
3. Acknowledge the compliment by
   a. Saying how it made you feel *or*
   b. Stating your feeling about the item that was complimented.

<u>SCENES TO USE IN ROLE PLAYS:</u>

1. Person A tells Person B he or she likes his or her shoes. Person B accepts the compliment.
2. Person B tells person C he or she likes the color of his or her shirt. Person C accepts the compliment.
3. Person C tells person D that he or she likes his or her jeans. Person D accepts the compliment.
4. Person D tells person E that he or she likes his or her haircut. Person E accepts the compliment.
5. Person E tells person A that he or she likes his or her hair style. Person A accepts the compliment.

<u>SPECIAL CONSIDERATIONS WHEN TEACHING THIS SKILL:</u>

This skill is best practiced in conjunction with the skill Giving Compliments. After group members have had the opportunity to practice giving compliments to the group leaders, it usually works well to go around the room and have each group member give a compliment to the person sitting next to him or her. The person receiving the compliment then has the opportunity to practice the steps for Accepting Compliments.

FRIENDSHIP AND DATING SKILLS

SKILL: Finding Common Interests

RATIONALE: One of the best ways to meet new people or develop friendships is to learn something about others. At the same time, sharing something about yourself also encourages the development of new relationships. Talking to another person about common interests that you may have is an easy and enjoyable way to learn more about each other.

STEPS OF THE SKILL:

1. Introduce yourself or greet the person you want to talk with.
2. Ask the person about what activities or hobbies he or she enjoys doing.
3. Tell the person about what activities or hobbies you enjoy doing.
4. Try to find a common interest.

SCENES TO USE IN ROLE PLAYS:

1. You want to get to know the new person at the day program.
2. You and your roommate want to do some activity together, but you do not know what each other likes.
3. You are interested in getting reacquainted with a family member who has just moved back into the area.
4. You are having lunch with a person you just met on your new job.
5. You are at a party and meet someone you would like to get to know better.

SPECIAL CONSIDERATIONS WHEN TEACHING THIS SKILL:

After group members have spent several sessions role playing this skill and feel relatively comfortable with it, group leaders can change the format of the group to one that is less structured. Group leaders can choose a topic to discuss relating to common interests and then facilitate the discussion. Members seem better able to talk about subjects that are related to things that happened before the onset of their illness. Topics that are particularly popular include favorite TV programs watched when a kid, games that you played as a kid, and music that you used to listen to when you were younger.

FRIENDSHIP AND DATING SKILLS

SKILL: Asking Someone for a Date

RATIONALE: There are times when you may find yourself attracted to another person; it could be someone you have just met or perhaps someone you already know. In either case, you may want to pursue dating that person. We have found that it is a little easier to ask someone for a date if you follow the steps listed below.

STEPS OF THE SKILL:

1. Choose an appropriate person to ask.
2. Suggest an activity to do together.
3. Listen to the person's response and do one of the following:
   a. If the person responds positively to your suggestion choose a day and time to get together. Be willing to compromise.
   b. If the person indicates that he or she is not interested in going out on a date, thank the person for being honest with you.

SCENES TO USE IN ROLE PLAYS:

1. There is a new person at your day program whom you would like to get to know.
2. You discover that you have a lot in common with a person at work and decide to ask him or her out.
3. There is a person with whom you volunteer that you would like to get to know.
4. You are at a party at a friend's house, and you meet someone whom you would like to ask out.
5. You decide to ask your new neighbor out on a date.

SPECIAL CONSIDERATIONS WHEN TEACHING THIS SKILL:

1. Some clients may have difficulty identifying appropriate people to date. Group leaders should spend time before practicing the skill helping clients identify what are some important factors to consider when choosing a potential date. For instance, clients can ask themselves questions such as "How well do I know the person?"; "Is this person available to date or is he or she involved in a relationship?"; "Is this someone who is not allowed to date me?" (e.g., a staff member is off limits); "What things do I have in common with this person?"
2. Group leaders need to remind clients that there is always the chance that the person they are asking may refuse their invitation. It is therefore important to be prepared for that possibility. Strategies for handling a possible rejection should be identified, such as remaining calm and not getting angry at the person. Also, clients can always talk to a friend or someone they trust afterwards and share their feelings about the incident.

FRIENDSHIP AND DATING SKILLS

SKILL: Ending a Date

RATIONALE: Dates don't last forever. Sooner or later it comes time to say, "Good-bye." There are many reasons it may be time to end the date, including completing the activity you had planned, running out of things to say, and sometimes even because you are having a bad time. Ending a date may feel awkward, but we have found that by keeping certain steps in mind, you can end a date more smoothly.

STEPS OF THE SKILL:
1. Thank the person for spending time with you.
2. If you enjoyed the date, tell the person that you would like to get together again.
3. Say, "Good-bye."

SCENES TO USE IN ROLE PLAYS:
1. It is time to end a date with a person from work. This was your first date with this person, and you had a very nice time.
2. It is time to end a date with a person whom you like very much. This has been your third date, and you are wondering how the person feels about you.
3. It is time to end a date with a person your friend fixed you up with. This was a blind date, and you did not have a very good time.
4. It is time to end a date with a person whom you like very much. You want to let the person know you had a great time, but you are not yet comfortable kissing.
5. It is time to end a date with a person whom you have been dating exclusively for several months.

SPECIAL CONSIDERATIONS WHEN TEACHING THIS SKILL:

It is customary for many people to end a date with a goodbye kiss when a good time has been had. Not everybody wants to end a date with a kiss, however. Some people prefer to just shake hands, while others are not comfortable with any physical contact. Clients will need to decide if they want to give or receive a kiss or a handshake and then judge if the other person is feeling similarly. Group leaders can help clients recognize clues that will help them determine how the other person is feeling so that they can make a decision as to what to do. Group leaders can also remind clients that, if they are having a difficult time figuring out what the other person is feeling, they can always ask the person directly. For example, a person might say, "I had a very nice time today and would like to kiss you good-bye. Is that okay with you?"

FRIENDSHIP AND DATING SKILLS

SKILL: Expressing Affection

RATIONALE: There are times when you may find that you like someone very much and want to let that person know how you feel. Letting someone know that you care about him or her can seem awkward or even a little scary. We have found that following these few steps can help to make expressing affection go a little more smoothly.

STEPS OF THE SKILL:

1. Choose a person whom you are fond of.
2. Pick a time and place where you can talk to the person in private.
3. Express affection using a warm and caring voice tone.
4. Tell the person why you feel this way.

SCENES TO USE IN ROLE PLAYS:

1. You have just finished a date with a person whom you like very much.
2. You have been dating this person exclusively for the past 4 months.
3. It is your grandmother's birthday, and you want to let her know how important she is to you.
4. It is Valentine's Day, and you just received flowers from a person you have dated a few times.
5. You want to let a friend know how much he or she means to you.

SPECIAL CONSIDERATIONS WHEN TEACHING THIS SKILL:

1. Group leaders should point out at the beginning of group that this skill focuses on the expression of verbal affection. However, group leaders can use this skill as an opportunity to have a frank discussion about the physical expression of affection if they are so inclined.
2. This skill requires that a group member be able to identify which people are appropriate to express affection to. It will be helpful for group leaders to discuss with members how to decide who is and is not an appropriate choice to express affection to.
3. Group leaders should remind group members that even when they choose an appropriate person to express affection to, their gesture may not be well received. It will be useful for group leaders to help members identify clues to look for that may indicate that the other person is uncomfortable and how to respond in those instances.

FRIENDSHIP AND DATING SKILLS

SKILL: Refusing Unwanted Sexual Advances

RATIONALE: Nobody should ever feel pressured into having sex when he or she does not want to. Sometimes people may feel pressured by someone they have just met, or perhaps by someone they know well or are currently dating. It is important to be able to make your feelings clearly known in a firm and direct manner.

STEPS OF THE SKILL:

1. Using a firm voice, tell the person that you are not interested in having sex.
2. Depending on your relationship with that person, explain why you feel that way.
3. If the person does not listen and continues to pressure you, leave the situation.

SCENES TO USE IN ROLE PLAYS:

1. A person you have just met wants to have sex with you.
2. A person that you have been dating for the last month pressures you to have sex. You like this person a lot but are not yet comfortable with the idea of becoming sexually involved.
3. A person at the day program who frequently gives you money and cigarettes now demands that you repay him or her by having sex.
4. Your partner that you are living with wants to have sex, but you are not feeling the same way at the moment.
5. A person you work with has helped you out and now tells you that you owe him. He or she starts pressuring you to have sex.

SPECIAL CONSIDERATIONS WHEN TEACHING THIS SKILL:

1. Before practicing this skill, group leaders should have a discussion with group members about the importance of never being pressured into doing something that you do not want to do. Group leaders can remind group members that if a person truly cares about them that person will respect their decision without putting them down.
2. Some group members have a difficult time distinguishing between what is real and what is not real. It is very important for group leaders to frequently remind members that this is just a role play and then talk about why it is important to practice this skill. If a group member seems to have a difficult time distinguishing between the two, then the role play should be stopped and be replaced by a general discussion about strategies for handling pressure to engage in sexual activity.

FRIENDSHIP AND DATING SKILLS

<u>SKILL:</u> Requesting That Your Partner Use a Condom

<u>RATIONALE:</u> When engaging in sexual activity, it is important to protect yourself from contracting sexually transmitted diseases. Requesting that your partner use a condom is one way to significantly reduce your risk of contracting a sexually transmitted disease. For women, it is also one important way to reduce your chances of having an unwanted pregnancy.

<u>STEPS OF THE SKILL:</u>
1. Choose a time and place where you and your partner can talk in private.
2. Tell your partner that you would like him to wear a condom.
3. Explain your reasons for making the request.
4. If he refuses, tell him that you will not engage in any sexual activity with him until he uses one.

<u>SCENES TO USE IN ROLE PLAYS:</u>
1. You want to have sex with a person you just met.
2. You want to have sex with a person whom you have been dating for the last month.
3. You want to have sex with a person whom you have been dating regularly for the last year.

<u>SPECIAL CONSIDERATIONS WHEN TEACHING THIS SKILL:</u>
1. It will be useful for group leaders to remind members that this request is best made before engaging in sexual activity. It is also better not to wait until the *moment* before they are about to engage in intercourse to make the request.
2. Some group members have a difficult time distinguishing between what is real and what is not real. It is very important for group leaders to frequently remind members that is is just a role play and then talk about why it is important to practice this skill. If a member seems to have a difficult time distinguishing between the two, then the role play should be stopped and replaced by a general discussion about strategies for requesting that a partner wear a condom.

FRIENDSHIP AND DATING SKILLS

SKILL: Refusing Pressure to Engage in High-Risk Sexual Behavior

RATIONALE: Engaging in high-risk sexual behavior can have serious consequences. High-risk sexual activity greatly increases your chances of contracting sexually transmitted diseases, including AIDS. Knowing how to refuse pressure to engage in high-risk sexual activities is one important step toward taking care of yourself and your health.

STEPS OF THE SKILL:

1. Tell your partner that you will not engage in the high-risk sexual activity.
2. Explain your reason for refusing to do so.
3. If you still want to engage in sex, suggest a different sexual activity that is safer.
4. If the person continues to pressure you, tell him or her that you need to leave.

SCENES TO USE IN ROLE PLAYS:

1. A person you have just met wants you to engage in a high-risk sexual activity.
2. A person you have been dating for about a month and like a lot pressures you to engage in a high-risk sexual activity. You want to have sex with this person but are not willing to put yourself at risk by giving in to his or her request.
3. Your partner, whom you have been involved with for over a year, thinks it might be fun try something new to spice up your sex lives. Unfortunately, what he or she has in mind is considered to be a high-risk sexual activity.

SPECIAL CONSIDERATIONS WHEN TEACHING THIS SKILL:

1. Before practicing this skill, group leaders should have the group generate a list of sexual behaviors that are considered to be high-risk for contracting STDs, especially AIDS (refer to Appendix A for a list). Group leaders will also need to have a discussion about how people contract AIDS and other STDs. They may also need to dispel any myths surrounding the transmission of these diseases as well as myths about who is likely to carry these diseases.
2. Some clients have a difficult time distinguishing between what is real and what is not real. It is very important for group leaders to frequently remind group members that this is just a role play and then talk about why it is important to practice this skill. If a member seems to have a difficult time distinguishing between the two, then the role play should be stopped and then replaced by a general discussion about high-risk sexual behaviors.

Medication Management Skills

MEDICATION MANAGEMENT SKILLS

SKILL: Making a Doctor's Appointment on the Phone

RATIONALE: Most people, at some time or another, need to see a doctor. Often it is up to the person who is not feeling well to make the appointment. We have found that making appointments goes more smoothly if people follow the steps presented below.

STEPS OF THE SKILL:

1. Identify yourself or give your name.
2. Tell the person that you would like to make an appointment to see the doctor.
3. Listen to the person's response. Be ready to provide any information that he or she may ask for.
4. Repeat back the time and date of the appointment given to you and then thank the person for his or her help.

SCENES TO USE IN ROLE PLAYS:

1. You need to make an appointment because you have been feeling sick for over a week and do not seem to be getting any better.
2. You realize that you need to make an appointment for your annual physical.
3. You think that your medication isn't working, so you call your doctor for an appointment.
4. You notice that you are experiencing some early warning signs of relapse and make an appointment to see your doctor.
5. You are experiencing side effects from your medication and want to make an extra appointment to see your psychiatrist.

SPECIAL CONSIDERATIONS WHEN TEACHING THIS SKILL:

1. Group leaders should help clients identify what information they are likely to be asked for when making a doctor's appointment (e.g., the nature of the problem, insurance information, etc.).
2. Group leaders should also remind clients that they will need to be specific but brief when describing why they want an appointment. Clients should also be reminded that it is important that they speak in a slow and clear manner so that they can be understood. In addition, clients should be warned of the likelihood that the receptionist may put them "on hold" for a while and that they will need to be understanding about this.

MEDICATION MANAGEMENT SKILLS

SKILL: Asking Questions about Medications

RATIONALE: It is important to understand why a doctor has prescribed a certain medication for us and how to take that medication properly. It is equally important to feel that the medication is being helpful. When people have questions about the medications that they are taking, they need to seek out someone who is knowledgeable and talk to that person about their concerns.

STEPS OF THE SKILL:

1. Choose a person to speak to, such as a case manager, a nurse, a doctor, or a family member.
2. Ask the person your question about medication. Be specific.
3. If you do not understand the person's answer, ask more questions.
4. Thank the person for his or her help.

SCENES TO USE IN ROLE PLAYS:

1. You are having trouble sleeping and are wondering if it is related to the new medication you are taking.
2. Your doctor has suggested that you begin taking a new medication but you have concerns about its possible side effects.
3. You want to stop taking your medication because you are feeling better.
4. You don't think that the current dose of medication you are taking is helpful and want to increase it.
5. You want to know if you can have a beer if you take the medication that has been prescribed.

SPECIAL CONSIDERATIONS WHEN TEACHING THIS SKILL:

1. It will be useful for group leaders to discuss with clients the importance of writing down any questions they may have (so they do not forget) before speaking to a specific person about their medication concerns.
2. Group leaders should also emphasize the importance of clients understanding the answers that they receive. Clients should be encouraged to ask more questions or even ask another person their question if they do not understand the answer they have received.

MEDICATION MANAGEMENT SKILLS

SKILL: Asking Questions about Health-Related Concerns

RATIONALE: Talking to others about our health can sometimes feel uncomfortable or scary. This may especially be true if we need to speak with a doctor or a nurse. It is important that we understand what is going on with our health, however. Asking questions of someone who is knowledgeable will enable us to better take care of ourselves.

STEPS OF THE SKILL:

1. Choose a person to speak to, such as a case manager, a nurse, or a doctor.
2. Ask the person your question.
3. If you do not feel comfortable with the person's answer or if you do not understand, ask more questions.
4. Thank the person for his or her help.

SCENES TO USE IN ROLE PLAYS:

1. You ask a staff member at the Community Residence about what to expect at your upcoming physical examination.
2. Your doctor just changed your medication dose, and you want to know how it will affect you.
3. You are having trouble sleeping and ask your doctor if he or she can prescribe any medication to help.
4. Recently you have noticed that you have gained some weight, and you want to do something about it. You ask your nurse about the best ways to lose weight.
5. You haven't been feeling well lately and want to see a doctor. You ask your case worker to make an appointment for you.

SPECIAL CONSIDERATIONS WHEN TEACHING THIS SKILL:

1. Before beginning to practice this skill, it may be useful for group leaders to spend some time helping members identify different people they might want to ask questions about health-related issues. This list might include people such as doctors, nurses, case managers, therapists, and family members.
2. It may also be of use to have the group generate a list of different health care providers, such as psychiatrists, dentists, physical therapists, gynecologists, and so forth, and then discuss what aspect of health they specifically focus on.

Vocational/Work Skills

VOCATIONAL/WORK SKILLS

SKILL: Interviewing for a Job

RATIONALE: Making a good first impression is important when trying to get hired for a job. Having an interview for a job provides a person with that opportunity. We have found that interviews are more likely to go smoothly when people have an idea about what will be asked of them and when they keep the following steps in mind.

STEPS OF THE SKILL:

1. Look at the person.
2. Shake the interviewer's hand and introduce yourself using a confident voice tone.
3. Tell the interviewer why you are interested in this job.
4. Answer any job-related questions the interviewer asks you.
5. Thank the interviewer for his or her time.

SCENES TO USE IN ROLE PLAYS:

1. You are interviewing for a volunteer position at your local nursing home.
2. You are interviewing for a job at the post office.
3. You are interviewing for a job at a landscaping business.

SPECIAL CONSIDERATIONS WHEN TEACHING THIS SKILL:

1. Group leaders should review with clients the most common questions asked during an interview. It will be important for clients to have ready answers for questions such as "What past experience or skills do you have that qualify you for this job?"; "What makes you interested in this job?"; and "What do you consider your strengths to be?"
2. Group leaders need to spend time discussing the importance of making a good first impression when going on an interview. It is useful to discuss grooming, hygiene, and appropriate dress.
3. Clients should be frequently reminded that maintaining eye contact and speaking in a firm, confident manner are very important and will help them make a good impression.

VOCATIONAL/WORK SKILLS

SKILL: Asking for Feedback about Job Performance

RATIONALE: Most people want feedback on their job performance at some point during their work careers. However, asking for that feedback may feel awkward or scary. We have found that people feel less awkward when they keep certain steps in mind.

STEPS OF THE SKILL:

1. Identify an area that you would like some feedback about.
2. Request feedback from the appropriate person. Say something like "I am interested in knowing how you think I am doing with _____; I would like to talk to you about it when you have a chance."
3. Listen carefully to the person's response, especially any suggestions that he or she may make.
4. Thank the person for his or her time.

SCENES TO USE IN ROLE PLAYS:

1. You have been at your new job for about a month and are wondering how your boss thinks you are doing.
2. You have been working on a project with a co-worker and ask for his or her feedback on your part of the project.
3. You have been feeling unsure about the progress that you have made on a new project and ask your supervisor for some feedback.
4. You have been given additional responsibilites at work and ask for feedback about how you are doing.
5. Recently your supervisor commented that you had been working too slowly. Since then you have tried to improve your time and are wondering if you are now working at an acceptable pace.

SPECIAL CONSIDERATIONS WHEN TEACHING THIS SKILL:

1. Some clients have little experience with working at a job as an adult and may not be able to readily identify what things people ask for feedback about. It will be helpful if group leaders spend some time helping clients identify appropriate things one might seek feedback about.
2. Group leaders may need to remind clients that often they will have to make an appointment or wait some time before a supervisor has the opportunity to speak with them. It is important that clients anticipate this so that they are able to respond without getting angry or upset.
3. It is also important that group leaders discuss with clients the importance of listening to a supervisor's feedback *without* interrupting or getting defensive.

VOCATIONAL/WORK SKILLS

<u>SKILL:</u> Responding to Criticism

<u>RATIONALE:</u> Receiving criticism from a supervisor can be an upsetting experience. Most people have been on the receiving end of criticism at work at some point or another. Knowing how to respond to that criticism can help make the experience more tolerable and even turn it into something productive.

<u>STEPS OF THE SKILL:</u>

1. Without interrupting or getting angry, listen carefully to what is being said to you.
2. Repeat back what the person said.
3. Ask the person what you can do to improve the situation.
4. If you do not understand what was said, continue to ask questions until it becomes clear.

<u>SCENES TO USE IN ROLE PLAYS:</u>

1. You have arrived late to work on several occasions, and your supervisor confronts you about it.
2. Your supervisor tells you that you are working too slowly.
3. Your boss tells you that he or she is unhappy with the quality of your work.
4. Your boss tells you that your dress does not meet the office dress code standards.
5. Your office-mate tells you that he or she is unhappy with how messy you keep your half of the office.

<u>SPECIAL CONSIDERATIONS WHEN TEACHING THIS SKILL:</u>

1. Group leaders should remind clients that no one likes to be the recipient of criticism. However, it is important to remain calm and listen carefully to what is being said so that you can remedy the situation.
2. Because receiving criticism is an upsetting event, group leaders may want to review with the clients ways to manage angry or upsetting feelings.

VOCATIONAL/WORK SKILLS

SKILL: Following Verbal Instructions

RATIONALE: Being able to follow instructions is a skill that is required in almost all settings, such as school, home, or on the job. It is especially important to be able to follow verbal instructions on the job, where having an accurate understanding of a particular assignment is essential to the overall functioning of the workplace.

STEPS OF THE SKILL:

1. Listen carefully to the person giving instructions.
2. If you are confused about what was said, ask the person to repeat the instructions.
3. Repeat back the instructions to the person.
4. Ask more questions if you still do not understand.

SCENES TO USE IN ROLE PLAYS:

1. Your job coach has just given you instructions about the best route to take to your job.
2. It is your first day on the job, and your supervisor instructs you to go to the orientation given for new employees. It is a large building, and you are not sure how to find the room.
3. You have just been asked to take on more responsibilities at work and are confused about what is expected of you.
4. Your supervisor has asked you and a co-worker to work on a project together. The supervisor has split the project responsibilities between the two of you; however, it is still not clear to you what you need to be doing.
5. Your vocational counselor has given you a rather complicated homework assignment. You realize that you need some clarification about it.

SPECIAL CONSIDERATIONS WHEN TEACHING THIS SKILL:

1. Many group members have trouble following instructions as a result of their symptoms and cognitive deficits. Therefore, it will be helpful to begin the role plays using simple instructions and then work up to harder ones. In addition, simple instructions should be given to group members who are very symptomatic or have severe cognitive deficits.
2. It may also be helpful for group leaders to help the members come up with strategies for remembering instructions, such as writing them down on a sheet of paper.

VOCATIONAL/WORK SKILLS

SKILL: Solving Problems

RATIONALE: All of us experience problems at one time or another. Problems can be big or small and can occur in any setting, including at work. Learning a systematic way of dealing with problems is an important skill needed to function in the world as well as to maintain and excel in our jobs.

STEPS OF THE SKILL:

1. Define the problem.
2. Use brainstorming to generate a list of possible solutions.
3. Identify the advantages and disadvantages of each solution.
4. Select the best solution or combination of solutions.
5. Plan how to carry out the best solution.
6. Follow up the plan at a later time.

SCENES TO USE IN ROLE PLAYS:

1. You have been put on probation at work because you frequently show up late in the morning.
2. You have been offered a job that you would like to take, but the hours conflict with your weekly therapy appointment.
3. You have a job as a maintenance worker in a cafeteria. Your supervisor tells you that you are working too slowly and asks you to figure out a way to improve your productivity.

SPECIAL CONSIDERATIONS WHEN TEACHING THIS SKILL:

1. Because this skill is somewhat more complicated and takes longer to practice than the other skills, it is taught using a somewhat different format. Instead of having each group member complete a role play individually, group leaders should present a scenario to the entire group and then assist them through the steps of the skill together. Teaching the skill in this format has two functions: (a) it keeps all members interested and involved, and (b) it provides the members with experience working together toward a common goal (which requires that they put to use some other skills that they have learned).
2. Step 2 requires group members to generate a list of possible solutions. During this step, group leaders need to emphasize the importance of writing down all ideas without judging whether or not they are good or bad. This technique is called "brainstorming."
3. The Problem-Solving Worksheet in Appendix A is helpful in teaching this skill.

VOCATIONAL/WORK SKILLS

SKILL: Joining Ongoing Conversations at Work

RATIONALE: There will be times at work when you may want to join a conversation that is in progress with some co-workers, such as during lunch or a break. Learning how to join a conversation without being rude or creating an awkward situation can be accomplished by simply following a few steps.

STEPS OF THE SKILL:

1. Wait for a break or a pause in the flow of the conversation.
2. Say something like "Mind if I join you?"
3. Say things related to the conversation topic.

SCENES TO USE IN ROLE PLAYS:

1. You are on your lunch break and see some people whom you would like to join who are eating their lunch and talking.
2. You are on a break and see some co-workers gathered around the vending machines. You decide to join them.
3. There has been a temporary power outage at work and you find yourself with nothing to do. You hear two people talking about the outage and are curious to find out what they know.

SPECIAL CONSIDERATIONS WHEN TEACHING THIS SKILL:

1. This skill requires that group members be able to make judgments about when it is appropriate to join a conversation. Some group members will have difficulty recognizing when there is a break or pause in the flow of the conversation. Therefore, it may be helpful to spend some time before beginning the role plays having group members observe the leaders talking and seeing if they are able to identify when the conversation flow has been broken.
2. This skill also requires that group members make judgments about when it is not okay to join a conversation. For instance, it may not be appropriate if the people talking look upset, angry, or serious. It would be helpful for the leaders to spend some time reviewing how people identify different affect.

Epilogue: Tips for Effective Social Skills Training

In the preceding chapters we have provided an extensive explanation and description of social skills training, and provided instructions and materials for conducting skills groups. The technique is fairly straightforward, and a clinician who has some facility at working with schizophrenia patients should have little difficulty mastering the intervention. However, some points need to be reiterated, and a few others need to be considered in order to maximize results.

1. *Teaching social skills is teaching, not group psychotherapy.* Most people working in mental health became interested in the field because they wanted to help people, and it is generally assumed that the way to help is through some form of verbal psychotherapy. Regardless of the specific brand, these approaches all assume that conversation about emotionally important issues is a central ingredient for change. That is absolutely *not* the case with social skills training. This is an educational, skill-building procedure. Conversation is a vehicle to transmit information and make people feel comfortable with one another, not to teach. As previously indicated, a piano or tennis instructor does not bring a group of students together to *talk* about striking the piano keys or the tennis ball and discuss how the students *feel* about it. The participants in social skills training are often *willing* to discuss their problems; sometimes they *prefer* talking to working at learning. Nevertheless, talking and self-exploration are issues for *other* groups. The leader must make up his or her mind before beginning whether he or she will be conducting a social skills group or doing a little social skills in the course of a more openended verbal psychotherapy. The former is the only way to really develop complex new behaviors. We suggest that the leader bring a check sheet with him or her into each session in which the lesson plan is outlined and that at

least 45 minutes of each 60-minute session be devoted explicitly to the plan (i.e., role playing and modeling). This type of imposed structure is the only way to achieve the goals of social skills training (we promise!!). The remaining time at the end, after the work is done, can be used for discussion, coffee and cookies, medication checks, or any other clinically or socially useful activity. However, learning is work and work gets done first, or it tends not to get done at all.

The level of organization referred to in Point 1, above, is particularly important for teaching. Prepare written materials (handouts and poster boards) in advance, come to sessions with a set of role play scenarios already prepared, and stick as close as possible to the script. When we suggest doing two to three role plays with each member we *mean* two to three brief role plays with each member, not one or two, sprinkled with conversation and differing wildly in content or length. Keep in mind that role plays are not vehicles to stimulate discussion *about* social situations or to rehearse a single, long-winded, idiosyncratic dialogue. Think of learning to serve in tennis by serving once, hitting a few volleys, talking about your grip, volleying a little, and then trying another serve versus hitting 10 serves in a row and getting corrective feedback after each shot. Finally, keep in mind that every group is a little different. Learning to be an effective leader requires that you practice implementing the structure with different groups whose members present somewhat different challenges.

2. *Learn to do social skills training.* Doing social skills training effectively is a skill. Consequently, the leader must learn how to do it in the same way that participants learn their new social skills. That means starting slowly, practicing, and securing feedback. Where possible, it would be very helpful to observe a skills group conducted by experienced skills trainers, or to watch videotapes. Short of that, skill can be bootstrapped by soliciting feedback from co-leaders or supervisors who are familiar with the goals. As with all new skills, it is important to start slowly. Select easy skills to teach, work with a co-leader, and set very minimal goals. Practice *doing* skills training, and don't worry too much about the outcome. Get used to role playing and to running a structured group. Become comfortable with the role of teacher and in keeping a group on task. Keep in mind that the structure (how you teach) is much more important than the content (what you teach). Most neophyte leaders function as if the opposite is true and spend too much time talking.

3. *Don't work in isolation.* In all likelihood, the participants in your groups will be receiving antipsychotic medications, have a case manager, and (potentially) one or more leaders. Keep in touch with your colleagues. Find out when the patient has been put on a new medication, or has received a major change in dosage. Learn how he or she is doing in other settings (is

this a particularly bad time for him or her? Is he or she showing prodromal signs of relapse?). Of special note is the issue of whether the member is giving you a hard time that he or she is not giving others or vice versa. Similarly, what is going on in the person's life outside of the treatment center? Are there conflicts at home? Do you need to be in touch with family members or residence managers to ensure that the member's new skills are being reinforced or to teach a specific skill needed to avoid conflict in the home (e.g., the member is fighting with a sibling or housemate, and you can teach a skill to alleviate the conflict). As a general rule, generalization of the effects of training will be enhanced to the extent that the skills you teach are (a) relevant to the person's immediate environment, and (b) are reinforced by the environment.

4. *Never, never underestimate the cognitive deficits of your members.* We have previously highlighted the problems schizophrenia patients face in memory, attention, and higher-level problem solving. This is one of the most important and most difficult points for most clinicians to understand. Clients with schizophrenia who are asymptomatic can appear to maintain lucid conversations, seem to learn and understand well, and respond affirmatively to questions about whether or not they understand. We have regularly observed such apparently well-functioning clients nod appropriately to instructions, parrot the leader's role-played responses, and be totally unable to generate an appropriate response when the situation is slightly changed. Whether they don't remember, are easily distracted, or are so concrete that they can't transpose ideas from situation A to situation B, they often lack the capacity to learn from continuities across situations. The only solutions to this dilemma that we have found to be effective are (a) impose as much structure as possible and minimize demands on abstraction (use prompts and handouts, identify simple commonalities across situations for the person to focus on, and keep instructions very, very simple and straightforward); and (b) practice, practice, practice (the more automatic the response is in situation X, the less the demand on working memory and analysis). Finally, do not ask if your participants understand: Have them demonstrate! Similarly, do not preach or lecture. Keep your instructions brief, and always use audiovisuals (handouts, posters) for *anything* you want them to remember. Finally, keep role plays brief and narrowly relevant to what you are trying to teach. It is typical of new leaders to get caught up in role playing, staying in role too long, and leading the interaction far from the few specific points the participant is supposed to practice. The longer the role play lasts, the greater the likelihood that the participants will forget what they are supposed to be focusing on.

5. *Although the subject is not directly related to social skills training, keep in mind that your members will be at high risk for HIV and AIDS.* The

techniques used for teaching safe sex and low-risk behaviors are very similar to the techniques described in this book for social skills training. We advise all social skills training leaders to consider including an HIV unit if members are not already learning the material elsewhere. Moreover, given the learning and motivational problems faced by individuals with schizophrenia, a refresher course would be appropriate even if they have had prior instruction. Training materials are readily available from the National Institutes of Health, National Institute on Drug Abuse, the Centers for Disease Control and Prevention, and other federal agencies. Useful Internet sources include www.nih.gov and www.nida.gov.

6. *Be positively reinforcing.* It is natural for most of us to tell others what they have not done or what they have done wrong when we are giving instructions. A key to making this intervention work well is to be consistently positive and reinforcing. Some new skills trainers interpret this caveat to mean that they must be bubbly and effusive and praise everything. To the contrary, a laid-back style will work fine as long as participants hear that they doing okay and that you and the other group members approve. Most people with schizophrenia have long histories of failure and frustration. Social skills training is one place that they can be assured of success because (a) the level of demand is geared to their capacity, not some abstract or unreachable standard; and (b) communications are always positive, emphasizing what they have done well, not what they have done poorly.

Even difficult group members (and some are difficult) can be controlled without much negativity and censure if the leader can focus on rules and the situation, rather than the person's bad behavior (e.g., "It is important that we don't make fun of one another here. Fred, if you are having trouble not laughing when Jon tries to talk, maybe you would like to take a brief break." "Steve, Susan may find it distracting when you touch her during group; why don't you come over here and sit next to me. Then it will be easier for you not to touch her."). Remember, you can't lose your temper, be sarcastic, or speak in an angry tone of voice and be an effective teacher. Group members will turn off or, if they are really testing you, will be reinforced for their inappropriate behavior. Of course, everyone must feel safe, including the leaders. If a member is really posing a threat, he or she should be asked to leave, and the overall positive tone must be temporarily suspended.

7. *Be persistent.* We believe that this manual provides all of the information needed for you to conduct effective skills training groups. However, we have not said it is easy. The leaders must do more homework than in other treatments in order to be adequately prepared. The intervention is fun for

both leaders and participants (it really is!!), but everyone works hard. There is no sitting back and letting others do all the work. Many times, it will seem easier to just talk about something or move on to a new topic, rather than repeat the same role play for what seems like the umpteenth time. Nevertheless, remember our tennis and music analogies. It's like the old joke: "How do you get to Carnegie Hall?" "Practice, practice, practice."

APPENDICES

Appendix A: Materials Useful to Group Leaders

SOCIAL SKILLS ORIENTATION FOR PROFESSIONALS

What Are "Social Skills"?

Social skills are the specific behaviors people use when interacting with others that enable individuals to be effective at achieving their personal goals. Situations such as having a casual conversation, making friends, expressing feelings, or obtaining something from another person all require the use of social skills.

What Are Some Examples of Social Skills?

Good social skills include both *what* is said during a social interaction and *how* it is said. When communicating with another person, the verbal content of the message, that is, the person's choice of words or phrases, is important. *How* that message is communicated can be just as important. For example, appropriate facial expressions, body language, eye contact, and a good, firm voice tone all help to communicate the message. Social skills training aims at improving both what people say during interactions and how they say it.

Why Are Social Skills Important?

People with psychiatric illnesses usually experience many problems in their relationships with others, including treatment providers, family members, and other clients. These problems result in difficulties in community adjustment and an impoverished quality of life. For many clients, poor social functioning is related to inadequate social skills. For example, clients may have difficulty starting a conversation, speak in a low monotone voice, or fail to establish eye contact. Helping clients to improve their social skills can enhance their social functioning in the community.

Where Do Social Skills Come From?

There are many possible causes of skill deficits in people with psychiatric illnesses. Some clients become ill before they have been able to fully develop their social skills. Others may have grown up in an environment in which they did not have good role models. Still others may have learned good social skills but later lost them as they developed their illness and withdrew from other people. Clients who have spent long periods of time in hospitals where there were few expectations placed on their behavior may be out of practice and need help relearning skills and knowing when to use them. Any combination of these possibilities can contribute to deficits in social skills.

Are All Problems in Social Functioning Due to Deficits in Social Skills?

No, social dysfunction can arise from other problems as well. Medication side effects can cause problems in social functioning. In addition, if the social environment in which the clients reside is not conducive and supportive to appropriate and assertive social behavior, social dysfunction will result.

What Is Social Skills Training?

Social skills training is a set of psychotherapeutic techniques based on social learning theory that has been developed to teach social skills to individuals. Social skills training uses the same methods that were developed over 20 years ago for assertiveness training. Social skills training involves several steps. The first step is to provide a rationale or help the client to understand why it is important to learn the skill. The second step is to demonstrate (model) the skill in a role play. The third step is engaging the client in a role play, and the fourth step involves providing feedback to the client and suggestions for improvement. Fifth, clients are encouraged to practice on their own.

How Often Should Social Skills Training Be Conducted?

As often as possible! It is preferable to have the social skills group meet at least two times per week, but clients can be reminded to practice the skills often, even on a daily basis. The more opportunities clients have to practice social skills, the better they get, and the more natural the skills become.

What Type of Social Skills Can Be Taught?

A wide variety of skills can be taught depending upon the clients' needs. Some of the most common skills to teach psychiatric patients include initiating and maintaining conversations, making requests of other people, expressing feelings, resolving conflicts, making friends, and being assertive.

How Can Staff Members Help Clients to Learn These Skills?

Staff members are as important to the success of social skills training as the group leaders are themselves. Staff members can help clients by knowing what skills are being taught, demonstrating these skills in their own interactions with clients (and each other), prompting and encouraging clients to use the skills in specific situations, and giving them positive feedback when they demonstrate good social skills. Furthermore, staff members can help clients learn better skills by engaging them in brief role plays conducted *outside* of the regular group sessions. This additional practice may help some clients bcome more familiar and comfortable with the skills, enabling them to use them on their own. In summary, staff members play a *vital* role in assisting clients to improve their social skills and are an extended part of the social skills training team.

SOCIAL SKILLS ORIENTATION FOR CLIENTS

What Is Social Skills Training?

Social skills training teaches people how they can better communicate their feelings, thoughts, and needs to others. It also teaches them how they can better respond to other people's feelings, thoughts, and needs. Social skills help people to get what they want more often and help them to avoid doing things that they do not want to do.

How Is Social Skills Training Different from Other Groups?

Social skills training is different from other forms of therapy groups. Group members do not sit around and talk about their problems. Instead, members spend group time trying out ways to actually solve their problems. They do this by practicing different skills during the group and then trying out these skills in real-life situations.

What Is Expected of Group Members?

Group members must be willing to keep an open mind. They must be willing to try new techniques designed to communicate with one other. Group members will learn about new skills and discuss how to use them in their lives. When they are ready, they need to practice the skills in group.

How Do Group Members Learn and Practice a New Skill?

Group members practice a new skill through role playing with the group leaders and then with each other. Role playing is similar to rehearsing for a play but more relaxed and fun. Group members are first given a handout that has the skill being taught broken down into a few easy steps. Next they watch the group leaders role play the skill with each other. (Role playing is acting in a pretend situation.) Finally, when members are feeling comfortable, they get to role play the skill. Nobody is ever forced to role play if he or she does not feel comfortable.

How Can Social Skills Training Help Me?

Social skills can help you communicate better with your friends, relatives, and bosses. They can help you talk to people you are interested in dating. You can focus on skills that will allow you to become more independent. Social skills training can help you improve the skills you need to achieve almost any goal you choose. Before the first session, each group member meets with a group leader. The leader helps the group member identify his or her own personal goals to work on in group.

PROBLEM-SOLVING WORKSHEET

Step 1: Define the problem.

Talk about the problem or goal, listen carefully, ask questions, get everybody's opinion. Then write down *exactly* what the problem or goal is:

_____

_____

Step 2: Use brainstorming to generate a list of possible solutions.

Write down *all* ideas, even bad ones. Get everybody to come up with at least one possible solution. List the solutions *without discussion* at this stage.

1. _____

2. _____

3. _____

4. _____

5. _____

6. _____

Step 3: Identify the advantages and disadvantages of each solution.

Quickly go down the list of possible solutions and discuss the *main* advantages and disadvantages of each one.

Step 4: Select the best solution or combination of solutions.

Choose the solution that can be carried out most easily to solve the problem.

_____

Source: Adapted from Mueser, K. T., & Gingerich, S. (1994). *Coping with Schizophrenia: A Guide for Families.* Copyright 1994 by New Harbinger Publications. Adapted by permission.

Step 5: Plan how to carry out the best solution.

List the resources needed and major obstacles to overcome. Assign tasks and set a timetable.

Step 1. _____

Step 2. _____

Step 3. _____

Step 4. _____

Step 6. Follow up the plan at a later time.
First focus on what you have accomplished. *Praise all efforts.* Then review whether the plan was successful and revise it as necessary.

SOCIAL SKILLS GROUP FORMAT

Instructions: This format is to be used for each skill group held. Group leaders should remind themselves of these 12 steps before the start of each group.

1. **Introduce New Group Members and Review Group Rules.**
   - When there is a new group member, have everyone introduce him- or herself.
   - Provide a *brief* overview or reminder of the group structure.
   - Elicit ground rules from "veteran" group members.

2. **Review Homework from Previous Group.**
   - Ask each group member to describe what he or she did for homework.
   - Praise *all* efforts no matter how small.

3. **Establish a Rationale for the Skill.**
   - Elicit reasons for learning the skill from group members.
   - Acknowledge all contributions made by group members.
   - Provide any additional rationales not mentioned.

4. **Discuss Steps of the Skill.**
   - Discuss the reasons for each step.
   - Check group members for their understanding of the reasons.

5. **Model the Skill Using a Role Play.**
   - Explain that you will demonstrate the skill in a role play.
   - Use two group leaders to model the skill.
   - Keep role play brief and to the point.

6. **Review the Role Play with the Group Members.**
   - Discuss whether each step of the skill was used in the role play.
   - Ask group members to evaluate the effectiveness of the role play.

7. **Engage a Group Member in a Role Play Using the Same Situation Modeled.**
   - Start with a member who is more skilled or is likely to be cooperative.
   - Request that the member try the skill in a role play with one of the leaders.
   - Ask the client questions to check his or her understanding of the goal of the role play.
   - Instruct the remaining group members to observe the client. Consider assigning each member a specific step or part of a step to observe.

8. **Provide Positive Feedback.**
   - Elicit positive feedback first from group members who have been assigned a specific step to observe.
   - Encourage feedback that is *specific*.
   - Cut off any negative feedback or criticism.
   - Praise all efforts.

9. **Provide Corrective Feedback.**
   - Elicit suggestions for ways the client could do the skill better.
   - Limit feedback to one or two suggestions.
   - Strive to communicate the suggestions in a positive, upbeat manner.

10. **Engage the Client in Another Role Play Using the Same Situation.**
    - Request that the client change *one* behavior during role play.
    - Check the client's understanding of the suggestions.
    - Focus on behaviors that are salient and changeable.

11. **Provide Additional Feedback.**
    - First focus on the behavior that was to be changed.
    - Consider using other behavior-shaping strategies to improve client skills, such as coaching, prompting, and supplemental modeling.
    - Be generous but *specific* when providing feedback.

Repeat Steps 7–11 with Each Member of the Group, Giving Everyone a Chance to Practice the Skill.

12. **Assign Homework.**
    - Give an assignment to practice the skill— use homework sheets.
    - Ask group members to identify situations in which they could use the skill.
    - When possible, tailor the assignment to each client's skill level.

CLIENT RULES FOR SOCIAL SKILLS GROUP

Instructions: A copy of these rules (poster size) should be posted in the room where the group is held so that they can be referred to as needed.

1. Stay on the Group Topic.

2. Only One Person May Speak at a Time.

3. No Name Calling or Cursing.

4. No Criticizing or Making Fun of Each Other.

5. No Eating or Drinking during Group.

GUIDELINES FOR GIVING CONSTRUCTIVE FEEDBACK

1. Be alert to clients using the skill, even if it is only for a brief moment.

2. Start by giving praise. Find the positive behavior to highlight. A good way to begin is "I really like the way you _____."

3. Be specific about what the client did well. For example, "I like the way you looked at me when you were talking."

4. *Avoid* critical comments and terms such as "wrong" or "bad."

5. Make suggestions for improvement on only one area at a time. Some clients may not be able to accept any suggestions at first; for them, stick to praise for what was done well.

GUIDELINES FOR COMMUNICATING WITH CLIENTS
WHO ARE EXPERIENCING SYMPTOMS

1. Speak slowly and clearly.

2. Make only a few statements at a time.

3. Periodically ask if the client understands what you are saying.

4. Ask the client to repeat back what you have just said.

5. If the client is not able to follow what you are saying, repeat the information using fewer words and sentences.

6. Ask the client to repeat back what you have just said.

HOMEWORK SHEET

Instructions: Homework assignments are designed to encourage group members to practice the skills they are currently learning in the social skills training group. The group leaders will give a specific assignment each week, which will be written on this form. Sometimes it is helpful for a staff member or family member to be assigned to initiate and assist practicing. The group leaders will review the complete homework sheets the following week.

Client: _____ Staff member or family member: _____

Assignment:

_____

_____

_____

_____

Date practiced: _____ Time: _____ Location: _____

Briefly describe what took place:

_____

_____

_____

_____

How did it go?

_____

_____

_____

_____

_____

FACTS ABOUT HIV AND GUIDELINES FOR SAFER SEX

Facts about HIV (the Virus That Causes AIDS)

1. HIV is transmitted through the exchange of certain body fluids (semen, vaginal discharges, and blood infected with the HIV virus).

2. HIV cannot be spread through casual contact such as shaking hands, hugging, sneezing, kissing, or sharing bathrooms and kitchens.

3. HIV cannot be spread through insect bites or by donating blood.

4. People infected with HIV usually look and feel healthy.

5. AIDS is caused by HIV infection.

6. There is no vaccine or cure for HIV and AIDS at this time.

Guidelines for Safer Sex Practices

The following guidelines should be used by everyone. *Anyone* who is sexually active and has not been in an *exclusively* monogamous sexual relationship since 1978 is at risk of contracting the HIV virus. Anyone who engages in unsafe sex practices with a partner who has been exposed to the HIV virus is also at risk of contracting AIDS. For example, people may have been exposed unknowingly to the virus through blood transfusions or intravenous drug use. It is important to note that following these guidelines will not guarantee safety from infection. However, strict adherence to them can greatly reduce the chances of infection.

1. Have sex only with a partner who is not infected, who has sex only with you, and who does not use needles or syringes.

2. Always use (or have your partner use) a latex condom and a spermicide if you do not know for sure that your sexual partner is uninfected. Use a new condom each time you engage in sexual intercourse—never use the same condom more than once.

3. Use a water-based lubricant with your condom to add safety. Do not use oil-based jelly, baby oil, or any other substance that is not water-based because it can cause the condom to break.

4. Avoid the exchange of blood, semen, and vaginal secretions during sexual activity.

SUPPLEMENTAL READING LIST

Bellack, A. S. (Ed.). (1989). *A clinical guide for the treatment of schizophrenia.* New York: Plenum Press.

Burns, D. D. (1980). *Feeling good: The new mood therapy.* New York: William Morrow.

Kavanagh, D. (Ed) (1992). *Schizophrenia: A practical overview.* London: Chapman & Hall.

Keefe, R. S., & Harvey, P. D. (1994). *Understanding schizophrenia.* New York: Free Press.

Liberman, R. P. (1972). *A guide to behavioral analysis and therapy.* New York: Pergamon Press.

Martin, G., & Pear, J. (1996). *Behavior modification: What it is and how to do it* (5th ed.). Upper Saddle River, NJ: Prentice Hall.

Mueser, K. T., & Gingerich, S. (1994). *Coping with schizophrenia: A guide for families.* Oakland, CA: New Harbinger.

Redd, W. H., Porterfield, A. L., & Anderson, B. L. (1979). *Behavior modification: Behavioral approaches to human problems.* New York: Random House.

Woolis, R. (1992). *When someone you love has a mental illness.* New York: Putnam.

Appendix B: Materials Related to Assessment

ATTENDANCE AT SOCIAL SKILLS GROUP

Date: _____ Leaders: _____

Topic: _____

Instructions: Leaders complete this form **immediately** after each group is held.

Group members	Time present	No. of role plays	Attentiveness*	Cooperation*	Performance*

*To rate Attentiveness, Cooperation, and Performance, use this scale:

1	2	3	4	5
Extremely poor		Average		Extremely good

RATING SCALE CRITERIA FOR PERFORMANCE, COOPERATION, AND ATTENTION DURING SOCIAL SKILLS GROUP

Performance

1. Requires tremendous amount of assistance to perform skill. Shows little or no ability to rehearse the skill without extensive therapist coaching.
2. Requires considerable coaching and/or redirection but is able to demonstrate some skill spontaneously. On average can follow only two of the four steps of the skill.
3. Needs some help or redirection, but on average can follow three steps of the skill.
4. Needs little corrective feedback following role plays. Follows at least three steps and needs help only in "fine-tuning" role plays.
5. No assistance necessary to follow the steps. May perform the role play in a creative, inventive way.

Cooperation

1. Only minimally willing to participate. Openly defiant and disruptive. Considerable time is taken to encourage client to participate.
2. Rather reluctant to participate, but shows some definite efforts. May answer questions when called upon, but refuses to role play.
3. Willing to do what is asked with no resistance. Answers questions and engages in role plays, but does not volunteer.
4. Actively participates, at least partly without prompting. May start off hesitant, but warms up quickly and displays some enthusiasm.
5. Easy to engage in discussions and role plays. Enthusiastic and volunteers to be involved in group activities. May spontaneously give supportive feedback to others.

Attention

1. Attending 0–20% of the time. May at times know what is being discussed, but usually is self-absorbed or preoccupied.
2. Attending 20–40% of the time. Fades in and out of awareness, but on average is following the group less than half the time.
3. Attending 40–60% of the time. About half the time the patient is following what is going on in the group and the other half is distracted, or acting bored.
4. Attending 60–80% of the time. Most of the time knows what is going on, although there may be a few lapses in attention.
5. Attending 80–100% of the time. Gives relevant and specific answers to questions.

Source: Douglas, M. S., & Mueser, K. T. (1990). Teaching conflict resolution skills to the chronically mentally ill. *Behavior Modification* 14 (4), 519–547. Copyright 1990 by Sage Publications. Reprinted by permission.

SOCIAL ADAPTIVE FUNCTIONS SCALE (SAFE)

Resident name:_____   Evaluation date: _____

Staff name: _____

Instructions: Complete for the *typical* behavior **during the past month**. Circle one response for each item. When considering a rating for a particular behavior, it is important to compare the resident's ability to that of a person in a nonpsychiatric population. Group leaders should complete this scale once every 3 months.

0. No impairment
1. Mild impairment
2. Moderate impairment
3. Severe impairment
4. Extreme impairment

1. Bathing and Grooming	0	1	2	3	4
2. Clothing and Dressing	0	1	2	3	4
3. Eating, Feeding, and Diet	0	1	2	3	4
4. Money Management	0	1	2	3	4
5. Neatness and Maintenance	0	1	2	3	4
6. Orientation/Mobility	0	1	2	3	4
7. Reading/Writing	0	1	2	3	4
8. Impulse Control	0	1	2	3	4
9. Respect for Property	0	1	2	3	4
10. Telephone Skills	0	1	2	3	4
11. Conversational Skill	0	1	2	3	4
12. Instrumental Social Skill	0	1	2	3	4
13. Respect and Concern for Others	0	1	2	3	4
14. Social Appropriateness/Politeness	0	1	2	3	4
15. Social Engagement	0	1	2	3	4
16. Friendship	0	1	2	3	4
17. Recreation/Leisure (Nonsocial)	0	1	2	3	4
18. Participation in House Social Activities	0	1	2	3	4
19. Cooperation with Treatment	0	1	2	3	4

TOTAL _____

Source: Adapted from Harvey, P. D., Davidson, M., Mueser, K. T., Parrella, M., White, L., & Powchik, P. (1997). The Social-Adaptive Functioning Evaluation (SAFE): A rating scale for geriatric psychiatric patients. *Schizophrenia Bulletin, 23,* 131–145.

1. BATHING AND GROOMING

0. <u>No impairment</u>. The person bathes and grooms him- or herself without prompting and assistance. He or she appears to be aware of and takes pride in his or her appearance.

1. <u>Mild impairment</u>. The person can perform most bathing and grooming tasks. *Occasionally*, he or she needs to be reminded to cut fingernails, shave, bathe, or comb his or her hair but, when prompted, corrects these problems.

2. <u>Moderate impairment</u>. The person can perform less complex grooming tasks (combing hair, showering) but may need assistance in performing more complex aspects of grooming (shaving, cutting fingernails). He or she <u>regularly</u> requires reminding to maintain grooming.

3. <u>Severe impairment</u>. The person does not initiate any activities of grooming. He or she is willing to be bathed and groomed but needs extensive assistance to perform the basic grooming tasks (showering, combing hair). He or she may insist on an unusual and eccentric style of hair arrangement or makeup.

4. <u>Extreme impairment</u>. The person is uncooperative and/or actively resists grooming and bathing, creating a health hazard.

2. CLOTHING AND DRESSING

0. <u>No impairment</u>. The person is able to dress him- or herself without help; he or she clothes appropriate for the season from among his or her possessions, and, if given funds or the opportunity, is able to purchase or appropriately select clothing.

1. <u>Mild impairment</u>. The person dresses him- or herself without prompting or assistance, but sometimes he or she appears sloppy (e.g., soiled or torn clothing, shirttails exposed, buttons or zippers are open, shoelaces are untied).

2. <u>Moderate impairment</u>. The person needs some prompting or assistance to dress him- or herself. He or she sometimes may dress in odd combinations of clothes (pants are on inside-out; wears multiple layers of clothing) or in seasonally inappropriate clothing (heavy coat in summer). The person may not realize when his or her clothes need to be cleaned.

3. <u>Severe impairment</u>. The person needs extensive assistance dressing but does not resist this assistance. He or she may often dress in odd combinations or seasonally inappropriate clothing. He or she may disrobe without realizing that the situation is inappropriate.

4. <u>Extreme impairment</u>. The person refuses to wear clothes or is so unresponsive that dressing is ineffective and, therefore, spends most of the time in pajamas or robe.

3. EATING, FEEDING, AND DIET

0. No impairment. The person is able to feed him- or herself without assistance and has specific food preferences. If given funds or opportunity, the person would be able to choose his or her own diet, buy additional food items, or prepare a simple and adequately nutritional meal.

1. Mild impairment. The person can use eating utensils and supplement the meals provided by the residence with food purchased at neighborhood stores. He or she is somewhat sloppy in eating habits and table manners and might choose an unusual diet if unsupervised (e.g., only sweets or only potato chips).

2. Moderate impairment. The person occasionally eats spontaneously but needs constant prompting in order to finish the meal. Use of eating utensils is poor, and use of hands instead of utensils is not unusual. He or she cannot independently care for all dietary needs.

3. Severe impairment. The person accepts food but needs to be supervised while eating. The person may occasionally refuse food, eat excessively, or eat nonnutritive, hazardous substances.

4. Extreme impairment. The person swallows food when fed, but supplements are necessary in order to survive (high-caloric, high-protein supplements or intragastric feeding). If unsupervised, the person might be at risk of choking.

4. MONEY MANAGEMENT

0. No impairment. The person is able to manage his or her own money without assistance. Person knows how much money he or she has, can count money, is capable of budgeting, and spends it accordingly.

1. Mild impairment. The person is able to manage his or her own money with some assistance. He or she may need some help in budgeting his or her money but is able to spend budgeted money without significant assistance.

2. Moderate impairment. The person needs considerable assistance budgeting, counting, and spending money. If unsupervised, he or she might spend money impulsively or give large sums away. However, he or she is capable of performing some or most of these activities *with the help of staff* prompting or monitoring (e.g., purchasing an item).

3. Severe impairment. Most aspects of money management need to be performed or closely supervised by staff members. The person is not capable of performing even the simplest of tasks involving money without assistance, but he or she wishes to have money or values what it can purchase.

4. Extreme impairment. The person is unwilling to participate in any aspects of money management and is uninterested in money or buying things. The person's money is completely managed by others.

5. NEATNESS AND MAINTENANCE ACTIVITIES

0. No impairment. The person keeps his or her room neat and helps staff in maintenance activities in the house.

1. Mild impairment. The person requires some prompting to keep his or her room neat. He or she sometimes helps out with maintenance in the house when asked by staff.

2. Moderate impairment. The person needs extensive prompting or actual assistance to keep his or her room clean.

3. Severe impairment. The person can only minimally participate in any "household" maintenance tasks. He or she can do some simple activities when prompted (e.g., picking up clothes from the floor), but otherwise staff must maintain his or her room.

4. Extreme impairment. The person does not assist in any "household" maintenance tasks.

6. ORIENTATION/MOBILITY

0. No impairment. Person is able to leave the house on his or her own and return at the appropriate and agreed-upon time.

1. Mild impairment. The person knows his or her way around the neighborhood and can leave the house unaccompanied, but he or she is sometimes late when arriving at destinations.

2. Moderate impairment. The person can usually leave the house unaccompanied, but he or she sometimes fails to arrive at a destination or fails to return on time. The person may know some parts of the neighborhood.

3. Severe impairment. The person can only leave the house when escorted and would otherwise fail to arrive at his or her destination. The person knows few parts of the neighborhood.

4. Extreme impairment. The person does not leave the house and shows no incentive to leave.

7. READING WRITING

0. No impairment. The person writes letters and reads (e.g., newspapers, books).

1. Mild impairment. The person writes little (e.g., a simple note, occasional brief letter), or reads a little (e.g., a brief newspaper article) on his or her own. The person needs help correctly addressing and mailing a letter.

2. Moderate impairment. The person reads and/or writes some if prompted, but rarely does so on his own initiative. The person cannot read beyond simple sentences.

3. <u>Severe impairment</u>. The person signs his or her name, or reads simple signs, but not more, even if prompted.

4. <u>Extreme impairment</u>. The person is essentially illiterate; he or she does not read or write at all, even if prompted, and does not sign his or her name.

8. IMPULSE CONTROL

0. <u>No impairment</u>. The person waits as necessary in order to have his or her needs met.

1. <u>Mild impairment</u>. Occasionally, the person is impatient (e.g., repeats the same demand, is excessively emphatic when making a request). His or her impulses can be controlled with simple reminders.

2. <u>Moderate impairment</u>. The person is sometimes intrusive if his or her needs are not met immediately. He or she may have loud outbursts but is not violent. Verbal commands or brief periods of time in a "quiet room" are adequate to maintain his or her impulses.

3. <u>Severe impairment</u>. The person often has problems with outbursts that require seclusion (e.g., at least once every week or two). Certain topics of conversation or certain situations are avoided to prevent these outbursts.

4. <u>Extreme impairment</u>. The person is prone to violent outbursts that require seclusion (e.g., several times per week) and is avoided by other persons and staff.

9. RESPECT FOR PROPERTY

0. <u>No impairment</u>. The person follows social rules regarding respect for others' property and adequately maintains his or her own property.

1. <u>Mild impairment</u>. The person maintains his or her property and respects the property of others, but he sometimes needs reminders to obey these social rules.

2. <u>Moderate impairment</u>. The person understands the difference between his or her property and that of others. He or she may occasionally take others' property but is willing to return it when requested. He or she sometimes may not notice or protest when someone takes his or her property.

3. <u>Severe impairment</u>. The person has a limited understanding of the distinction between his or her property and that of others and often disobeys social rules regarding property (e.g., he regularly takes others' property or gives his or her own away). The person responds to prompts to follow conventional rules regarding property (e.g., giving others' property back when instructed to).

4. <u>Extreme impairment</u>. The person does not follow social rules respecting others' property or maintaining his or her own and does not respond to prompts to follow these rules.

10. TELEPHONE SKILLS

0. <u>No impairment</u>. The person uses the telephone appropriately, including directory assistance.

1. <u>Mild impairment</u>. The person dials most telephone numbers without assistance but needs help in using directory assistance.

2. <u>Moderate impairment</u>. The person uses the telephone but consistently needs assistance in dialing.

3. <u>Severe impairment</u>. The person needs extensive assistance using the telephone (e.g., dialing, speaking into the receiver, speaking loudly enough, knowing when to hang up).

4. <u>Extreme impairment</u>. The person refuses or is incapable of using the telephone, even when extensive assistance is offered.

11. CONVERSATION SKILL

0. <u>No impairment</u>. The person converses with others in a socially appropriate, skilled manner (e.g., choice of topic, level of self-disclosure, good eye contact, and voice loudness).

1. <u>Mild impairment</u>. The person has fairly good skills when conversing with others. His or her choice of conversational topic or self-disclosure may occasionally be inappropriate, or his or her nonverbal skills (eye contact, interpersonal distance) or paralinguistic skills (voice tone, loudness) may need some improvement. Feedback is successful in getting the person to alter his or her behavior.

2. <u>Moderate impairment</u>. The person has some ability to engage in conversations with others (e.g., can talk for several minutes with another person), but often demonstrates poor skills (e.g., choice of topic, nonverbal, and paralinguistic skills). Feedback produces only small improvements in these skills.

3. <u>Severe impairment</u>. The person has great difficulty sustaining any conversation for more than a very brief period (e.g., 30 seconds–1 minute). People have difficulty following the person's conversations, which may revolve around delusions or lead nowhere in particular. Person appears not to listen to others but can briefly engage other people in conversations. Feedback is ineffective at improving the person's ability to converse.

4. <u>Extreme impairment</u>. The person is incapable of engaging in even very brief conversations, even when prompted. Person is mute, speaks in a garbled fashion, has severely disordered syntax, or is so preoccupied with delusions that even brief conversations are impossible.

12. INSTRUMENTAL SOCIAL SKILLS

0. <u>No impairment</u>. The person understands the house rules and roles of staff and is able to ask for specific services from appropriate staff members in a socially skillful

manner. Person regularly attains the instrumental (tangible) goals of his or her interactions.

1. Mild impairment. The person is often able to achieve the instrumental goals of his interactions. The person may occasionally ask an inappropriate person for something. Social skill problems may occasionally limit the person's ability to achieve instrumental goals (e.g., the person demands something rather than requests it; he or she stands inappropriately close to the other person; he or she speaks in a low voice tone.

2. Moderate impairment. The person sometimes achieves the instrumental goals of his or her interactions with others, but his or her success is often hampered by poor social skills (e.g., lack of specificity, prominent deficits in nonverbal and paralinguistic skills). The person may misperceive social roles (asking the cook for change in medication). Despite these limitations, the person tries regularly to obtain instrumental goals.

3. Severe impairment. The person rarely attains instrumental goals of social interactions because of poor social skills and misperception of social roles. The person approaches others occasionally to achieve instrumental goals.

4. Extreme impairment. The person never approaches others to achieve instrumental goals.

13. RESPECT AND CONCERN FOR OTHERS

0. No impairment. The person shows appropriate respect and concern for others' feelings in his or her interactions, even during emotionally charged conflicts.

1. Mild impairment. The person occasionally shows inappropriate disregard for others' feelings (e.g., during a conflict). When prompted, the person can demonstrate more appropriate respect.

2. Moderate impairment. The person sometimes appears unaware of how others may feel about what he or she says (e.g., insulting others).

3. Severe impairment. The person sometimes makes crude and inappropriate comments. He or she makes lewd sexual comments or crude racial slurs without regard to how these remarks are perceived by his audience.

4. Extreme impairment. The person frequently makes crude and inappropriate comments without regard to how they are perceived by others.

14. SOCIAL APPROPRIATENESS/POLITENESS

0. No impairment. The person's interactions with others are well-mannered and polite. Even in emotionally charged situations, he or she usually conducts him- or herself in a thoughtful and considerate fashion.

1. Mild impairment. The person is sometimes socially awkward but is usually polite.

He or she may occasionally be impolite (e.g., asking an intrusive question, not responding to a greeting) but responds when given feeback about such behaviors.

2. Moderate impairment. The person often fails to demonstrate common polite behaviors (e.g., making greetings, getting out of someone's way, responding to simple requests such as turning down the radio) and is sometimes socially inappropriate. When the person is given feedback about his or her behavior, some small improvements are possible.

3. Severe impairment. The person is almost never polite and is often socially inappropriate. Attempts to correct his or her behavior are largely unsuccessful.

4. Extreme impairment. The person is socially inappropriate nearly all the time. His or her behavior as well as speech are characterized by unacceptable social conduct.

15. SOCIAL ENGAGEMENT

0. No impairment. The person both initiates social interactions with others on a regular basis (e.g., several times per day) and is responsive to interactions initiated by others. Social interactions are not limited to very brief periods but may extend to longer periods of time (e.g., more than 15 minutes).

1. Mild impairment. The person both initiates social interactions with others and is responsive to others, but interactions tend to be shorter or occur less frequently.

2. Moderate impairment. The person regularly participates in social interactions, but he or she usually reciprocates social interactions, rather than initiates them.

3. Severe impairment. The person usually avoids social contacts. He or she rarely initiates social interactions, and when others initiate the interaction, he or she is only minimally responsive. Most interactions are quite brief.

4. Extreme impairment. The person actively refuses to interact with others and may leave the room when someone enters. He or she may react with fear or aggression if forced to interact.

16. FRIENDSHIPS

0. No impairment. The person has friendly relationships with others inside and outside the house. At least one of these friendships goes beyond "acquaintance," and the nature of the friendship is close, stable, long-lasting, and mutually rewarding.

1. Mild impairment. The person has several acquaintances but has difficulties forming and maintaining close, stable friendships. The person may interact preferentially with staff members instead of peers. Or, he or she may have friendships that are based on abnormal content or motivation. For example, the person exploits or is being exploited sexually, financially, or the relationship is based on inappropriate or unusual attractions.

2. <u>Moderate impairment</u>. The person may seek out and spend time with one other person, but without meaningful interaction (e.g., sitting silently). The person may seek out a staff member with whom he or she attempts to be friendly.

3. <u>Severe impairment</u>. The person has one or two acquaintances with whom he or she maintains some contact, but these relationships are maintained solely on the initiative of the other person.

4. <u>Extreme impairment</u>. The person has no contacts with either peers or staff members.

17. <u>RECREATION/LEISURE (NONSOCIAL)</u>

0. <u>No impairment</u>. The person has well-developed, specific interests or hobbies (e.g., knitting, running, reading, crossword puzzles) that he or she participates in *more than once* a week.

1. <u>Mild impairment</u>. The person has definite interests or hobbies, to which he or she devotes regular, but less than frequent, time (once a week or less).

2. <u>Moderate impairment</u>. The person has some specific interests, but involvement in activity is irregular (once or twice a month).

3. <u>Severe impairment</u>. The person has some superficial interests (favorite TV program or magazine; follows a sports team) that he or she engages in.

4. <u>Extreme impairment</u>. The person has no superficial interests or hobbies. He or she may spend his or her free time involved in nondiscriminating TV viewing or sitting around smoking cigarettes.

18. <u>PARTICIPATION IN HOUSE SOCIAL ACTIVITIES</u>

0. <u>No impairment</u>. The person takes appropriate and selective advantage of social activities offered by the house staff and appears to enjoy them.

1. <u>Mild impairment</u>. The person often participates in social activities organized by the house staff, but occasional prompting is needed.

2. <u>Moderate impairment</u>. The person participates in some social activities organized by the house staff, but he or she often needs to be prompted and occasionally leaves before the activity is completed.

3. <u>Severe impairment</u>. The person passively and reluctantly participates in occasional social activities organized by the house staff, but rarely or never on his own accord.

4. <u>Extreme impairment</u>. The person refuses to participate in social activities organized by the house staff.

19. <u>COOPERATION WITH TREATMENT</u>

0. <u>No impairment</u>. The person fully cooperates with the treatment plan and implementation. He or she understands the benefits and the risks of the treatment and is

an active participant in his or her treatment (e.g., requests a specific medication). The person is able to accurately report adverse effects from medication or intercurrent medical illnesses.

1. Mild impairment. The person is fully compliant with treatment and other suggestions or reasonable requests, but he or she does not actively participate in the treatment plan and occasionally overemphasizes or underemphasizes adverse effects of medication or intercurrent medical illnesses.

2. Moderate impairment. The person is compliant with most suggestions but occasionally refuses treatment or other reasonable requests. He or she may often complain of medical problems that have no physiological explanation.

3. Severe impairment. The person is only selectively compliant with treatment suggestions. Medical illnesses or psychotic symptoms may be exacerbated because of noncompliance with medication or other suggestions.

4. Extreme impairment. The person refuses to comply with treatment to the extent that severe health problems result. He or she may need to be restrained or medicated by force or with court intervention.

References

Anderson, C. M., Reiss, D. J., & Hogarty, G. E. (1986). *Schizophrenia and the family: A practitioner's guide to psychoeducation and management.* New York: Guilford Press.

Andreasen, N. C. (1982). Negative symptoms in schizophrenia: Definition and reliability. *Archives of General Psychiatry, 39,* 784–788.

Bandura, A. (1969). *Principles of behavior modification.* New York: Holt, Rinehart & Winston.

Bellack, A. S., Blanchard, J. J., & Mueser, K. T. (1996). Cue availability and affect perception in schizophrenia. *Schizophrenia Bulletin, 22,* 535–544.

Bellack, A. S., & Morrison, R. L. (1982). Interpersonal dysfunction. In A. S. Bellack, M. Hersen, & A. E. Kazdin (Eds.), *Interpersonal handbook of behavior modification and therapy* (pp. 717–748). New York: Plenum Press.

Bellack, A. S., Morrison, R. L., Mueser, K. T., Wade, J. H., & Sayers, S. L. (1990). Role play for assessing the social competence of psychiatric patients. *Psychological Assessment: A Journal of Consulting and Clinical Psychology, 2,* 248–255.

Bellack, A. S., & Mueser, K. T. (1993). Psychological treatment for schizophrenia. *Schizophrenia Bulletin, 19,* 317–336.

Bellack, A. S., Mueser, K. T., Wade, J., Sayers, S. L., & Morrison, R. L. (1992). The ability of schizophrenics to perceive and cope with negative affect. *British Journal of Psychiatry, 160,* 473–480.

Corrigan, P. (1995). Wanted: Champions of psychiatric rehabilitation. *American Psychologist, 50,* 514–521.

Davis, M., Eshelman, E., & McKay, M. (1995). *The relaxation and stress reduction workbook* (4th ed.). Oakland, CA: New Harbinger.

Drake, R. E., Bartels, S. J., Teague, G. B., Noordsy, D. L., & Clark, R. E. (1993). Treatment of substance abuse in severely mentally ill patients. *Journal of Nervous and Mental Disease, 181,* 606–611.

Drake, R. E., & Mueser, K. T. (Eds.). *Dual diagnosis of major mental illness and substance abuse disorder II: Recnt research and clinical implications* (New Directions in Mental Health Services No. 70). San Francisco: Jossey-Bass.

Eckman, T. A., Wirshing, W. C., Marder, S. R., Liberman, R. P., Johnston-Cronk, K., Zimmermann, K., & Mintz, J. (1992). Technique for training schizophrenic patients in illness self-management: A controlled trial. *American Journal of Psychiatry, 149,* 1549–1555.

Falloon I. R. H., Boyd, J. L., & McGill C. W. (1984). *Family care of schizophrenia.* New York: Guilford Press.

Gingerich, S., & Bellack, A. S. (1995). Research-based family interventions for the treatment of schizophrenia. *The Clinical Psychologist, 48,* 24–27.

Gray, J. A., Feldon, J., Rawlins, J. N. P., Hemsley, D. R., & Smith, A. D. (1991). The neuropsychology of schizophrenia. *Behavioral and Brain Sciences, 14,* 1–84.

Hatfield, A. B., & Lefley, H. P. (Eds.). (1987). *Families of the mentally ill: Coping and adaptation.* New York: Guilford Press.

Hatfield, A. B., & Lefley, H. P. (1993). *Surviving mental illness: Stress, coping, and adaptation.* New York: Guilford Press.

Hersen, M., & Bellack, A. S. (1976). Social skills training for chronic psychiatric patients: Rationale, research findings and future directions. *Comprehensive Psychiatry, 17,* 559–580.

Hersen, M., Bellack, A. S., & Turner, S. M. (1978). Assessment of assertiveness in female psychiatric patients: Motoric and physiological measures. *Journal of Behavior Therapy and Experimental Psychiatry, 9,* 11–16.

Kavanagh, D. J. (1992). Recent developments in expressed emotion and schizophrenia. *British Journal of Psychiatry, 160,* 601–620.

Keefe, R. S., & Harvey, P. D. (1994). *Understanding schizophrenia.* New York: Free Press.

Lefley, H. P., & Johnson, D. L. (Eds.) (1990). *Families as allies in treatment of mentally ill: New directions for mental health professionals.* Washington, DC: American Psychiatric Association Press.

Martin, G., & Pear, J. (1996). *Behavior modification: What it is and how to do it* (5th ed.). Upper Saddle River, NJ: Prentice Hall.

McFarlane, W. R., Lukens, E., Link, B., Dushay, R., Deakins, S., Newmark, M., Dunne, E. J., Horen, B., & Toran, J. (1995). Multiple family groups and psychoeducation in the treatment of schizophrenia. *Archives of General Psychiatry, 52,* 679–687.

McKay, M., & Fanning, P. (1987). *Progressive relaxation and breathing* [audiocassette]. Oakland, CA: New Harbinger.

Miller, W. R., & Rollnick, S. (1991). *Motivational interviewing: Preparing people to change addictive behavior.* New York: Guilford Press.

Morrison, R. L. (1990). Interpersonal dysfunction. In A. S. Bellack, M. Hersen, & A. E. Kazdin (Eds.), *International handbook of behavior modification and therapy* (3rd ed., pp. 503–522). New York: Plenum Press.

Mueser, K. T., Bellack, A. S., Douglas, M. S., & Morrison, R. L. (1991). Prevalence and stability of social skills deficits in schizophrenia. *Schizophrenia Research, 5,* 167–176.

Mueser, K. T., Bellack, A. S., Douglas, M. S., & Wade, J. H. (1991). Prediction of social skill acquisition in schizophrenic and major affective disorder patients from memory and symptomatology. *Psychiatry Research, 37,* 281–296.

Mueser, K. T., Doonan, R., Penn, D. L., Blanchard, J. J., Bellack, A. S., Nishith, P., & deLeon, J. (1996). Emotion recognition and social competence in chronic schizophrenia. *Journal of Abnormal Psychology, 105,* 271–275.

Mueser, K. T., Drake, R. E., Clark, R. E., McHugo, G. J., Mercer-McFadden, C., & Ackerson, T. (1995). *Toolkit for evaluating substance abuse in persons with severe mental illness.* Cambridge, MA: Evaluation Center at HSRI.

Mueser, K. T., Fox, M., Kenison, L., & Geltz, B. (1995). *Better living skills group: Treatment manual.* Unpublished manuscript, Darthmouth Medical School.

Mueser, K. T. & Gingerich, S. (1994). *Coping with schizophrenia: A guide for families.* Oakland, CA: New Harbinger.

Mueser, K. T. & Glynn, S. M. (1995). *Behavioral family therapy for psychiatric disorders.* Boston: Allyn & Bacon.

Nikkel, R. E. (1994). Areas of skill training for persons with mental illness and substance use disorders: Building skills for successful community living. *Community Mental Health Journal, 30*(1), 61–72.

Prochaska, J. O., DiClemente, C. C., & Norcross, J. C. (1992). In search of how people change: Applications to addictive disorders. *American Psychologist, 47,* 1102–1114.

Sayers, S. L., Bellack, A. S., Wade, J. H., Bennett, M., & Fong, P. (1995). An empirical method for assessing social problem solving in schizophrenia. *Behavior Modification, 19,* 267–289.

Seidman, L. J., Cassens, G. P., Kremen, W. S., & Pepple, J. R. (1992). Neuropsychology in schizophrenia. In R. F. White (Ed.), *Clinical syndromes in adult neuropsychology: The practitioner's handbook* (pp. 381–449). New York: Elsevier.

Skinner, B. F. (1938). *The behavior of organisms: An experimental analysis.* New York: Appleton-Century-Crofts.

Skinner, B. F. (1953). *Science and human behavior.* New York: Macmillan.

Torrey, F. (1995). *Surviving schizophrenia: A family manual* (3rd ed.). New York: Harper & Row.

Ziedonis, D. M. (1992). Comorbid psychopathology and cocaine addiction. In T. R. Kosten & H. D. Kleber (Eds.), *Clinician's guide to cocaine addiction: Theory, research, and treatment* (pp. 337–360). New York: Guilford Press.

Ziedonis, D. M., & Fisher, W. (1994). Assessment and treatment of comorbid substance abuse in individuals with schizophrenia. *Psychiatric Annals, 24,* 477–483.

Index

Page numbers in italics indicate reference entries.

Ackerson, T., *281*
Activities of daily living, 19
Adolescence, 5
Affective states, 7
Alcohol abuse, 142–151
  four-stage model, 143, 144
  integrated treatment, 142–145
  motivation to change, 145–147
  troubleshooting, 142–151
Alogia, 9
Anderson, C. M., 167, *279*
Andreasen, N. C., 9, *279*
Anergia, 9
Anger management
  curriculum menu, 98
  curricular skill sheet, 202
  lesson plans, 99, 100
Anhedonia, 9
Anxiety (*see* Social anxiety)
Anxiety-reduction strategy, 23
Assertiveness skills
  behavioral repertoire, 18
  curricular skill sheets, 197–206
Assessment, 21–43
  general issues, 22–24
  and goal setting, 108–110, 121
  interview techniques, 24–26
  materials for, 266–278
  of progress in group, 119–121
  role-playing tests, 26–43
  Social Problem-Solving Battery in, 30–43
Attendance
  assessment scale, 267

highly symptomatic clients, 130–132
  positive reinforcement for, 130, 131
  in residential settings, 131, 132, 166
Attention deficits
  and information processing, 8
  rating scale criteria, 268
  role play, impact of, 133, 243
  social development interference, 5
  social perception, impact of, 13
Auditory hallucinations, 132

Bandura, A., 44, *279*
Bartels, S. J., 143, *279*
Behavioral observation
  role-playing tests, 26–43
  and Social Problem-Solving Battery, 30–43
Behavioral repertoires, 13–17
Bellack, A. S., 4, 6–8, 13, 22, 26, 30, 106, 126, 134, 139, 167, *279–281*
Bennett, M., 30, *281*
Better Living Skills Group, 144, 145
Blanchard, J. J., 13, *279, 281*
Boyd, J. L., 79, *280*

Cassens, G. P., 8, *281*
Children, attention deficits, 5
Clarification skills, 16
Clark, R. E., 143, *279, 281*
Client selection, 87
Close-ended questions, 14, 15
Coaching, 75–77

Cognitive impairments
  and comprehension difficulties, 132
  role-play consideration, 243
Co-leader groups, 86, 116
Communication skills, 155–157
Community living skills, 209–214
Compromise and negotiation skills, 191
Concrete thinking, 15
Conflict management, 95, 191–194
Conversational skills
  curricular skill sheets, 179–187
  overview, 14, 15
  questioning strategies in, 14, 15
  rating scale assessment, 274
  reinforcement in, 15
  timing factors, 17
Corrective feedback (*see* Feedback)
Corrigan, P., 163, 279
Couples, skills training for, 78, 79
Cultural issues, 105, 106
Curriculum menus, 97–101
Curriculum planning, 93–107

Dating skills
  behavioral repertoire, 18, 19
  curricular skill sheets, 217–226
Davidson, M., 269
Davis, M., 162, 279
Deakins, S., 280
Deep breathing exercises, 162, 163
deLeon, J., 280
Delusions
  and disruptive group behavior, 134, 135
  role of, in comprehension difficulties,
    132
DiClemente, C. C., 143, *281*
Discrimination modeling, 74, 75
Distractibility, 133
Doonan, R., 280
Douglas, M. S., 8, 139, *280*
Drake, R. E., 142, 143, 146, 279, *281*
Drug abuse, 142–151
  four-stage model, 143, 144
  integrated treatment, 142–145
  motivation to change, 145–147
  troubleshooting, 142–151
Drug refusal skills, 206
Dual Diagnosis Relapse Prevention, 146
Dually diagnosed clients, 142–151
  integrated treatment model, 142–145
  motivation to change, 145–147

Dunne, E. J., *280*
Dushay, R., *280*

Eckman, T. A., 20, 279
Emotional cues, 13, 17
Employment skills
  behavioral repertoire, 19
  curricular skill sheets, 235–240
Environmental factors, 7, 8
Eshelman, E., 162, 279
Expressed emotion, 79
Expressing angry feelings, 106
Expressing positive feelings
  curricular skill sheet, 217
  rationale, 48
  steps in, 94
Expressing unpleasant feelings
  curricular skill sheet, 201
  homework assignments, 64, 69–71
  modeling of, 73
  rationale, 48
  steps in, 94
  training steps, 50, 51
Expressive skills
  categories of, 10
  schizophrenia deficits, 10–12
Eye contact
  conversational skill characteristics, 15
  discrimination modeling, 75
  prompting techniques, 77
  schizophrenia deficits, 11

Facial expression, 11
Falloon, I. R. H., 79, 158, 161, 167, 280
Families
  expressed emotion in, 79
  self-help organizations, 168
  skills training for, 78, 79
  stress reduction role, 159–163
  support function, 154–158, 167, 168
Fanning, P., 162, 280
Feedback
  by clients, 126, 127
  guidelines, 259
  in role plays, 55, 56
  staff training in, 166, 167
Feeling statements
  function of, 57
  in role plays, 57, 58, 70, 71
Feldon, J., 8, 280

Fisher, W., 146, *281*
Fong, P., 30, *281*
Fox, M., 144, *281*
Friendship skills
  curricular skill sheets, 217–226
  rating scale assessment, 276

Geltz, B., 144, *281*
Generalization
  assessment of, 120, 121
  effect of "social skills training team,"
    90–92
  homework assignments, function of, 63
  programming of, 46, 47
  as ultimate test of skills training, 46
Gingerich, S., 155, 157, 159, 163, 167, 280,
    281
Glynn, S. M., 79, 155, 158, 161, *281*
Goal setting
  assessment, role in, 108–110, 121
  and client preparation, 88, 89
  dually diagnosed, 146
  homework assignments relationship, 114,
    115
  and tailored skills training, 110–115
Gray, J. A., 8, 280
Group leaders
  selection of, 85
  training, 86, 87
Group psychotherapy, 241, 242
Group skills training, 80–92 (*see also* Role
    playing)
  advantages, 80
  client selection for, 87
  composition of, 81, 82
  curriculum planning, 93–107
  duration of, 82
  group psychotherapy comparison, 241,
    242
  structural guidelines, 81–84

Hallucinations, 134, 135
Harvey, P.D., 155, 269, 280
Hassles, 153
Hatfield, A. B., 168, 280
Hemsley, D. R., 8, 280
Hersen, M., 4, 22, 280
Heterosocial skills
  behavioral repertoire, 18, 19
  curricular skill sheets, 217–226

High-functioning clients
  homework assignments, 115
  role-play structure, 112, 113
  role-play tailoring, 117
  troubleshooting, 139–143
History taking, 24, 25
HIV-risk behavior, 226, 243, 244, 262
Hogarty, G. E., 167, 279
Homework assignments
  noncompliance, 127–129
  rationale, 63
  review of, 67–72
  role-playing step, 63–65
  and skills training transfer, 46, 47, 63
  tailoring of, 114, 115
Homework Sheet, 261
Horen, B., 280
House rules, 159

Independent living skills, 19
Individual differences, 108–122
  assessment, 108–110
  and goals, 110–115
  and homework assignments, 114, 115
  role-play structure considerations,
    112–114
Individual skills training, 78
Information processing
  and attention deficits, 8
  and problem solving, 8, 9
Inpatient programs
  social learning milieu, 163–167
  staff training, 164–166
Insight-oriented therapy, 123, 124, 241
Interpersonal anxiety (*see* Social anxiety)
Interpersonal history, 24, 25
Interview assessment
  interpersonal history, 24, 25
  observational data in, 25, 26
  and significant others, 26

Job interviews
  behavioral repertoire, 19
  curricular skill sheet, 235
Johnson, D. L., 168, 280
Johnston-Cronk, K., 279

Kavanagh, D. J., 79, 280
Keefe, R. S., 155, 280

Kenison, L., 144, 281
Kremen, W. S., 8, 281

Lefley, H. P., 168, 280
Lesson plans, 97–101
Liberman, R. P., 279
Life event stress, 153
Likert scales, 28
Link, B., 280
Listening skills
  behavioral repertoire, 16
  curricular skill sheet, 179
  steps in, 94
Low-functioning clients
  attendance problems, 130–132
  comprehension difficulties, 132, 133
  distractibility, 133
  homework assignments, 115, 127, 129
    noncompliance, 127–129
  role-play structure, 113
  role-play tailoring, 116, 117, 130–138
  social withdrawal, troubleshooting,
    135–137
Lukens, E., 280

Making requests skill, 94
Marder, S. R., 279
Martin, G., 155, 280
McFarland, W. R., 167, 280
McGill, C. W., 79, 280
McHugo, G. J., 281
McKay, M., 162, 279, 280
Medication management
  behavioral repertoire in, 19, 20
  curricular skill sheets, 229–231
Memory problems
  role-play impact, 243
  and schizophrenia, 8
Mercer-McFadden, C., 281
Miller, W. R., 146, 280
Mintz, J., 279
"Mock meeting" training, 147
Modeling
  definition, 45
  negative feeling statements, 73, 74
  of problem solving, 102
  and role plays, 45, 51–53, 73–75
Morrison, R. L., 7, 9, 22, 26, 139, 279, 280
Motivation
  among dually diagnosed clients, 145–147

and homework noncompliance, 128
  schizophrenia deficits, 7
Motivation-Based Dual Diagnosis Treatment,
  146
Motivational Enhancement Therapy, 146
Mueser, K. T., 6, 7, 8, 13, 26, 79, 106, 139,
  142, 144, 146, 155, 157–159, 161,
  163, 269, 279–281

National Alliance for the Mentally Ill, 168
Negative assertion skills, 18
Negative reinforcement, 45
Negative symptoms
  and attendance problems, 130
  causes, 9
  as neurobiological constraint, 9
  and social withdrawal, troubleshooting,
    135–137
Negotiation skills, 191
Neurobiological factors, 8, 9
Newmark, M., 280
Nikkell, R. E., 145, 281
Nishith, P., 280
Noncompliance
  homework assignments, 127–129
  and medication management skills, 19, 20
Nonverbal behavior
  discrimination modeling, 75
  schizophrenia deficits, 11
  social perception training, 106
Noordsy, D. L., 143, 279
Norcross, J. C., 143, 281

Observational data
  in interview assessment, 25, 26
  role-playing tests, 26–43
  and Social Problem-Solving Battery, 30–43
Open-ended questions, 14
Overlearning, 45

Paralinguistic behavior
  discrimination modeling, 75
  prompting technique, 77
  schizophrenia deficits, 11
Parental report, interview data, 26
Parrella, M., 269
Pear, J., 155, 280
Penn, D. L., 280
Pepple, J. R., 8, 281

Personal space, 12
Positive assertion skills, 18
Positive reinforcement
    by clients, 126, 127
    definition, 45
    and group attendance, 130, 131
    guidelines, 259
    importance of, in social skills training, 45,
        244
    in role plays, 55, 56
    staff training in, 166, 167
Positive symptoms
    and attendance problems, 130
    definition, 9
    and disruptive group behavior, 134, 135
Posture, 12
Powchik, P., 269
Problem solving
    curriculum planning, 102, 103
    role-playing assessment of, 30–43
    schizophrenia deficits, 8, 9
    skills training steps, 102
    worksheet, 254, 255
Prochaska, J. O., 143, 281
Prompting technique, 77
Proximics, 12
Psychoeducation, 79
Psychotic symptoms
    and disruptive group behavior, 134, 135
    role of, in comprehension difficulties, 132
    and social functioning, 6, 7

Questioning strategies, 14, 15

Rawlins, J. N. P., 8, 280
Receptive skills, 12, 13
Reframing, 161, 162
Reinforcement (see also Positive reinforce-
        ment)
    conversational strategy, 15
    in social skills training, 45
Reiss, D. J., 167, 279
Relapse prevention, 152–169
    families in, 154–158
    and staff member support, 154–158
    stress management techniques, 159–163
    supportive environment, role of, 154–169
Relaxation techniques, 162, 163
Residential settings
    social learning milieu, 163–167
    staff training, 164–166

Response-Generation Task, 30–43
    procedural aspects, 40, 41
    in Social Problem-Solving Battery, 30
    target scenes, 41–43
Response latency, in conversation, 15, 17
Role-Play Task, 30–43
    procedural aspects, 31, 32
    in Social Problem-Solving Battery, 30
    target scenes in, 32–40
Role playing
    as assessment tool, 26–43
    behavioral observations of, 26–43
    client reluctance problem, 125, 126
    coaching technique, 75–77
    corrective feedback, 56, 57
    generalization, 29, 30
    high-functioning clients, 116, 117,
        130–138
    homework assignment step, 63–65
    and individual goals, 112–114
    low-functioning clients, 116, 117, 130–138
    positive feedback, 55, 56, 58
    rehearsals, 53, 54
    in social problem solving, 30–43
    and social skills modeling, 45, 51–53,
        73–75
    steps in, 51–66
Rollnick, S., 146, 280

Safe sex behavior, 226, 243, 244, 262
Sayers, S. L., 26, 30, 279, 281
Seidman, L. J., 8, 281
Self-report data, 25
Sexual relationships
    behavioral repertoire, 18, 19
    curricular skill sheets, 224–226
Shaping, 45
Significant others, interview data, 26
Situational specificity
    and assessment, 22, 23, 25
    and interview data, 25
    social skills factor, 4
Skill sheet guidelines, 95–97
Skinner, B. F., 44, 281
Smith, A. D., 8, 280
Social Adaptive Functions Scale, 269–278
Social anxiety
    assessment, 23
    role-playing tests, 28
    social skill relationship, 23
Social environment, 7, 8